British Government

A reader in policy making

This reader presents over seventy case studies of policy making in Whitehall and Westminster ranging from the pits closures to the *Satanic Verses* affair. Simon James combines newspaper coverage, official documents, academic analysis and the recollection of participants to explore:

- the various ways in which policy originates and is shaped within Whitehall;
- the different modes of parliamentary control, the problems of implementation and policy review;
- the role of civil servants in developing policy;
- the role of the Prime Minister and cabinet;
- the impact of the European Union.

Designed as a textbook for undergraduates, *British Government: a reader in policy making* provides a vast range of source material and analysis that will be of value to students of British politics and public policy.

Simon James is a Research Fellow of the Institute of Contemporary British History, and the author of *British Cabinet Government* (Routledge 1992).

British Government

A reader in policy making

Simon James

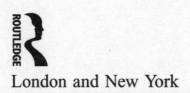

London and New York

First published 1997
by Routledge
11 New Fetter Lane, London EC4P 4EE

Simultaneously published in the USA and Canada
by Routledge
29 West 35th Street, New York, NY 10001

© 1997 Simon James

Typeset in Times by LaserScript, Mitcham, Surrey
Printed and bound in Great Britain by
Clays Ltd, St. Ives PLC

British Library Cataloguing in Publication Data
A catalogue record for this book is available from the British Library

Library of Congress Cataloging in Publication Data
British Government: A reader in policy making/[edited by] Simon James.
  Includes index.
  1. Political planning – Great Britain. 2. Great Britain –
Politics and government. I. James, Simon.
JN318.B75   1997
320.941 – dc20   96–24794

ISBN 0–415–11303–2 (hbk)
ISBN 0–415–11304–0 (pbk)

To Kier Hopley

Contents

Acknowledgements

The contents of this book owe much to my conversations with Kier Hopley over innumerable pints of beer in innumerable London pubs. He has kindly allowed me to adapt the section of the introduction on the origins of policy from a seminar he gave to RIPA International, and has made many helpful suggestions for subjects to include and where to find public material on them. Since he is a serving civil servant, I should stress that he has adhered strictly to the requirements of official propriety, and that all opinions and omissions are mine. This book is dedicated to him.

Caroline Wintersgill of Routledge commissioned the book, and has given me much encouragement and guidance. I am indebted to her, and to her ever-helpful colleague James Whiting, who saw it through to publication.

Family, friends and colleagues have shown their usual tolerance towards a writer. I am grateful to Hilary Douglas, who suffered more than most; to Sophie (again); and to Harriet and Alex Ingles for their kind hospitality while I wrote the introduction.

I acknowledge with thanks the permission of the following for permission to reproduce material of which they hold the copyright:

Guardian Newspapers for extracts from the *Guardian*, the *New Statesman* and *New Society*, as individually acknowledged in the text;
the Economist Newspaper Ltd for extracts from two articles acknowledged in the text;
Newspaper Publishing plc for extracts from the *Independent* as acknowledged in the text;
the *Financial Times* for extracts from that newspaper as acknowledged in the text;
Solo Syndication for extracts from the *Daily Mail*, as acknowledged in the text;
Times Newspapers Limited for extracts from *The Times* and the *Sunday Times*, as acknowledged in the text;
Ewan Macnaughton (with particular thanks to Mrs Helen White) and the *Daily Telegraph* for extracts from news articles from the *Sunday Telegraph* and *Daily Telegraph*, as individually acknowledged in the text;

Blackwell Publishers for an extract from *Who Are the Policy-makers* by Sir Edward Playfair;

Reed Consumer Books for extracts from *Inside the Think-Tank* by Tessa Blackstone and William Plowden;

David Higham Associates for extracts from *The Castle Diaries 1964–70*;

the BBC and the Rt Hon. J. Enoch Powell for extracts from *Whitehall and Beyond*;

the BBC, David Dimbleby and Sir John Hoskyns for extracts from *David Dimbleby in Conversation with Sir John Hoskyns*;

the Public Records Office for extracts from the minutes of the Home Affairs Committee of the Cabinet (Crown copyright);

Public Policy and Administration for an extract from *Some Reflections on Cabinet Government* by the Rt Hon. Edmund Dell;

Curtis Brown Ltd for extracts from Tony Benn's diaries *Office without Power: 1968–72* and *Against the Tide: 1973–76*;

Curtis Brown Ltd and William Plowden for extracts from *The Motor Car in Politics*;

the Local Government Chronicle and Tony Travers for extracts from *Implementing the Council Tax*;

Rodney Brooke, Secretary of the Association of Metropolitan Authorities, for extracts from the Association's Annual Report for 1993;

John Hall of the London Boroughs Association for extracts from *The Parking Story* by David Hurdle and Ian Keating;

Guy Stapleton and the Cabinet Office for extracts from *Beyond the Thin Green Line*;

Sir Jonah Walker-Smith for an extract from *The 1922 Committee* by Sir Derek Walker-Smith, originally printed in *The Times*;

Sir Michael Edwardes for extracts from *Back from the Brink*;

Dr Garret Fitzgerald and Macmillan Publishers for extracts from *All in a Life*;

HMSO for permission to reproduce extracts from the following Crown copyright documents: 'Report of the Committee on Homosexual Offences and Prostitution' (Cmnd 247), 'The Civil Service Code' and 'Questions of Procedure for Ministers'

the Rt Hon. Lord Wakeham for extracts from *Cabinet Government*;

George Cardona for *One Step Ahead of 'Yes Minister'*, originally printed in *The Times*;

the Rt Hon. Edmund Dell for an extract from *Collective Responsibility: Fact, Fiction or Façade*;

the *Political Quarterly* for extracts from *The Genesis of the Race Relations Bill* by Keith Hindell;

the Incorporated Council for Law Reporting for extracts from the judgements of Lord Fraser and Lord Diplock in the GCHQ case;

Butterworths for extracts from Lord Denning's judgement in *Congreve v. the Home Office*.

Introduction

This book is written for A level students and undergraduates studying the making of policy in British central government. It provides a series of case studies of policy making by the civil service, ministers, the cabinet and its committees, parliament, the European Union, pressure groups and the courts. Most case studies are compiled from newspaper coverage, but some are drawn from official documents, academic studies and ministerial diaries.

Surprisingly, this is an unusual venture. Books on central institutions tend to describe them in the abstract, or illustrated only with sketchy examples and a few case studies. This must be dispiriting for students, who presumably study politics because it is a live subject that unfolds before them daily. Yet it can be very difficult to relate the abstractions in textbooks to the untidy reality displayed on the television screen. And, unlike their teachers, students will have a small bank of political memories on which to draw: at the time of writing most undergraduates will have no recollection of political life before Margaret Thatcher, and many A level students will not recall much before John Major. Case studies both bring the study of politics to life and offer students an historical perspective. The studies in this book cover a span from the late 1950s to the early 1990s.

In theory it is a good idea to leave students to dig out case studies for themselves. In practice, sources are fragmentary and their reliability varies; the research resources available, especially to A level students, are limited; and – the biggest barrier – students don't know where to look. The case studies in this book took a year to compile, and some are drawn from pretty esoteric sources.

THEORETICAL PREMISE

This type of book presupposes that the author has some view about the theory of how policy is made, and how the British political system works. There is no shortage of theories on offer, ranging from differing models of rational or incremental behaviour to various forms of organisational dominance. I will not rehearse them here, but students will find a helpful outline of them in chapters 2 and 3 of the reader edited by Greenaway, Smith and Street (see Further Reading, page 15). As they point out, many of these theories are incompatible with one another, and many concentrate on specific aspects of the policy making process: some focus on the political impetus that gives rise to policy change, some on the processing of the decision through central government, others on policy implementation.

The model of policy making on which this book is based could be described as an 'open institutional' approach. It is 'institutional' in the sense that it examines policy mainly in terms of the various actors and institutions who influence its development, and particularly the formal institutions of central government: ministers, the cabinet and its committees, civil servants and parliament. This is a fairly traditional approach, which has the advantage of being easily intelligible to students who tend to start the study of government by looking at institutions. But it sets this approach in the framework of the concept of 'policy communities', which argues that the development of a policy is determined in large part by the existence around it of a grouping of interested actors: parliamentarians, vested interests, pressure groups, local government, the news media and other external influences. And these two combined approaches have to be seen in the overall context of what a computer analyst would call an 'open systems' approach: that is, policy making is not a sealed, secret activity insulated from the rest of society, and it is open to any person or group to try to influence a policy.

That last point, however, needs some qualification. Anybody can attempt to alter government policy, and this book gives two examples of 'outsiders' who succeeded in doing just that: Christopher Bailey, who successfully had his ship repair business excluded from nationalisation legislation (4.b.3) and Andrew Congreve, a London solicitor who successfully challenged the Home Office's policy on television licence fees. But for the most part, if you have not gained acceptance as a member of one of the regular policy communities, it is very difficult for you to get in on policy making. You are not automatically consulted by departments on new developments; you do not have the regular contacts with the department that enable you to feed in new ideas and pick up early warning signals; ministers' and officials' consideration of policy options will not be conditioned by the thought of what your reaction might be. A good example of this exclusion of 'unaccepted' groups was the difficulty of relations between Muslim groups and the Home Office over the law of blasphemy (2.b.4): while these groups obtained access to officials and ministers, they were not plugged into the Home Office's regular policy community in the same way as, say, the police or penal reform groups.

THE POLICY MAKING PROCESS

What is a policy? The working definition adopted in this book is: a course of action which the government has taken a deliberate decision to adopt. This should be distinguished from a government's philosophy. A government comes into office with a certain set of ideas and values – its philosophy – and the government's policies are the practical plans through which that philosophy is translated into practice. So the Labour government came to power in 1974 with the philosophical intent of greater social equality; increasing state pensions (see 2.a.1) was one policy contributing to that aim.

Governments rarely write policy on a clean slate. You have to set out from where you are: the starting point for Fowler's reform of social security was the existing system (2.a.3). Governments also have to work within the framework of society as a whole, with all the restrictions and pressures that this imposes. In particular, this puts policy making at the mercy of external events: a drought, a bus strike, a shortage of skilled engineers, an epidemic of German measles, a run on the pound. As a result, policy making is an untidy business. A policy may be painstakingly constructed over years, or cobbled together in hours. And it is made in different ways on different subjects: the decisive way in which the government devised – and then scrapped – unit fines (5.a.3) contrasts with the bumbling prevarication over the 1964 race relations bill (2.a.2).

None the less, it is possible to chart a 'policy process', the various stages through which a policy will pass as it develops. There are six stages, which are as follows.

A subject becomes an issue

At any one time there are hundreds of subjects under public debate: should cannabis be legalised? should passengers in the back seats of cars be compelled to wear safety belts? should we subsidise opera? But while these may be discussed in pubs and on the radio, only some of these subjects are 'issues' in the policy sense: that is, subjects that are politically live, and which attract the attention of policy makers. Whether a subject is, in this sense, an issue can probably best be gauged by the amount of coverage it gets in parliament and in the news media. It does not have to attract enormous attention: controversy about most issues is carried on through minor coverage in the inside pages of newspapers, or through parliamentary questions. But to be 'an issue', a subject does have to create some ripples in the political world.

Issues come and go: nuclear disarmament was highly controversial in the 1960s, died away in the 1970s, revived in the 1980s, and subsided at the end of that decade. Whether to ban fox hunting is a subject that occasionally flares up, but tends to die away again fairly quickly. On the other hand, Liberty (formerly the National Council for Civil Liberties) has for years fought to overcome general public apathy towards civil liberties issues with little success.

The issue gets on to the policy agenda

At any particular time there exists a policy agenda: those issues on which the government either wants to act or feels compelled to act. Given that policy in

Whitehall is very much based on individual departments, it is probably truer to say that each department maintains its own policy agenda. The pressure groups that cluster round each department spend a lot of time trying to persuade ministers that they ought to accept on to the policy agenda whatever issue the group is concerned with. They are only sometimes successful – look, for example, at the mixed success of environmental groups over recent decades. As a result, the governing party's agenda at any moment takes on only a minority of the issues that may be live at that time.

In the end, whether a matter gets onto the policy agenda depends on a mixture of:

- its intrinsic importance: the industrial implications of British Airways' purchase of a new generation of aircraft were too important to be ignored (3.b.1);
- circumstances: is it in tune with the preoccupations of the department?;
- the extent to which it can attract public or parliamentary support and news coverage, like the Police Federation's campaign for side-handled batons (4.c.1);
- luck.

The government investigates the issue

If the issue does get on to the policy agenda, the department responsible for this area gathers the facts and the views of those active in the field. This usually involves extensive discussion and consultation with the groups and organisations most involved in the issue (the 'policy community' – a concept explained below). The development of government policy towards London's parking problems (2.b.3) is a good example of such consultations. Sometimes this stage of the task is delegated to an outside inquiry, like the Annan Committee on broadcasting (2.b.1). Occasionally it is done in secret, like the 1985 social security review (2.a.3). Since most policy is incremental, building on past policy decisions, the civil servants involved are usually well familiar with the issues, and with the more prominent figures in the policy community.

The government takes a decision

Having gathered the data, officials identify the options and put a paper – a 'submission', in the jargon of Whitehall – to ministers. This is a rather mysterious phase of the process, difficult for the outsider to penetrate. The problem of the 'black box' within which such decisions are made is discussed in more detail below.

Very often a decision will go outside the purview of a single department: the Concorde case study (1.d.2) shows how a decision can cut across departmental boundaries. In case of disagreement, or if the issue is intrinsically controversial, the issue will go to cabinet committee or to the cabinet itself, and there is a fair likelihood of the Prime Minister getting involved. Section 1.d. sets out a variety of case studies examining how policies are thrashed out at that level.

The stage of legislation and legitimisation

Many policy decisions can be taken using ministers' existing powers. But many significant initiatives require legislation, and while the government can usually rely on its majority in the Commons and the forbearance of the Lords, in recent years there have been some notable government defeats in parliament, such as those on the shops bill and proposals to charge for school transport (6.b.2 and 6.c.1).

There can also be a 'legitimisation' stage, when a proposal does not formally require parliamentary approval, but is put to parliament for its views – perhaps on a motion proposed by opponents of the policy. At this point again the government can usually rely on its majority, but there have been cases when opposition from the government's own backbenchers has forced the withdrawal of a policy; for example the sale of British Leyland and the closure of thirty coal mines (6.b.3 and 6.b.4).

There has also been a growing tendency for policy decisions to be challenged in the courts. The development of the process of 'judicial review' allows a policy's opponent to challenge the lawfulness of a decision. It does not allow decisions to be challenged because people simply don't like them: the challenge has to be on the grounds of impropriety or unreasonableness (a point explained in 6.d). But the widespread use of judicial review effectively adds another possible stage to the policy process.

Policy implementation and review

These tend to be two sides of the same coin. There is little in the way of systematic policy evaluation in the British system: departments usually just implement a policy, and then leave it alone unless it seems not to be working. Only when implementation fails is a policy seriously reviewed. Consequently the study of implementation is largely the study of failures, and some of these – the community charge, the unit fines system – are described in Chapter 5. Attempts at radical review of existing policy by the Central Policy Review Staff are illustrated in the same section: its success was, at best, mixed. But when policy is reviewed, the process starts again: any perceived inadequacy of the policy becomes an 'issue', Whitehall starts talks with the policy community, and so forwards. The policy process is linear, but there is a well-established 'feedback loop'.

FOUR DYNAMIC FORCES

Within this working model, there are four main dynamic forces:

- the partisan dynamic – the political direction injected into policy by the governing party;
- the administrative dynamic – embodied in the civil service, responsible for carrying out existing policy and advising on the feasibility of policy changes;
- the public dynamic – the most difficult to define precisely, and taking the form of public opinion, often reflected in parliamentary pressure and media interest;
- the 'interest' dynamic – made up of bodies outside government who have some stake in seeking to influence policy.

The partisan force is embodied principally by ministers, collectively through the cabinet and its committees, and individually as heads of departments with the final authority to decide policy. They give political direction by imposing new policies or altering the course of existing policies. The government's political supporters in parliament and in the country are also part of this partisan force, but their role is much less important. Departments exercise an exceptionally powerful hold on the policy process. As a result, once a politician becomes a minister he or she becomes distanced from political colleagues outside the government. The contribution of parliamentary backbenchers to this 'partisan dynamic' is at best indirect: see for instance the agitation by Conservative backbenchers for Employment Secretary James Prior to introduce tougher laws against secondary strikes (2.a.5). The contribution of the party machine is negligible: while in opposition the party machinery plays a significant part in devising policy initiatives for a return to government, but once the party leaders are back in power, the party's central bureaucracy has virtually no influence on policy.

The administrative dynamic is provided mainly by the civil service. On major issues of policy officials respond to ministerial priorities – introduce a pay policy, privatise this industry – and their duty is to advise on the implementation of policy pledges. That can lead to civil servants arguing the toss with ministers: for example, when Labour ministers decided to introduce security of tenure for tenants of furnished accommodation, officials opposed this on the grounds that it would lead to a drying up of relets. Ministers told them to go ahead anyway, and it was done (3.a.2). (Events in this case proved the officials right.) A more dramatic example of this type of conflict was Tony Benn's conflict with both his own officials and the Prime Minister over his industrial policy (3.c.2).

To that extent the administrative dynamic usually acts as a restraint on the partisan dynamic: the practical caution of officials tempers the ideological enthusiasm of ministers, although ultimately what the minister says goes. This does not mean that officials will always oppose change: for example, they were pleased at Labour ministers' plans in 1974 to nationalise shipbuilding, which they saw as the best way of solving the industry's problems. But officials' support or opposition is based on practical considerations.

On many more technical issues, however, the initiative for change is likely to come from officials. A vast amount of the business of any department consists of administering policies which may not interest ministers very much but which are needed to keep the wheels of daily life turning. When an existing policy is not working properly and requires repair, officials will take the initiative. So regularly officials will put to ministers such thrilling proposals as an updating of building regulations, an improved system for administering agricultural fertiliser grants, or a revision of the law on trespass.

Departments have a very powerful hold on the policy process. Wherever the initiative for a policy comes from, and whatever information and advice is gathered to inform the decision, the actual processing of the decision is firmly in the hands of the civil servants responsible for that area. They will compile the data, identify the options and put a package of advice to the minister. Once the decision is taken, they will co-ordinate its implementation. Naturally, controlling the channels through which policy passes gives officials considerable influence over the policy's content: while they cannot invariably impose their own solution, they will make sure that their concerns and preferred option feature prominently in the advice put to the minister.

This tight grip on policy is exercised principally by the 'policy core' of the civil service: the relatively small number of officials who work in or around Whitehall. The bulk of civil servants work in agencies: semi-independent bodies with responsibility for the executive tasks of government, like running job centres or issuing passports. Their task is to carry out policy rather than to help shape it, although their chief executives must, in practice, offer advice to ministers – for instance, no change to arrangements for paying income support would be made without the advice of the chief executive of the Benefits Agency. Much business is also in the hands of non-departmental public bodies (once known as 'quangos') who often have specific advisory duties – for example, the Social Security Advisory Committee. But this advice always passes through the filter of the civil servants in the department.

The 'public' dynamic is a rather incoherent amalgam of pressures of broader public opinion, usually reflected in parliament and the news media. This can take a variety of forms. Rare but formidable is a sharp revolt of general public opinion against a government policy, like the revulsion against the proposed closure of thirty coal mines (6.b.4) which moved many citizens to action by writing to the press and lobbying their MPs. More common but still pretty hard to deal with is a campaign organised by a pressure group which attracts support from a sizeable section of public opinion, such as the campaign by doctors against their proposed new contracts (1.f.1). Most common is a pressure group campaign which attracts some press attention and parliamentary support but does not necessarily generate public sympathy: for example, the protests from many divorced fathers against the Child Support Agency (5.a.4), which attracted only mixed and rather passive sympathy from the wider public.

The 'interest' policy dynamic comes from what are generally called pressure groups. Here there is a helpful distinction between sectional groups and promotional groups. Sectional groups seek to protect the interests of a particular segment of society: for example the Society of Motor Manufacturers and Traders exists to protect the interests of car makers. Promotional groups try to promote causes for philosophical reasons: for instance the prison reform work of the Howard League for Penal Reform. If you like, sectional groups are selfish and promotional groups are altruistic; but remember that a lot of people depend on the car industry for their living.

The government machine could not ignore pressure groups if it wanted to. If the government, say, ignored the warnings of environmental and conservancy groups and abolished many of the laws protecting endangered species of wildlife, these groups would raise merry hell in the press and would stir up protest in parliament, forcing ministers and officials to pay attention to their objections anyway. In practice, government departments go to exceptional lengths to consult major pressure groups on forthcoming proposals, by consulting them and to some extent involving them in policy making.

Although this consultation makes a virtue of necessity, it also helps Whitehall. Firstly, early consultation acts as a political litmus test: it shows whether a proposal is likely to stir up a row. Secondly, it allows a generalist civil service to draw on the knowledge and expertise of outside interests, particularly on the professional expertise of sectional interest groups whose members are workers in the field: the Department of Health, for example, consulted very closely with the Association of Directors of Social Services when introducing the Children Act of 1989. Thirdly, consultation may help protect the government against judicial review: not only is there an obligation – explicit or implicit – to consult people affected by a policy (see for example the GCHQ case at 6.d.4) but if the government's decision is challenged in the courts, the minister is in a slightly stronger position if he or she can say, 'But we consulted the people affected before taking the decision, and took their views into account.' Consultation, however, also works to the advantage of the pressure groups. As their relationship with the government develops, with frequent meetings between the two sides, the group can seize opportunities to bring its own objectives to the attention of the department and to get these subjects on to the government's policy agenda.

Four particular aspects of the policy making process merit closer examination: the origins of policy; policy communities; the Whitehall 'black box'; and the role of parliament.

THE ORIGINS OF A POLICY

It is helpful to classify the different sources from which a policy may arise.

1   Political sources, in which ministers decide to launch an initiative (as distinct from ministers taking a decision on a matter brought to them by the department or outsiders). The main manifestations of this are:

- *Manifesto commitments*: the simplest and most unarguable kind of initiative, when a party wins an election on a manifesto pledging it to cut or increase taxes, nationalise or privatise an industry, or, as exemplified in this book, to increase retirement pensions (2.a.1).
- *Proposals from party working groups*: British political parties are poorly funded and have meagre research capacities. A lot of worthy if unglamorous work is done behind the scenes by unpaid advisers – often academics, local government luminaries or business people – sympathetic to the party. Sometimes their work feeds directly into the manifesto: in the 1960s the Conservatives in opposition set up a network of policy groups whose work was translated through the manifesto straight into legislation. More often a party enters into a manifesto commitment without properly working out what it entails, and the new government has to turn to the research work of a party group to flesh it out. The development of the 1964 race relations bill (2.a.2) illustrates this.
- *Individual ministerial preference*: a new minister coming to a department in the middle of a government's term of office can create the impetus for change. One example, examined in 2.a.5, is the replacement of the moderate James Prior by the more radical Norman Tebbit at Employment in 1981. Another good example is the attitude of three successive trade and industry secretaries towards the idea of a levy on blank cassette tapes to compensate tape manufacturers for 'home taping' of records: Norman Tebbit favoured it, but he was replaced by Leon Brittan, who did not. When Brittan resigned, his successor Paul Channon revived the idea; but when Channon went the initiative was dropped again.
- *Mid-term revision by the government of its policies*: inevitably problems arise in the course of a government's life that the election manifesto has not catered for. Two good examples are the Fowler review of social security policy (2.a.3) and the genesis of the community charge (2.a.4).

2   Departmental sources, when civil servants ask ministers to take a decision on an issue. There can be various reasons for this:

- *The 'departmental view'*: a term that describes the combination of ethos, beliefs, received wisdom and bitter experience that any cohesive organisation develops, and which colours the advice that officials will offer their minister. Section 3.c.2 illustrates the scepticism shown by Department of Industry officials in 1974 towards Tony Benn's industrial policy.
- *Cyclical decisions*: some issues require decisions to be taken every year, such as pay increases for public sector workers and public spending allocation.
- *The need for repair*: in the course of administration, civil servants may conclude that outdated provisions must be updated, or that machinery that is not working properly should be overhauled. So periodically the Department of Trade and Industry assembles a package of revisions to commercial law;

some aspect of local government or the Health Service is reorganised; and assorted minor measures come forward on every subject from school crossing patrols to dog licences. Often this leads to a gradual and sometimes over-cautious reaction to problems, such as the government's piecemeal reactions to London's traffic problems in the 1950s (2.b.4).

3   Interest groups have a significant role in initiating some areas of policy. On many subjects there exists what has been termed a 'policy network' in which Whitehall agencies are closely linked to other groupings with an interest in the field who become involved in shaping the policy. See for example the close collaboration between the government and the local authority associations on any development affecting local councils (1.f.2) and the immediate access enjoyed by a powerful professional group like the doctors (1.f.1).

4   International obligations increasingly impinge on government policy. By far the most extensive influence is that of the European Union, whose directives on everything from lawnmower noise to competition policy are binding on the British government (see for example its impact in the field of alcohol duties, 4.a.2). But there are other international constraints: formal alliances like NATO, and informal commitments like the government's agreement not to introduce legislation in contravention of the European Convention on Human Rights.

5   Outside developments: the government was led by technological developments to grapple with the question of a fourth television channel (2.b.1) and had to take an interest in British Airway's aircraft purchasing policy in 1978 because of its impact on British industrial prospects (3.b.1).

6   Force majeure: occasionally some outside event puts ministers in a position where they must take action. For example, new scientific evidence over 'mad cow disease' compelled the government to order the mass slaughter of cattle in 1996.

7   Government-sponsored inquiries are often set up to provide policy advice to the government: see the Annan Inquiry on broadcasting (2.b.1) and the Wolfenden Report on sexual offences (2.b.2).

8   Parliament influences policy in a variety of ways. Occasionally the influence is direct and creative: the promotion of a private member's bill, such as Margaret Thatcher's bill on public access to council meetings (2.b.5) or the report of the Home Affairs Select Committee that brought about the repeal of the 'sus' law (2.b.6). Sometimes it is direct and negative: the Commons' rejection of the 1986 shops bill (6.b.2) and the Lords' refusal to allow charging for school transport (6.c.1). Most commonly, the influence is exercised by bringing pressure on the government to abandon a measure under threat of defeat, such as the sale of British Leyland (6.b.3).

9   The news media exercise influence on policy in two ways. Either they act as a conduit for interest group pressures – the campaign to keep Bart's Hospital open (4.c.2) – or contribute to pressure for a change in policy, notably in the

huge wave of hostile coverage (reflecting public feeling) of the community charge (5.a.1) and the coal mines closure crisis (6.b.4).

Two restraints are also worth noting. The courts, despite the absence of a written constitution, have come increasingly to review and declare invalid government policy and draw limits to ministerial discretion and the royal prerogative (6.d). And public finance is a perennial restraint on government policy: the need to hold down spending was at the root of the Wilson government's conflict over postponing the school-leaving age (3.b.3). It should also be noted that a policy decision can take the form of a decision to do nothing, notably the government's decision to do nothing about the blasphemy laws in the light of the Salman Rushdie *Satanic Verses* affair (2.b.4) or alternatively of reluctance to do anything on a contentious issue until public opinion moves round to accept it, like the Wolfenden Report's recommendations on homosexual offences (2.b.2).

In practice the genesis of a policy tends to lie in a combination of influences. For instance the shops bill saga originated in a Home Office review of a law fallen into disrepair, leading to a committee of inquiry, then to intense pressure group activity exploiting media coverage, culminating in the Commons' rejection of the bill (6.b.2). The row over the Child Support Agency began as a policy review within Whitehall with public expenditure undertones, broke as a major fuss in the media, was taken up in parliament and pursued in depth by a select committee (5.a.4). In all of the examples given below, various influences appear in differing permutations.

POLICY COMMUNITIES

The importance of pressure groups in British politics has been recognised for decades. In 1979, Richardson and Jordan's innovative study *Governing under Pressure* suggested the concept of policy communities to analyse their influence. They argued that around every main area of policy – defence, welfare, criminal justice and so on – there develops a community of interests concerned with the issue: a community dominated by the Whitehall department responsible for the issue, but including a vast range of interested groups and bodies. Rhodes subsequently elaborated this insight, arguing that there is a typology of what he termed 'policy networks': some, for example, based functionally on departments, like transport; others on specific issues that cross departmental boundaries, like local government finance; 'producer networks', like indus-trialists; professional networks like the medical world; and so on.

These two concepts between them certainly provide a helpful framework for understanding the role of pressure groups and Whitehall's crucially important relations with them. Subsequently there has been earnest and sometimes heated debate between British political scientists about how far this insight can be developed and whether it is possible to measures the relative influence of actors within policy communities, and so on. It will suffice for students of this book to grasp the concept of policy communities as explaining a basic truth about the way public policy is shaped. I would argue, however, that in reading the case studies below a helpful distinction can be made between policy communities and issue networks. At the 'macro' level, there exist policy communities, as Richardson and Jordan described them, which encompass a broad area of policy focused upon a particular department or, occasionally, a major cross-departmental function like local government or industry. But within such broad policy communities, at the 'micro' level, distinct issue networks spring up on particular subjects. For example, the policy community surrounding the Home Office comprises a wide constellation of interests: police forces, prison governors, landowners, local councils, local authorities, refugee groups, civil liberties bodies and so on. But on the specific issue of reforming the parole system, officials will deal with a much narrower circle of contacts: mainly the Parole Board, prison governors and the various prison reform pressure groups.

The essential point is that around any Whitehall department there is a cluster of pressure groups, like satellites revolving around a planet. While Whitehall carefully reserves for itself the final word, extensive consultation ensures that the network concerned with any issue has a good opportunity of influencing that policy's development and content. This can lead to the development of a symbiotic relationship between the department and certain major pressure groups. The close link between the Ministry of Agriculture and the National Union of Farmers is a textbook example. Similarly Maurice Kogan's *Politics of Education* (based on interviews with ministers) observed that in the 1960s the Department of Education and Science would make no serious move without first consulting the local education authorities and the teachers' unions. Such close links have come in for a lot of criticism: in particular the Conservatives sharply attacked the close relationship that developed between Labour governments and the trade unions over incomes policy in the 1970s, and that relationship was brusquely curtailed by Mrs Thatcher's government.

Yet Richardson and Jordan, in a follow-up study of pressure groups in 1987, found that the practice of consultation was alive and well. In the local government field, for instance, the 1990s find the policy communities thriving as a consequence of government reforms. Indeed the principle of consultation has actually been further entrenched by the development of judicial review. In recent years one popular ground for challenging a decision in the courts has been 'unfair procedure', and failure to consult interested parties can constitute unfairness (6.d.4).

It is strange. Ministers wield extensive powers, the civil service has a potent policy making capacity and parliament usually approves ministers' proposals. Britain ought to be a model of centralised decision making. Yet few decisions are taken without painstaking consultation beforehand.

INSIDE THE 'BLACK BOX'

Of all the stages in the policy making process, the most impenetrable is the stage at which the crucial decisions are actually taken. This stage, at which civil servants marshal the arguments and advice, and ministers take the final decisions, is a very private one. It is referred to sometimes by students of politics – and frequently by government lobbyists – as the 'black box'. The outputs of policy are usually well publicised; ministers, who make frequent parliamentary statements and employ teams of press officers, go to great lengths to publicise their decisions. Similarly a lot of policy inputs are public. Much information is actually published by the government: for instance, the mass of statistics published by the Central Statistical Office. A lot of the data that feed into policy are published by government-sponsored bodies: committees of inquiry, or national inspectorates. Much information is published by independent sources: commercial and industrial data, or scientific research. Pressure groups, whose views are so important an ingredient in policy making, are normally only too keen to publicise their arguments. And on some issues the framework for discussions is set by a public report, like the Law Commission report on the law of blasphemy (2.b.4).

Within this 'black box', the basic constitutional roles are familiar: ministers set policy aims, officials advise on how to fulfil them, ministers then decide, and officials execute. Civil servants may be apt to argue the toss a bit but, in essence, that is how the system works. So the minister sets out the broad policy objective – for instance, nationalising the shipbuilding industry – and takes the decisions on the main practical issues of implementation: excluding ship repair firms; running the nationalised industry through a board of industrialists rather than direct from the department, and so on. The civil servants provide the strategic analysis of the issues (these are the main problems you will have to address in privatising shipbuilding; this is the international commercial context; these are the organisational problems of the industry); unravel the technical details (what do we do about shipbuilding firms' existing debts? what about their workers' pension rights?); draft the legislation and arrange its passage through parliament; square the financial details with the Treasury; negotiate with owners and unions; and prepare innumerable drafts of the cabinet memoranda, parliamentary statements, press releases and letters that will be needed.

It is impossible to understand policy making in Whitehall without appreciating the volume of detailed work attached to even a minor policy issue. Given the press of business on ministers, the civil servants must handle most of this. As a result, ministers could become marginalised from policy making; but, if recent ministerial diaries are anything to go by, officials are scrupulous to a fault about clearing with ministers any significant document, including parliamentary answers, press notices and letters to MPs – so scrupulous, indeed, that ministers are severely overloaded with work.

The policy community will of course be deeply involved in the policies preoccupying the inhabitants of the black box. Civil servants will turn to it for advice and information, and sound its members out informally on the feasibility of different ideas. Leading pressure groups will visit ministers to put their views. But even these privileged semi-insiders have trouble discerning the process by which policy is being made within the department: what stage it has reached, and what the main participants are thinking. A certain degree of detachment will still be maintained by Whitehall, which remains reluctant to disclose how ministers' minds are moving: which options are being most closely studied and which discarded; the main criteria that are being used in discussion; the wider framework of considerations within which the decision is being taken; and the timetable to which discussions are proceeding.

Here it is worth considering how government lobbyists (both pressure groups and professional 'for hire' lobbyists) go about their work. When they set out to make a case to Whitehall, the main things they try to find out are:

- *The timetable to which a subject is to be handled*: how far have civil servants got in their analysis? When will ministers be taking the crucial decisions?
- *The participants*: is the matter being handled by a junior minister, or by the secretary of state personally? Which team of officials within the department is leading on the work on the issue, and which other teams in the department have an interest? What outsiders are involved, and to what extent?
- *Ministerial preoccupations*: where does the issue fit into ministers' priorities? How interested are they in the issue? Do they see it as part of a wider problem – for example, are they likely to view your campaign to gain help for widget manufacturers as only a small part of the overall problem of assistance for industry?
- *Civil service priorities*: which, although led by ministers' priorities, will not be identical. Officials may perceive an issue to have an intrinsic importance even though it lacks political appeal to ministers, and so bring it to their attention.
- *The cross-departmental interest*: to what extent are other departments, including the Treasury, involved? Is Number Ten showing an interest?
- *The political sensitivity* that Whitehall perceives the issue to have, which will affect the level of ministerial interest, public presentation of the issue, and ministers' vulnerability to pressure from backbenchers.
- *The issue's vulnerability to other considerations*: these could be rational – for example, a decision not to close an uneconomic weapons plant for reasons of national defence – or 'irrational' – in the strict sense of the word – like the decision to bail out the unviable Chrysler car plant at Linwood in 1975 because of the government's fear that closure would fuel support for the Scottish Nationalists.

PARLIAMENT

Where does this leave parliament? It has never governed; it has only restrained and influenced government. Until the late seventeenth century it met only briefly and sporadically, and its efforts focused on rectifying government actions of which it disapproved: 'redress before supply'. Today parliament essentially acts as a brake on governmental actions of which it disapproves: a few case studies of this are examined in 6.b and 6.c. But since parliament now meets for nine months of the year the timescale of restraint is shorter. Given the high speed of communications and the speed with which an issue can become a politically live subject, MPs have an important role in pressing ministers to change government policy because of public or constituency concerns.

Richardson and Jordan argued that MPs had become mere conduits for the views of pressure groups, 'scavengers for issues'. That is a gross exaggeration. There is a trace of truth in it: pressure groups certainly seek to recruit MPs to speak on their behalf in parliament. But to suggest that this is more than a minor part of their role is to ignore their primary duty to their constituents, their attachment to their party, and their independence of thought. The parliamentary pages of any newspaper provide reassuring examples of the independence and bloody-mindedness of many backbench MPs.

Some of the case studies that follow look at the role of specific actors and institutions in policy making; others illustrate the different factors and pressures that shape a policy's evolution.

Overall, however, they are grouped in a way that broadly reflects the different stages of policy evolution described above. Chapter 1 is an introductory section sketching out the roles of the main institutional actors involved. Chapter 2 looks at different ways in which policy originates. Chapter 3 looks at the Whitehall 'black box', and Chapter 4 at the various external influences on policy. Chapter 5 considers implementation and policy review, and Chapter 6 the control exercised by parliament and the courts.

FURTHER READING

There are two good theoretical chapters in J. Greenaway, S. Smith and J. Street, *Deciding Factors in British Politics: A Case Studies Approach* (London: Routledge, 1992). The best full-length study of the policy making process for students is B. Hogwood's *From Crisis to Complacency: Shaping Public Policy in Britain* (Oxford: OUP, 1987).

On policy communities, J. Richardson and A. Jordan's pioneering *Governing under Pressure: The Policy Process in a Post Parliamentary State* (Oxford: Martin Robertson, 1979) probably overstates the role of pressure groups; the same authors' *Government and Pressure Groups in Britain* (Oxford: Clarendon, 1987) puts matters in a slightly better perspective. *Beyond Whitehall and Westminster: The Sub-central Governments of Britain* (London:

Unwin Hyman, 1988) by R. Rhodes gives a sophisticated typology of policy networks.

On the operations of the core executive, see S. James, *British Cabinet Government* (London: Routledge, 1992) and P. Hennessy's *Whitehall* (London: Fontana, rev. ed. 1990).

1 The actors

The first chapter of this book introduces the main participants in Whitehall policy making: the civil service, whose role has come under question in recent years; ministers and the Prime Minister; the cabinet and its committees where policy conflicts are played out; the institutions of the European Union, which have come to influence so greatly policy making in Britain; and the various types of interest and pressure groups that cluster round central government attempting to influence its decisions.

1.a THE CIVIL SERVICE

1.a.1 'The duties of civil servants'

Civil servants' obligation of political impartiality and responsibility to ministers has long been recognised as an element of the British unwritten constitution, but only very recently has the government given it formal standing by entrenching these principles in the new Civil Service Code, published in 1995.

> The constitutional and practical role of the Civil Service is, with integrity, honesty, impartiality and objectivity, to assist the duly constituted Government, of whatever political complexion, in formulating policies of the Government, carrying out decisions of the Government and in administering public services for which the Government is responsible.
>
> Civil servants are servants of the Crown. Constitutionally, the Crown acts on the advice of Minsters and, subject to the provisions of this Code, Civil Servants owe their loyalty to the duly constituted Government.
>
> Civil servants should conduct themselves with integrity, impartiality and honesty. They should give honest and impartial advice to Ministers, without fear or favour, and make all information relevant to a decision available to Ministers. They should not deceive or knowingly mislead Ministers, Parliament or the public.
>
> Civil servants should conduct themselves in such a way as to deserve and retain the confidence of Ministers and to be able to establish the same

relationship with those whom they may be required to serve in some future Administration. They should comply with restrictions on their political activities. The conduct of civil servants should be such that Ministers and potential future Ministers can be sure that confidence can be freely given, and that the Civil Service will conscientiously fulfil its duties and obligations to, and impartially assist, advise and carry out the policies of the duly constituted Government.

Civil Servants should not without authority disclose official information which has been communicated in confidence within Government. . . .

Civil servants should not seek to frustrate the policies, decisions or actions of Government by declining to take, or abstaining from, action which flows from Ministerial decisions. Where a matter cannot be resolved by the procedures set out in paragraphs 11 and 12 above [i.e. reference to superiors within the department, and if necessary appeal to the Civil Service Commissioners] on a basis which the civil servant concerned is able to accept, he or she should either carry out his or her instructions, or resign from the Civil Service. Civil servants should continue to observe their duties of confidentiality after they have left Crown employment.

(*The Civil Service Code*, London: HMSO, 1995,
paragraphs 1, 2, 5, 9, 10 and 13)

1.a.2   'The man of spirit': a permanent secretary disagrees

For many years, however, there has been a current of thought among senior civil servants that their role is more complex and ambiguous than this formulation allows. As long ago as 1964 Sir Edward Playfair, formerly Permanent Secretary of the War Office, cast a quizzical eye over the subject.

The civil servant must present the alternatives but he must come down on one side or the other; otherwise the Minister is left floating. The Minister must be presented with a definite proposal; he may or may not agree with it, but it concentrates the civil servant's mind and his own; it shows for one thing that the proposal has been thought about seriously.

When dealing with the normal kind of Minister of which I am talking, I would be sending in to him a number of files on all kinds of questions, some of them quite small matters, some of them quite big, some a particular aspect of something very big. I am now talking about the daily routine; for the really big issues there would be a lot of sitting round the table, discussion and so forth. I would go in daily and the Minister would go through my pile of files; normally he would agree with them but every so often he would come to one and say: 'No, I do not agree with this at all – I want to phrase it quite differently' or 'I don't want to take this line' or 'I want to do the opposite'. Human instinct on those occasions makes one want to stand up for the views one has expressed, particularly as one has tried to express them fairly definitely; but I always regarded it as my duty to support the Minister and not to supplant him. It was my job to give him every help – because his burden was so heavy that he should be spared all unnecessary disputes. Therefore on those occasions I turned my tongue three times round in my mouth and said to myself: 'Does it matter a damn how this is decided?' If it did then I would say so and argue my case; and, as the Minister knew me to be a man who did not waste arguments, he would always pay attention. I am not concerned with which way the matter was eventually decided, but only with the fact that he would pay attention. But in nine cases out of ten it was a matter of presentation. In others his view depended on his relations with his fellow Ministers, or the matter was trivial and all that mattered was that something should be decided. In those cases, which were the majority, I would not argue but would accept the Minister's view, preferably giving him credit for having seen something which had escaped me, so as to make him feel happy.

That is the way I think a Permanent Secretary should behave – with total subordination and a rather consistent attempt to consider what the Minister really needs. But I think no man of spirit can do this for long and that is one reason among many why I believe, and have urged on successive heads of the Civil Service, that all Permanent Secretaries should be compulsorily retired after five years in the rank; otherwise the mechanism begins to seize up under the strain and they start deteriorating in one way or another. Some people are coming round to my way of thinking; but so far, I am bound to say, I have met with little support, at least among Permanent Secretaries.

(Sir Edward Playfair, 'Who are the Policy-makers?', *Public Administration*, vol. 43, autumn 1965)

1.a.3 'Political objectives and administrative methods': the views of a mandarin

In his BBC Reith Lectures in 1983, Sir Douglas Wass (former joint Head of the Home Civil Service and Permanent Secretary to the Treasury) mused on the issue:

The line which separates the politically committed and publicly responsible Minister from the politically neutral permanent official is drawn at a particularly high level in Britain. In practically no other country is there so little change in the administrative apparatus when a new government takes office. Officials who advise in favour of a particular policy, and devise means of implementing it, cheerfully accept the same responsibilities in regard to the diametrically opposite policy when the government of the day changes. Foreigners find this incomprehensible and wonder how our civil servants can retain the commitment and the dedication they need to do their job in the face of such sharp political shifts in direction. And many of our own citizens ask whether senior civil servants are not all modern equivalents of the Vicar of Bray.

. . . The presumption on which the system operates is that the Civil Service is unswervingly dedicated to the democratic parliamentary process and to the paramountcy of ministers in decision-taking. The professional ethic it has embraced requires it to give unqualified loyalty to its departmental ministers and to seek to the best of its ability to put the government's policies into execution. In advising Ministers it should take their political objectives as given and regard it as its duty to secure those objectives in the most efficient and publicly acceptable way.

. . . But, even granted a large measure of mutual trust, the senior official cannot always escape his own value judgements and preserve intact his neutrality on policy objectives. You will remember my saying that policy objectives are issues for ministerial choice and decision. They are at the heart of politics. But, true as that is, it is sometimes difficult for civil servants to stand back and not seek to influence decisions on those objectives. Long exposure to a problem may have led them to the conclusion that a certain policy course is in some sense 'right' for the country and that any other course is 'wrong'.

This amounts to what one of my predecessors, Lord Bridges, once described as the departmental view: an opinion about policy which is widely shared at official level throughout the whole department. It may be difficult for permanent officials to avoid coming to this sort of conclusion. They are, after all, greatly experienced in policy analysis and evaluation. They are usually highly intelligent people with a strong sense of public service and a commitment to the long-term well-being of the country. These are commendable characteristics, but they carry with them the risk that the political sense of officials may be unduly sharpened and lead them to overstep the boundaries of their proper role. While most civil servants have no difficulty recognising the limits to their authority, many are confronted at some point in their careers with a minister who wishes to do something they consider to be thoroughly inefficient if not perverse. Now a good official will not normally take a single apparently perverse decision by his minister as the final word: he will seek to bring him round to his own way of thinking. Indeed, if his professional conscience drives him to argue for a course of action which – within the framework set by ministers – he believes to be right, it is positively his duty to face any unpopularity he may be courting. A wise minister will respect an official who does this, and realise that an apparently tiresome adviser may be the best safeguard against his own folly.

(Sir Douglas Wass, *Government and the Governed*, BBC Reith
Lectures 1983, London: Routledge & Kegan Paul, 1984)

1.a.4   'Pretty pessimistic, pretty cynical': a critic of the civil service

The early 1980s witnessed an outbreak of sharp criticism of the civil service. From the left Tony Benn accused them of subverting the last Labour government (see 3.a.1); from the right Margaret Thatcher regarded the civil service as a product of the postwar consensus she abhorred. (None of this has prevented ex-ministers of both parties from praising individual civil servants lavishly in their memoirs.) The scepticism, if not outright hostility, of the radical right towards Whitehall found its spokesperson in 1982 when Sir John Hoskyns, who had just resigned after three years as head of Margaret Thatcher's policy unit in Downing Street, warned in a television interview with David Dimbleby that the government's radicalism would be blunted unless it reformed Whitehall.

DIMBLEBY   Did you find that when you came into Downing Street, with a Prime Minister who had radical policies she wanted to pursue, that the Civil Service was actively hostile to the pursuit of those policies?

HOSKYNS   I wouldn't say actively hostile. What I would say – and it's a matter of judgement – is that they were pretty pessimistic, pretty cynical and generally feeling well, you know, this woman'll soon learn; she's never had high office before; she'll soon realise that everything is almost impossible and there isn't much we can do about anything and we'll just have to wait for her to calm down and realise that.

DIMBLEBY   What effect does that attitude have, then?

HOSKYNS   Well it means, obviously, that they're not going to – I'm talking really now about an attitude, I think, very much at the upper levels of the Civil Service; I don't think that's necessarily the attitude at the sort of 30/early 40 year olds – but it does mean, obviously, that they aren't going to motivate their people to really sweat like hell to try and find answers to difficult problems because, deep down, they don't really think there are any.

DIMBLEBY   How did you feel this in reality. I mean, when you were there in Downing Street, trying to make sure that the Thatcher policies were put through. How did you come up against this barrier of the Civil Service?

HOSKYNS   It's difficult to put one's finger on it. What happens is that, at meetings to discuss difficult problems – sometimes on even things as crucial as the Budget, sometimes on legislation – there would be simply people round the table who were saying, you know, we've tried all these things before; or, you know, they tried that in 1973 but it didn't work and they tried, you know, Jenkins tried this in 1968 (or something) and it didn't work; and so there is never the feeling – which I've experienced a lot in business – of excitement; of brain-storming. Producing some sort of half-baked ideas out of which, suddenly, people begin to see that maybe we've got something here; maybe there is a way of doing it. They never got into that mode . . . in terms of organisation, there is no part of the Civil Service which is really set up to take the objectives – that is the over-riding key objectives – of the incoming Government and say we're working out, for you, the detailed strategy for how we're going to get there; which is not a simple business. That can't be done unless there's an organisation whose job it is to do it – and the Cabinet Office is a co-ordinating body, it isn't a goal-seeking body in that way – and it also can't be done unless you can bring into it, first, people with a political commitment to trying to get it done; and, second, a richer mixture of talents and experience.

. . . I'm not really talking about something like the American [system] where, by definition, all the top jobs change. I'm saying that you do need to bring in quite a lot of new people – and I'm talking about really quite large numbers – otherwise it won't make any difference to the culture. Some of them, I think, could, in certain Departments, be in Permanent Secretary positions or in very senior Civil Service positions or, perhaps, working absolutely in tandem with a civil servant who knows exactly how the machinery of that Department runs and the outsider would be working in the innovative policy design area.

DIMBLEBY   These outsiders; what's their role meant to be?

HOSKYNS   It's really, I think, as much as anything, to prevent the Minister feeling so isolated and so lonely that, in the end, he simply does, without question, what his officials tell him; sometimes that might be right, sometimes it'll be wrong. What he's got to have, I think, is some people around him who are politically sympathetic and competent in that field (of transport or whatever it may be) with whom he could really sit down, you know, at the end of the day with a whisky and soda and say, now, how are we doing. If he doesn't have that, then I think he's likely to be just a sort of puppet, really, of the machine. They may not think they are but I think many of them do end up operating rather like that.

DIMBLEBY   There is an old argument – well known to you I'm sure, as well – which is that the Civil Service does act as a kind of ballast in Britain because you have a political system that produces pendulum swings of policy and that the Civil Service by sort of being somewhere in the middle there, at least prevents the extreme, on either side, actually achieving the sort of results that they'd want and it minimises the swing of policy which is one of the curses – people always say – of the way that Britain has been governed. You're not sympathetic to that?

HOSKYNS   Well I don't think that's really a legitimate role. If the country has highly polarised political parties and, therefore, this big swing – which certainly has been the case in the last 10 years although probably not much before that – then, you know, that is a fact of life and that is what is there and that is what people do or don't vote for. You could change that only through constitutional reforms – I happen to be in favour of electoral reform; I don't regard it as a panacea; I do regard it as, perhaps, a very important enabling measure which would make other things possible. But I think that it's quite wrong – I know exactly what you mean – but I think it's wrong to say that the civil servants should have a legitimate role of, so to speak, defining some middle ground (by their own judgement) and then saying – no matter whether it's Mrs Thatcher going that way or Tony Benn going that way – we've decided that this is really what is best for Britain. That is quite wrong. That is not an apolitical position, is it? They are then political.

(from 'David Dimbleby in Conversation', BBC1,
7 December 1982)

1.a.5   Should we politicise the civil service?

The civil service hates the idea of politicising senior posts, and it is no surprise that Sir Douglas Wass took the opportunity in his lectures to deploy the arguments against it.

It would lead to the sort of administrative chaos which so often marks a new administration in the United States. It has been my experience to work with the senior members of several American administrations and I have always been struck by the time it takes them to settle into the unfamiliar environment of Washington and to learn the craft of executive government. This is in no way to criticise them. As businessmen or academics they cannot be expected to know how to run a government department any more than a civil servant can be expected to manage an industrial concern without a lot of training and experience. The mechanics, the procedures and methods of government, the constraints of the administrative process, all these things are new to outsiders; and because they are not familiar with them they make mistakes which experienced hands would not. One of the virtues of the British system is that we change governments smoothly, without the violent dislocation which is a feature of the Washington scene. It is the senior Civil Service's job to make sure that the transition takes place without a hitch, and it is to its credit that the record has been so good.

But there is another reason for hesitating before we politicise our top administrative posts, and it is this. The time-horizon over which policy is formulated would become markedly biased towards the short-term. One of the advantages of a permanent cadre of heads of departments is that their very permanence inclines them to take the long view of the problems they are dealing with. They have to live with the consequences of decisions, often for many years. By contrast a minister's average stay in office is no more than about two years, and the political system under which he operates forces him to seek quick returns on anything he does. I saw many examples of ministerial indifference to reforms where the pay-off would have come only after a lengthy interval. Let me illustrate the point with an example. For many years officials in several departments have been concerned about the inefficiencies and misallocations generated by our system of housing finance, with its restrictions, its subsidies, its tax exemptions and so on. This system was originally justified fifty and more years ago by the considerable social benefits (what economists call 'externalities') which come from good housing, compared with the benefits to be derived from alternative ways of spending money. But as time passed, the trade-off between housing and other objectives of policy has changed, and with it the optimal balance of policy. But it has always been difficult to interest politicians in reform because of the slow rate of social pay-off, compared with the short-term political costs of change.

(Sir Douglas Wass, *Government and the Governed*, BBC Reith Lectures 1983, London: Routledge & Kegan Paul, 1984)

1.b   MINISTERS

1.b.1   The minister arrives

One of the reasons that new ministers can find Whitehall life bewildering is that each department has a large volume of ongoing business that requires ministerial attention.

Incoming ministers, particularly just after an election, naturally see their role primarily as implementing the party manifesto. Civil servants make elaborate preparations to implement election promises; but in addition during the month of the election campaign a backlog of continuing business will have built up, and officials also press this on the minister, as James Prior discovered when he became Secretary of State for Agriculture in 1970:

> As soon as I arrived in my office, Basil Engholm [Permanent Secretary] came to meet me and talk over the immediate problems facing the Government. Urgent decisions were needed to tackle an outbreak of brucellosis and there was a scare that rabies had spread to Britain. The necessary meetings were set up, and then Basil left, handing me as he went a huge book which was the Ministry's briefing for the new Minister.
>
> During an election campaign the civil servants in every Department or Ministry prepare two sets of briefs to present to the incoming Minister after the election. One set is prepared for a Conservative Minister, another for a Labour Minister. The briefing provides a detailed analysis of how the Party's relevant manifesto commitments for the Department concerned might best be implemented, the costs involved, and so on. In addition, there is a thorough update on all the key aspects of the Department's work which has to be carried on regardless, whichever Party happens to win the election.
>
> I suspect that many new Ministers, suddenly finding themselves responsible for a Department of State, could be totally overawed by the officials' detailed briefing. Fortunately, in my first Cabinet post I knew my subject as a farmer better than most of my officials and so had few qualms about being too dependent on their advice or being overwhelmed by the volume of work.

(James Prior, *A Balance of Power*, London: Hamish Hamilton, 1986)

1.b.2 A minister's first impressions

To most ministers, their first few days in Whitehall are a culture shock. When in 1964 Labour returned to power after thirteen years in opposition, Richard Crossman became a minister for the first time, as Secretary of State for Housing and Local Government. After the first week he summarised his initial impressions:

> My Minister's room is like a padded cell, and in certain ways I am like a person who is suddenly certified a lunatic and put safely into this great, vast room, cut off from real life and surrounded by male and female trained nurses and attendants. When I am in a good mood they occasionally allow an ordinary human being to come and visit me; but they make sure that I behave right, and that the other person behaves right; and they know how to handle me. Of course, they don't behave quite like nurses because the Civil Service is profoundly deferential – 'Yes, Minister! No, Minister! If you wish it, Minister!' – and combined with this there is a constant preoccupation to ensure that the Minister does what is correct. The Private Secretary's job is to make sure that when the Minister comes into Whitehall he doesn't let the side or himself down and behaves in accordance with the requirements of the institution.
>
> . . . At first I felt like someone in a padded cell, but I must now modify this. In fact, I feel like somebody floating on the most comfortable support. The whole Department is there to support the Minister. Into his in-tray come hour by hour notes with suggestions as to what he should do. Everything is done to sustain him in the line which officials think he should take. But if one is very careful and conscious one is aware that this supporting soft framework of recommendations is the result of a great deal of secret discussion between the civil servants below. There is a constant debate as to how the Minister should be advised or, shall we say, directed and pushed and cajoled into the line required by the Ministry. There is a tremendous esprit de corps in the Ministry and the whole hierarchy is determined to preserve its own policy. Each Ministry has its own departmental policy, and this policy goes on while Ministers come and go. And in this world, though the civil servants have a respect for the Minister, they have a much stronger loyalty to the Ministry. Were the Minister to challenge and direct the Ministry policy there would be no formal tension at first, only quiet resistance – but a great deal of it. I am therefore always on the look-out to see how far my own ideas are getting across, how far they are merely tolerated by the Ministry, and how far the Ministry policies are being imposed on my own mind.
>
> (Richard Crossman, *The Diaries of a Cabinet Minister: Volume I: Minister of Housing 1964–66*, London: Jonathan Cape, 1975)

1.b.3   An ex-minister looks back

After six years and three cabinet posts, Crossman devoted a series of lectures in the United States to the British government system. Here he reflects on a minister's role as a catalyst for change in a department.

May I just list for you the uses of a Minister to a Ministry? There are four functions we have. (1) We have to win the battle in the Cabinet. The Cabinet Minister goes to the Cabinet as the champion of his Department and, therefore, goes supplied with a departmental brief. Where expenditure is concerned, a Department is usually well enough briefed to give him the arguments which the Chancellor is going to use, and the reply to them. (And, no doubt, the Chancellor has been briefed in the same way against him!) He is there to fight the battle of the Department in the absence of the Department.

The Department is at his mercy because no official is allowed to be present at the Cabinet meetings, apart from the Cabinet Secretariat. One of the ways Ministers' reputations are established in Whitehall is through their success or failure in winning victories in the Cabinet. . . .

(2) The Minister is there to present the departmental case to Parliament. Civil servants don't pretend to be expert on handling Parliament. They sit there in their little box, ready to brief us as we answer questions and handle debates. They really rely on the Minister to look after them in Parliament.

(3) Our job is to look after them in the country, to go around opening new buildings and attending banquets, performing in a minor way the jobs which endear our monarchy to the public. This is a Minister's representational role, to represent the Queen on official occasions. And that is very useful to the Ministry – as well as to the party.

(4) Lastly there is decision-taking. There's a whole mass of routine decisions, departmental decisions, decisions which are not to do with politics, and which have to be taken regularly and quickly. Therefore, a Minister who is available to give a decision in twenty-four hours is essential to a Ministry.

. . . The greatest danger for a radical Minister is to get too much going in his Department. Because, you see, Departments are resistant. Departments know that they last and you don't. Departments know that any day you may be moved somewhere else and they can forget you. It does not pay you to order them to change their minds on everything. For one thing, they can't. There's a limit to the quantity of change they can digest.

Select a few, a very few issues, and on those issues be bloody and blunt because, of course, you get no change except by fighting. I know there are people who believe you can achieve things in Whitehall without a battle with your Department. Well, it hasn't been my experience, and a very good thing too. If I want to change something and they have got their own departmental policy, they are bound to say, 'Look, before we are going to change our departmental mind for a temporary Minister, he must show that he really means it. First of all, he must be able to answer all our arguments; secondly, his will-power must be sufficient so that when we refuse to do anything week after week he must notice it, he must send for us he must bully us.' There must be a fight and a triumph.

(Richard Crossman, *Inside View: Three Lectures on Prime Ministerial Government*, London: Jonathan Cape, 1972)

1.b.4   What purpose do ministers serve?

Few politicians seem to step aside momentarily from political life to consider the precise purpose of a minister in a government department. An exception is Enoch Powell. His ministerial career was modest – he is better known for his resignations from office than for his tenure of it – but in 1964 he reflected on his experience, with particular reference to his four years as Minister for Health, in a radio interview with Norman Hunt.

POWELL   There is a good deal of popular misconception, you know, about ministers and policy decisions. I think a large section of the public imagines the competent minister bustling into his office on a Monday morning with a neatly written list of the new policies which he is going to put into force. In real life nearly all policy decisions emerge out of an existing situation. I don't say that the answer is thrust upon you, but the problem and the necessity of taking the decision emerges from life itself, and I would say that this is even true in the extreme instance of a new government moving in after a decisive General Election in which they've defeated their opponents. They would still find most of the decisions they were taking had arisen out of a pre-existing situation.

HUNT   How far in the light of the facts which the civil servants have presented you with can you go outside that range of advice in making your final decision?

POWELL   As far as the facts of life permit. You may for example come to the conclusion that you haven't got enough information or that the information, unintentionally no doubt, is slanted one way. In that case you will seek other information. You may feel that although the information is complete, the deduction which you intend to draw from it, either for reasons of political ideology, personal idiosyncrasy or just because you come to a different view, will not be that of your department. But any wise minister, any competent minister, will not just disagree with his department by crossing out 'yes' and writing 'no' on the papers. If he finds himself in disagreement with the advice which is tendered to him, he will seek to probe the reasons both in his own mind and in the departmental mind, by a process of discussion. It would be a very foolish minister who just overset the advice that he was tendered without having worked back to the constituents of that advice, and having decided that the alternative which he wanted to adopt was soundly based and rationally defensible.

. . . There is a great advantage in being new to a department, and this is why it is important that ministers should not stay too long in departments. The impact of a minister is always greatest (and his value I believe is always greatest) when he comes fresh from outside and can say: 'Good Lord, is that what you've been doing? Well, I'm afraid you won't go on doing that under me.'

HUNT   When he comes fresh from outside like that, does he really know enough about what's happening in the department to be able to be a new broom in that sense against all the very able civil servants who really do know what's best for the department?

POWELL   Well, naturally, you can't make such a remark as that which I have just imagined unless you are going to go on from that to discover the facts. And you will expect the department to explain to you why it is that this is happening and what all the attendant facts are. But any Minister should be coloured in his approach to decisions which have any political flavour or over-tones by the general policy of his government and his party. I don't think there's any difference in that respect between a new government and an old government.

(*Whitehall and Beyond*, London: BBC, 1964)

1.c   THE PRIME MINISTER

1.c.1   'Make your own waves': James Callaghan on the premiership

The job of a departmental minister is fairly easily defined, but that of the Prime Minister is not. James Callaghan, after serving successively as Chancellor, Home Secretary and Foreign Secretary, found life as premier eerily quiet:

For the first day or two while I was making governmental changes there was a constant stream of Ministers coming and going, but once that was complete I sat back and realised I had nothing to do. Ministers were busy with their Departmental work; the telephone did not ring for, generally speaking, people do not telephone the Prime Minister – the Prime Minister telephones them; replies to hundreds of letters of congratulations were being drafted elsewhere; the Cabinet Secretariat was efficiently arranging the meetings of Ministerial committees and my next appointment seemed to be a meeting of the Cabinet in two days' time.

In all my previous Departments private secretaries would have arrived in the room as soon as I set foot in the door, bearing piles of official papers to read and files with urgent problems for immediate decision. For a brief period as I sat in the Cabinet Room I savoured the suspicion that as everyone else was doing the Government's work, I could be the idlest member of the Administration if I was so minded. It was of course an illusion, although I never went to the other extreme and believed that a Prime Minister must be a workaholic. . . .

In my experience the work-load was greater both as Chancellor and as Foreign Secretary. To a large extent the Prime Minister makes his own pace. It is the Prime Minister himself who takes the initiatives, who pokes about where he chooses and creates his own waves. Ideally he should keep enough time to stand back a little from the Cabinet's day-to-day work, to keep in touch with Parliamentary and outside opinion, and to view the scene as a whole, knowing full well that periods of crisis will occur when this will be impossible.

(James Callaghan, *Time and Chance*, London: Collins, 1987)

1.c.2 Two premiers contrasted: James Callaghan and Margaret Thatcher

The extent to which Prime Ministers intervene in the work of departments varies greatly. Michael Edwardes, chairman of the troubled nationalised car manufacturer British Leyland (BL) perceived a great difference between James Callaghan and Margaret Thatcher.

I can think of few people easier to work with than the last Labour Prime Minister. James Callaghan is a relaxed but formidable man. In his quiet way he was persuasive and effective. He was a great delegator, even if some thought he delegated too much. I don't find this criticism compelling, for a Prime Minister paints on a very broad canvas, and how can Ministers operate effectively unless they are given authority to do their jobs supported by broad direction from the Prime Minister and with his ultimate backing? And how can a Prime Minister provide broad direction, if embroiled in detail? . . . I found him firm and decisive, and he never involved himself in minutiae.

While I was not in agreement with the philosophy of the Callaghan Government, I appreciate its very real management qualities. Having worked closely with both Labour and Conservative Governments, I found that we had a more workable relationship with the former. Not because they were easier to persuade – indeed they were at least as tough about providing funds – but rather because we knew where we stood with them. Whereas the present administration is heavily centred on Downing Street, the Callaghan Government was surprisingly decentralised: Ministers seemed to have more delegated authority.

[Margaret Thatcher] was the exact opposite of James Callaghan. Everything of any conceivable political consequence was referred to Number 10 – not only the strategic decisions on funding, but even matters such as the Chairman's remuneration. Moreover, this was no rubber-stamping process. Recommendations on other matters were frequently overturned. Quite apart from the Prime Minister's direct role in this, her general attitude to the sponsoring and spending Departments encouraged the central parts of the

Whitehall machine – such as the Treasury and the Central Policy Review Staff (the Think Tank) – to indulge their penchant for 'second-guessing' the judgements of other departments. I cannot judge whether she was right to delegate authority sparingly to her Ministers – but it certainly tended to undermine their credibility, and turn the already complex process of securing the right decisions from the Government into a fine art.

This was brought home to Edwardes with particular force during the negotiations over BL's 1981 corporate plan, which required a £990 million subvention from central government.

Having agreed the principles with senior Ministers, I was amazed to hear by telephone on Friday evening, 23rd January, that the Prime Minister had got her teeth into the various draft statements which were due to be issued publicly on the 26th January and that she had made extensive changes which once again raised major issues of principle, for she wanted privatisation to have precedence over recovery of the business. . . . It seemed that having decided in the appropriate ministerial Committee to support our funding, the Prime Minister must have separately summoned officials to Number 10, apparently without any collective Ministerial presence, to tell them of the significant changes in the business objectives she wanted them to negotiate with me – changes which in our view would have eroded the authority of the BL Board to carry through the recovery programme. In our view the act of privatising could severely inhibit recovery of the business. At my Saturday afternoon meeting with Sir Peter Carey [Permanent Secretary at the Department of Industry], his great ingenuity at drafting, as well as hours of argument, had to be employed to meet the Prime Minister's wishes as far as possible without undermining the Board's authority. Then we had 24 hours of waiting while the outcome of our discussions was sent out to Chequers for approval.

(Michael Edwardes, *Back from the Brink*, London: Collins, 1983)

1.d   THE CABINET AND ITS COMMITTEES

1.d.1   *Questions of Procedure for Ministers*

In 1992 the government published for the first time *Questions of Procedure for Ministers*, the internal Whitehall handbook which codifies much current constitutional and executive practice. The following extract defines the business that should come to cabinet and its committees, and sets out the purpose of the extensive cabinet committee system that has grown up since the Second World War.

Cabinet and Ministerial Committee business

Cabinet and Ministerial Committee business consists, in the main of –

(i) Questions which significantly engage the collective responsibility of the Government, because they raise major issues of policy or because they are of critical importance to the public.

(ii) Questions on which there is an unresolved argument between Departments.

Matters wholly within the responsibility of a single Minister and which do not significantly engage collective responsibility as defined above need not be brought to the Cabinet or to a Ministerial Committee unless the Minister wishes to have the advice of colleagues. A precise definition of such matters cannot be given; in borderline cases a Minister is advised to seek collective consideration. Questions involving more than one Department should be examined interdepartmentally, before submission to the Cabinet, so that the decisions required may be clearly defined.

Ministerial Committees

The Cabinet is supported by Ministerial Committees which have a two-fold purpose. First they relieve the pressure on the Cabinet itself by settling as much business as possible at a lower level; or failing that, by clarifying the issues and defining the points of disagreement. Second, they support the principle of collective responsibility by ensuring that, even though an important question may never reach the Cabinet itself, the decision will be fully considered and the final judgement will be sufficiently authoritative to ensure that the Government as a whole can be properly expected to accept responsibility for it. When there is a difference between Departments, it should not be referred to the Cabinet until other means of resolving it have been exhausted, including personal correspondence or discussions between the Ministers concerned.

If the Ministerial Committee system is to function effectively, appeals to the Cabinet must clearly be infrequent. Chairmen of Committees are required to exercise their discretion in advising the Prime Minister whether to allow them. The only automatic right of appeal is if Treasury Ministers are unwilling to accept expenditure as a charge on the reserve: otherwise the Prime Minister will entertain appeals to the Cabinet only after consultation with the Chairman of the Committee concerned. Departmental Ministers should normally attend in person meetings of Committees of which they are members or to which they are invited; unless they make it possible for their colleagues to discuss with them personally issues which they consider to be important, they cannot – except where their absence is due to factors outside their control – expect the Prime Minister to allow an appeal against an adverse decision taken in their absence.

(*Questions of Procedure for Ministers*, London: Cabinet Office, 1992, paragraphs 3 to 5)

1.d.2   Ministers in committee: Concorde

As observed in the Introduction, British government is very much departmental. Departments are internally cohesive and flexible: it is fairly easy to clear your lines with colleagues working in the same building, who you know reasonably well. But another department will have different priorities, perhaps a different ethos, and will be marked by the outlook of a different Secretary of State. Consequently co-ordinating policy between departments can be marked by quite severe conflicts.

As a result, in the process of policy making in Whitehall, ministers act primarily as spokespersons for their departments. That is not terribly surprising: in the eyes of the public and parliament, and for that matter in his or her own eyes, a minister is first and foremost 'Secretary of State for X'. Defence Secretaries get little credit for going along to committee meetings and demonstrating a mastery of local government finance or divorce law, but when a defence issue comes up they will be expected to show a grasp of their own subject and defend their territory. This behaviour displays itself particularly in cabinet committee meetings. Churchill observed that the cabinet system could work only if every minister 'fought his corner'. But personal and political considerations come into play as well. Joel Barnett was Chief Secretary to the Treasury, with the unpopular job of keeping the lid on public spending, in the Labour government of 1974–9. His book on Treasury life sketches the inner workings of a committee on the Concorde aircraft project. (It should be noted that at this time Industry and Trade were two separate departments.)

> The Prime Minister had set up a small Cabinet Committee with the Lord Chancellor, Lord Elwyn-Jones, in the chair and including among its members, apart from Tony Benn [Industry Secretary] and myself, Peter Shore, then Secretary of State for Trade, and Sam Silkin, the Attorney-General, who was to deal with the many legal problems arising out of our agreement with the French. Tony wanted to maintain the project and keep open the possibility of building more than the sixteen that were in course of production. I was strongly against even building the sixteen.
>
> I knew I was in for a battle, as Tony and Peter were old political friends and allies in the anti-Common Market campaign. Peter would obviously be reluctant to disagree with Tony if he could help it, though he was among the most impartial of Cabinet Ministers (unlike some others, he could be relied on to make his judgement on the facts). Concorde was produced near Bristol, and Tony [then MP for Bristol South-West] was well aware of the consequences for thousands of his constituents if it were to be scrapped. This is not to say that he did not genuinely feel that the project should continue on its own merits, but I am sure that he would be the first to concede that he was influenced by his constituency affiliation. The battle between us went on for many months, but even Tony, stalwart fighter that he is, had to

concede the central fact that all the rest of the committee had come to accept, notably that nobody other than the British and French actually wanted to buy the thing. Though I failed to stop the Concorde programme altogether, the 'ceiling' of sixteen planes remained firmly in place.

(Joel Barnett, *Inside the Treasury*, London: André Deutsch, 1982)

Here the dynamics of the committee were largely departmental, with the Treasury against the spending, and Industry and Trade both in favour; but the constituency and factional angles added a certain spice. The Prime Minister wisely appointed a neutral chairman. The compromise outcome was no particular surprise, when you consider that the project had been under way for so long, and was effectively a trade-off between political tolerability (Concorde was a prestige project and jobs were at stake) and the need to minimise the financial cost.

1.d.3   Ministers in committee: the community charge

Ministers may be driven mainly by their departmental interests, but are capable of raising their eyes from their parochial concerns when the political stakes are high and they will have to justify a controversial policy to the public and, especially, to their constituents. A good example was the discussion held on 20 May 1985 in E(LF) – the local government finance sub-committee of the economic affairs committee of cabinet – under Margaret Thatcher's chairmanship to discuss proposals from Environment Department ministers to introduce a community charge, to become famous as the 'poll tax'. While the Environment Secretary at the time was Patrick Jenkin, the prime mover behind the policy was his junior minister, Kenneth Baker, who recorded in his memoirs colleagues' reactions at the committee.

Keith Joseph [Education Secretary] supported the whole concept, saying, 'Accountability means paying and we need a system that relies less on heavy-handed intervention.' Nick Ridley [Transport Secretary] questioned whether the uniform business rate was the best tax for the commercial sector. George Younger [Scottish Secretary] asserted yet again that we must do something because of the political pressure in Scotland and was adamant that, 'We must abandon the present rating system.' David Young [Minister without Portfolio], too, was in favour but warned against the tax being too regressive. Norman Fowler [Health and Social Security] said that if we delayed, 'We will be criticised for inaction. Press ahead.' Nick Edwards [Welsh Secretary] made the useful point that, 'We must cushion the North/South divide and must not overdo the transfer of resources.' Grey Gowrie [Arts Minister] said it was a 'great plunge to move away from taxing property and should be done with very great care indeed'. Willie Whitelaw [Leader of the Lords] said that as the charge would carry all the weight of increased expenditure locally, 'It must be capable of fine-tuning and rebates will be necessary.' As a former

Home Secretary he also saw no difficulty in having two registers – one for electors and one for chargepayers.

There were, however, some who were less keen on the community charge. Leon Brittan [Home Secretary] was very cool and tried to defend the 1982 changes which he had introduced as Chief Secretary. This was quite sharply dismissed by the Prime Minister. Peter Rees, as Chief Secretary, questioned the methods of registration and felt that the forecasts of gainers and losers spelt trouble.

The main opponent was Nigel Lawson [Chancellor of the Exchequer], who had submitted a paper from the Treasury which recommended that the Government should 'take over complete responsibility for the financing and some aspects of the management of education'. Keith Joseph opposed this and defended local government's role in education. . . . The Prime Minister finally said to Nigel, 'I can see you are against the proposals. Is that right?' He nodded. Then she said, 'I can't have the Treasury being so negative'. But Nigel just ploughed on with his objections. Finally Margaret said, 'Very well. I will do one study and the Treasury can do its own. Then we can compare them and discuss it again.'

(Kenneth Baker, *The Turbulent Years*,
London: Faber and Faber, 1993)

Three aspects of this meeting are worth noting. Firstly, while some of the ministerial contributions recorded by Baker were inspired by departmental interests (notably the Treasury/Education clash) most were general observations on practical and political issues, drawn from ministers' own experience and practical sense. In that sense the discussion was more a political litmus test than a technical argument. Secondly, although the Treasury is usually a very powerful player in such discussions, on this occasion it was out-gunned by the determination of the Prime Minister to back Environment ministers. Lawson was furiously hostile to the community charge: his paper circulated to the Committee (extensively quoted in his memoirs) attacked the poll tax as 'completely unworkable and politically catastrophic', but his opposition broke on the Prime Minister's determination that the system must change, and his position was in any case weakened because what was under discussion was the tax-raising power of local government, not of the Exchequer. Indeed, if a Chancellor were to be overruled by colleagues on a major point of Exchequer taxation he would either be compelled to resign or be so weakened as to become a lame duck.

The third point is that, although in theory the Chancellor was given the chance to present alternative proposals, in practice the weight of opinion in favour of the community charge expressed at this meeting had decided the issue. His idea for a 'modified property tax', circulated in August 1985, got nowhere: Margaret Thatcher described it in retrospect as having 'most of the defects of the existing system and some more as well', and other colleagues offered no support. A September meeting of E(F) confirmed the principle of the community charge. Thereafter, the argument was about practicalities rather than principles, and Lawson had to make do with the eventual satisfaction, when the tax failed, of saying 'I told you so'.

1.d.4   A cabinet minister on cabinet meetings

Committees, then, are a vital and decisive part of the system. Where does this leave the cabinet? Until the 1980s it served mainly as a court of appeal, to which ministers who had lost at committee could bring their case. Although the weekly cabinet meeting received brief reports on foreign affairs and an outline of next week's parliamentary business, and undoubtedly discussed key events, appeals took up most of its time. Margaret Thatcher, less tolerant of dissent, more or less prohibited appeals, but allowed the cabinet a weekly discussion of home affairs. As a result it reverted rather to the practice of its nineteenth-century forebears: a gathering of political colleagues talking through the main events of the moment, discussing more than deciding.

Lord Wakeham, Leader of the House of Lords and chairman of key cabinet committees under Margaret Thatcher and John Major, described how the system worked in the early 1990s.

> At the top is the Cabinet itself. That includes the full range of policy interests, at home and overseas, and is the forum in which the various parts of Government come together, find out what is going on in other parts of the forest, and develop their collective identity. That is a very important role. I think many commentators who bemoan what they see as the decline of the Cabinet as a decision-taker fail to appreciate its significance as the cement which binds the Government together.
>
> But the Cabinet is large – with 22 members – and is a bit unwieldy for discussing detailed matters. So most policies are settled through more specialised committees, perhaps with a brief report to Cabinet to keep other colleagues abreast of decisions if that is thought appropriate. There are some topics, of course, where all Ministers are involved and there is no option but to take them in full Cabinet. The pre-budget discussions are the obvious example.
>
> . . . On matters [decided by committee] which are of sufficiently wide interest and importance, there would normally be a brief oral report to Cabinet on the following Thursday so that all Cabinet Ministers are aware of the decision and have an opportunity to raise any new points if they wish to do so. On very rare occasions, there will be a full discussion in Cabinet of an issue that has already been considered by a Cabinet committee. In this case, the initial discussion in Cabinet committees serves the purpose of a 'trial run', identifying the main issues and concerns that need to be fully explored in the subsequent Cabinet discussion.
>
> (Lord Wakeham, 'Cabinet Government', *Contemporary Record*,
> 8(3), Winter 1994)

1.e   THE EUROPEAN UNION

1.e.1   Co-ordinating Whitehall policy towards Europe

Membership of the EU has made a huge difference to British government. Domestic law is subservient to EU legislation; regulation by the commission reaches into many spheres of British life, and many ministers and officials spend much time negotiating with the Commission and other EU states. Some idea of the impact on Whitehall life (and a useful insight into the work of the official machine that supports ministerial committees) is given in this article by Guy Stapleton, a civil servant who served in the European Secretariat of the Cabinet Office.

> While every Whitehall Department is responsible for the implementation of EC obligations and formulation of policy in its own field, the range and complexity of Community business and the extent to which this interacts with domestic policies, often across departmental boundaries, pose special problems of coordination in reaching policy decisions. Strategy and tactics have to be blended in a way which provides both long-term consistency and a capacity for rapid response. The Community dimension needs to be given its proper weight in all relevant aspects of home and foreign policy, especially where Community rights and obligations are concerned. Ministers, Departments and Parliament also need to be kept abreast of developments in Brussels, Luxembourg and Strasbourg. The European Secretariat is the core of the Whitehall machinery which exists to make sure these needs are met.
>
> Essentially, it supports the Foreign and Commonwealth Secretary who has the task of overall coordination, under the Cabinet, of British policy towards the Community. It also advises the Lord Privy Seal, as Leader of the House of Commons, and the Lord President in the Lords on the procedures under which Parliament considers Community matters in accordance with recommendations of the Scrutiny Committees. It offers information and advice to Departments on questions of policy coordination affecting the Community. But most of the time of members of the Secretariat is spent as chairmen and secretaries of interdepartmental committees at official level, and in providing the secretariat for discussions of Community affairs between Ministers.
>
> In doing so, they first, with the help of Departments, look ahead over a period of three to four months and try to identify those issues which are going to require collective discussion by Ministers. Then they plan over a period of three weeks, firmly for the first week and more provisionally for the later weeks the items for Cabinet and Cabinet Committees. They talk to Departments to discover the points of difficulty. Then the day before the meeting they provide a handling brief for the Prime Minister or other Ministerial Chairman to help in steering the discussion. This explains the main issues, suggests how the discussion might be handled, and, most important of all, highlights very clearly those matters on which decisions

need to be reached. They attend the meeting, writing all the time in foolscap folio books with ruled lines – there is no truck with modern technology – and within 24 hours circulate the minutes, summarising the discussion only briefly but taking great care to formulate the conclusions as clearly as possible, since they are the basis on which action is taken.

But, of course, a good deal of this coordination work is carried on by officials, with only the more important issues, and those on which agreement cannot be reached, needing to be resolved by Ministers. This is especially true of European Community affairs, where there is an extensive and well-used structure of committees at official level. Ensuring that potential problems are caught in time means keeping in close touch with a wide range of contacts throughout Whitehall, and sometimes calls for a certain amount of cajolery to resolve differences or persuade protagonists to come round the conference table. And a lot of time is spent at that table. I must myself have chaired around 300 meetings during my time in the Secretariat, most being of the official committee on European questions which takes the bulk of European policy issues – and which has the dubious distinction of being the Cabinet Office Committee with the most meetings each year – or of its working groups dealing with legal questions and British staff in the Community, and must have attended at least an equal number of other people's meetings.

Apart from the time you spend in committee, two of the most striking features of life in the Secretariat are the very tight deadlines – a week may be a long time in politics, but twenty-four hours is likely to be all you get in 70 Whitehall – and the enormous range of subjects. A glance at my diary in June and July, for example, shows that in those two months I took meetings dealing with subjects as varied as the protection of workers from noise, extra-territorial jurisdiction, state aids, counterfeit goods, customs duty on aircraft, and origin marking. I see that I also attended meetings on such topics as the internal market, the proposed European research coordination agency, and preparations for the European Council. But other Secretariat meetings I wished I could have attended discussed considerably more intriguing items such as the taxation of firearms and horses and the import of obscene life size rubber dolls!

(Guy Stapleton, 'Beyond the Thin Green Line', *MAFF Bulletin*, October 1985)

1.f PRESSURE GROUPS AND POLICY COMMUNITIES

1.f.1 A professional interest group: the doctors

As the Introduction explained, most departments have particularly close ties with certain pressure groups whose work is closely interrelated with the concerns of the department. The complexity of this relationship was well illustrated by the 1989 conflict between Kenneth Clarke, when Health Secretary, and the general practitioners over the introduction of a new GPs' contract. The department was taking a tough line with a professional group without whose participation, however, the Health Service could not operate; while the doctors were furious but knew that they stood to gain more by negotiation with the department than by mass resignations.

The lights burned late on Thursday in the conference room of Richmond House, the Department of Health's Whitehall headquarters. On one side of the lozenge-shaped table sat leaders of Britain's 32,000 family doctors; down the other sat Kenneth Clarke, the health secretary, his deputy David Mellor and a clutch of civil servants.

At stake was the whole progress of Clarke's attempts to reform the NHS. For weeks some of his most senior cabinet colleagues had been privately questioning his tactical judgement in taking on the doctors at the same time as he was tackling reform in the hospitals. They feared the wrangle with GPs would derail the reform programme.

The anxieties of the cabinet were as nothing compared to those of Tory backbenchers. Under a bombardment of correspondence from furious GPs they were approaching a state of panic.

Thursday's deal marked the culmination of seven years of hard thought and tough talking over the future of the family doctor service. The long haul began when the rapidly-growing budget for GPs came under Treasury scrutiny in the summer of 1982.

The Department of Health and Social Security, as it then was, maintained that the service was 'demand-determined' (everyone who turned up at the surgery was treated) and therefore could not be cash-limited like the hospital service (which was rationed by the waiting lists).

The Treasury disagreed. Sir Geoffrey Howe, then chancellor of the exchequer, told a meeting of the Royal Society of Health in April 1982 that there should be a way to 'limit the cost of the family practitioner service without endangering the standards of care that the services provide'.

Under pressure from the Treasury, the DHSS commissioned Binder Hamlyn, a firm of accountants, to examine the problem. Its report, delivered a year later, was never published. But by the summer of 1984 Clarke, then junior minister of health, was at work on a green paper on the service. Due for publication in the autumn of 1984 it, too, never saw the light of day. Instead, after innumerable revisions, it finally emerged in April 1986 (Primary Health Care – an agenda for discussion) to be followed in November 1987 by a white paper (Promoting Better Health).

Formal negotiations with the BMA on the white paper proposals began in March last year. There have been more than 20 meetings, well over 100 hours of negotiations with 33 papers produced by the department and five by the BMA.

In February of this year, Clarke – by now secretary of state for health – finally ran out of patience. The white paper on the wider NHS reforms, Working for Patients, had just been published and some of its proposals cut across the deal with the GPs. Clarke urgently needed to get the new contract signed and sealed.

Over the heads of the BMA negotiators he wrote to every GP in the country explaining what the new contract involved and threatening to impose it if agreement could not be reached.

The GPs erupted; in packed meetings around the country they gave vent to their opposition; patients were regaled with grim warnings of what the new contracts would mean to them. Nothing like it had been seen since 1966 when the government tried to withhold a GP pay rise and provoked widespread threats of resignation.

The temperature rose as insults flew. A senior BMA figure compared Clarke to Dr Goebbels; Clarke referred in a speech to 'doctors feeling nervously for their wallets'.

But the strength of opposition, and Clarke's need of the BMA's co-operation in implementing the wider NHS reforms, meant a negotiated settlement was essential.

The turning point came on Thursday of last week when the BMA's national conference of GPs backed away from any immediate threat of resignation over the contract. A more conciliatory mood was immediately evident on Clarke's side and the concessions already given to Scottish GPs provided the basis for a new deal.

Over the seven years in which the contract has been under discussion the emphasis has shifted from cutting the cost of the family doctor service to securing better value for money. The aim has been to give more power to the patients both to judge the quality of the service and to control the way in which the money is paid out.

Patients will find it easier to choose and change doctors and a larger element of the GP salaries will depend on the number of patients on their lists.

Doctors' protests that this would mean less time spent with each patient were challenged by Clarke. He wants GPs to hire more nurses and other staff to do the routine work, freeing them to practise the kind of medicine for which they have been expensively trained and for which they are highly paid.

But the doctors won concessions that will help GPs with small lists, especially women wanting to work less than full time, who might otherwise have been forced to give up practice.

The new contract also provides an assortment of carrots and sticks to ensure that doctors devote more time to prevention, with payments for running clinics to help people stop smoking, control their drinking, lose weight and reduce stress. They will be paid extra if they achieve certain targets for vaccinating children and screening women for cervical cancer, but will lose if they don't.

They will also be paid more for doing minor operations in the surgery, taking the pressure off local hospitals, but less if they contract night calls out to agencies rather than doing them themselves.

The BMA believes the new deal has taken 'a lot of the sting of competitiveness' out of the contract which might otherwise have 'put GPs out of business'.

'This is not a climb-down; it's a retreat to a carefully prepared position,' one Tory MP said yesterday. 'These were areas we were always prepared to negotiate on. Clarke has done a pretty good job. And the timing is irrelevant. The Vale result [the government had just lost the Vale of Glamorgan by-election] would have been not much different if we had the deal a few days earlier. And if we had done that the government would have been criticised for being cynical.'

Whitehall sources said Clarke had made significant concessions, but had not given an inch on the principle of his proposals that general practice should become more responsive to patient need and offer better value for money.

(*Sunday Times*, 7 May 1989)

1.f.2   An institutional interest group: the Association of Metropolitan Authorities

Good examples of 'institutionalised' interest groups and their work are the local authority associations, who over the years have built up close links not only with the Department of the Environment, which has responsibility for local government, housing and planning, but also with departments responsible for overseeing other local government services, notably the Department for Education, the Home Office (policing, fire and emergency planning), the Department of Health (social services) and the Department of Transport. The AMA represents urban authorities. These extracts from the AMA's 1993 annual report give some idea of its role, its successes and frustrations, and the technical complexity of much government lobbying.

Housing

The main priority for the year was the Government's Housing and Urban Development Bill and, in particular, its proposal to extend compulsory competitive tendering to housing management. The Association was successful in persuading the Government to restrict the scope of Compulsory Competitive Tendering (CCT) to the landlord activities of local authorities, excluding housing benefit, homelessness assessment and the strategic and enabling role, and in delaying the introduction of CCT from 1995 to 1 April 1996. The Association is also pressing for a framework for CCT which gives adequate room for tenant consultation and tenant involvement in setting service standards and choosing the contractor. The Bill proposed to remove the 'tenants' veto' which would have given tenants the right to prevent the appointment of a contractor they did not want, and together with tenants' organisations across the country, the Association strenuously opposed this attack on tenants' rights, though without success. Negotiations are continuing on the role that tenants will be able to play.

Education

Intense lobbying by the AMA ensured several key victories in the Lords [on the education bill], including ones which gave LEAs a planning role and a duty to provide nursery places for children with special education needs. The Governmnent simply ignored their Lordships and guillotined debate even more in the Commons.

Education Secretary John Patten did climb down, however, over the removal of surplus school places. Last year he demanded LEAs [local education authorities] inform him how they intended to remove surplus places in schools drawn to his attention by the DFE [Department for Education]. AMA led a campaign which demonstrated that the DFE calculations were wrong and that, in any case, it was unwise to remove too many places when there will be an extra 125,000 children in school next year alone. LEAs were encouraged not to respond to the DFE until Mr Patten agreed to meet. Two meetings took place in June with Junior Minister Eric Forth and he has accepted AMA's case for a rethink of procedures.

Europe

The major victory of the year was on the Maastricht Bill when an amendment tabled with the other local authority Associations and the LGIB [Local Government Information Bureau] was carried in the Commons. Elected councillors will now occupy all of the UK places on the new Committee of the Regions, thus giving British local authorities a direct voice in European policy-making. The Associations are now waiting to hear whether the Government accepts the joint nominations submitted. The Committee is scheduled to start work in early 1994.

Social services

Throughout the year the AMA highlighted the fact that community care was seriously underfunded to the tune of £135 million. . . . This only confirmed the widespread view that the Government regards community care as a cost-cutting rationing process which has little to do with consumer choice. The Association said all of this in its evidence to the Commons Select Committee on Health whose report recommended, among other things, that unmet need should be monitored. But the Government – which until now has claimed that community care represents a needs-based approach – now says it can't define need and so cannot monitor when it is unmet.

Planning and economic development

A notable success in the year was the Government's climb-down on forcing local authorities to set up contaminated land registers. The abandoned scheme, contained in 1990 emergency planning legislation, had blighted sites which might not have been contaminated and hurt the local economies of many AMA authorities. There will now be a review of the powers and duties of public authorities for tackling contaminated land, in which the Association will take part.

Police

Government plans to reform police authorities and cut the councils' involvement in how their communities are policed have been condemned on numerous occasions by all three local authority Associations. The White Paper showed the Government had ignored these protests. . . . Accountability to a police authority, of whom two-thirds are locally elected councillors, helps secure local confidence in policing – particularly at difficult times as during the miners' strike. The Home Secretary's plan to appoint the chairman and five others gives him unprecedented power, while leaving the new authorities neither accountable to the local community nor to the Minister. Constitutionally the White Paper is a half-way step to nationalising the policing service – which would leave every element of the criminal justice system in the hands of the Government of the day. This, as the Associations have said, would be very bad for democracy.

(Association of Metropolitan Authorities, *Annual Report*, London: AMA, 1993)

2 Initiating policy

2.a POLICY INITIATED BY THE GOVERNMENT

The Introduction listed the various sources from which policy originates. This chapter offers a selection of case studies: firstly policies originated by the government, then examples of policy originated by external agencies.

2.a.1 The party manifesto: the 1974 pensions pledge

The most obvious mainspring of policy change is the party manifesto. This now plays a large part in general elections: parties go to some length to devise lists of promises that they will execute once in office. This is rather peculiar: in many European countries party manifestos are much vaguer documents, containing more statements of principle than concrete promises; and very few British electors read manifestos before voting. Nor do manifestos have legal force. In 1981 the Court of Appeal ruled that, although the Labour Party had won that year's elections to the Greater London Council with a promise to cut public transport fares, this did not give it carte blanche: the Council had to work within the existing legal framework set down by parliament, and consider properly the financial consequences of the policy.

For all that, the manifesto is a key document; there are those in all parties anxious to hold their leaders to their promises. Labour Party rank and file activists can be quite keen on this: in the 1970s Harold Wilson, under pressure from left-wingers accusing him of backsliding, used to proclaim that 90 per cent of the promises in the 1974 Labour manifesto had been fulfilled. (For the purpose of this bizarre calculation, a promise to retain the pint as a unit of measurement ranked equally with an undertaking to hold a referendum on membership of the European Community.) In the Conservative Party, where the manifesto is devised by the leadership with limited contribution from the rank and file, it is still regarded with some circumspection: Lord Wakeham (who served in the Thatcher and Major cabinets) reckoned that 'the manifesto is a very powerful practical constraint. You depart from it at your peril, and only if the case for doing so will be generally understood and accepted to be overwhelming.'

A party coming into power from opposition will usually have a number of commitments that it will wish to implement immediately, to prove its credentials. When Margaret Thatcher's government took office, for example, it immediately raised police pay and cut taxes. When Labour came to power in February 1974, it did so with a promise to raise old age pensions substantially, from £7.75 to £10 for a single person and from £12.50 to £16 for a married couple. Benefits for widows, the sick and the unemployed would rise in line with this. The estimated cost was £2,000 million.

The minister responsible for pensions was the new Secretary of State for Health and Social Security, the formidable Barbara Castle, who wanted pensions increased as soon as possible. She had already ridden roughshod over her officials' practical objections:

> We had a two-hour mass meeting with officials to discuss the uprating [of pensions and other benefits]. The brief officials had given me said that, with an effort, they could get the increase into payment by 1 September. Brian and I told them that this was politically unacceptable. After a lot of arm-twisting they agreed they might advance the date to 22 July, though they told us there was a lot of discontent among the staff about the pressure of work. They warned that, with such a date, a number of pensioners might get their increases in arrears. Tant pis, was all we said, and they went away a bit dazed. All I have to do now is to get it through Cabinet. I already know the Chancellor is talking about an autumn uprating and Jim [Callaghan] has said that that is all we promised at the election.
>
> (Barbara Castle, *The Castle Diaries 1974–76*, London: Weidenfeld and Nicolson, 1980 (6 March 1974))

Usually the two hurdles that a new policy must surmount are funding from the Treasury and approval by parliament. Sure enough, the Chancellor, Denis Healey, tried at Cabinet to postpone the pensions increase. But he hardly stood a chance given the political stakes.

> [Michael Foot, Employment Secretary] was very helpful, saying he was briefed by his Department to support me because an early date like July would be important for the Social Contract [the government's wage restraint agreement with the trade unions]. Peter Shore [Trade] backed me too. But the best effort came from Bob Mellish [Chief Whip], who said vigorously that his was the sort of point on which we had got to behave politically. There might be – and he hoped there would be – an election at any time. Were we to go into it with the pensioners still not having got their increase? Typically, Shirley [Williams, Prices], Reg Prentice [Education] and Jim [Callaghan, Foreign Secretary] suggested that we might go for 1 September as an intermediate date for the uprating, but Harold [Wilson] clearly was on my side. He suggested that the needs of demand management might change: we might even be faced with an increase in unemployment before too long. There

were three decisive factors: first, the effect on the TUC and the need to win support for the Social Contract; secondly, the possibility of an early election; thirdly, the fact that we might need an autumn Budget to expand demand. At this Roy [Jenkins, Home Secretary] came in to say that, as a former Chancellor, he believed he should support the Chancellor, but he wanted to ask him whether he really stood firm on this. Here Fred [Peart] passed me a note: 'Stand firm, you will win.' And sure enough, to my astonishment, Denis's opposition collapsed. He was prepared to 'concede', adding that he rejected 1 September as a 'soggy compromise'. I could have hugged him! I went away to receive the bewildered congratulations of the Department.

(Castle, *The Castle Diaries* (14 March 1974))

As to the second obstacle, in this case parliament made no objection: given the electoral importance of the measure there was no problem finding space for it in the legislative timetable, and the opposition would not incur the odium of opposing increased pensions. The necessary bill passed all its Commons stages on 10 April and became law shortly afterwards.

2.a.2   The 1964 race relations bill

The pensions uprating was easy: the policy was straightforward, and once the money was agreed Barbara Castle was home and dry. All too often, however, parties in opposition enter light-heartedly into promises without thinking through the practical details. In part this is due to the paucity of their research resources: there is no Department of the Opposition, nor can civil servants be called on to advise on administrative practicality, cost or legal details. Politicians in opposition must rely on the spare-time advice of friendly academics (expert in theory but not necessarily in administrative practice) or the thinly stretched resources of party researchers: usually young, overworked and ill-paid. And manifesto commitments are written primarily with the aim of winning the election: the emphasis is on rhetoric rather than feasibility. There is a certain amount of truth in W. C. Fields's cynical observation: 'Campaign resolutions are nothing more than overgrown New Year's resolutions: they are thrown together at the last minute, with never a thought as to how they may be gracefully broken.'

The consequences showed painfully when Labour won the 1964 election. Despite thirteen years in opposition, a lot of policies were poorly thought out and failed to get off the launching pad. Richard Crossman, who despite having been opposition spokesman on education was unexpectedly made Minister of Housing and Local Government, found himself in charge of a manifesto commitment to introduce rent controls, and discovered that although the Labour Party had committed itself to the policy five years earlier 'there is only one slim series of notes by Michael Stewart [Labour Housing spokesman] on the kind of way to do it on the files. . . . That's all there is. Everything else has to be made up on the spot.'

An equally unedifying episode at this time was the race relations bill, whose genesis is charted in the following article by Keith Hindell. It too was a manifesto promise announced some years earlier. A number of bills to outlaw discrimination had been proposed by Labour MPs in the 1950s, and there had been a certain amount of study of the subject in opposition, but all this work was fragmentary and incoherent.

At the beginning of 1964 the Shadow Cabinet and the Society of Labour Lawyers were both asked by the National Executive Committee to draft proposals for legislation.

Three members of the Shadow Cabinet (Sir Frank Soskice, Douglas Houghton and Gilbert Mitchison) drafted a Bill and a memorandum which Soskice presented to the N.E.C. Study Group on Race Relations in June 1964. The Committee concerned itself mainly with the question of incitement – what was the best way of defining it? what was the best method to use to control it without infringing too much on the rights of free speech? how could the law best catch a major fascist figure and yet not be too irritating to the general public? where was a suitable law whose general principle Parliament had already accepted? After a great deal of careful and erudite thought the committee concluded that the Public Order Act of 1936 should be enlarged to make it illegal to publish a defamatory libel of an individual or a group with the intention of provoking hatred or disorder. . . . [The Committee's draft Bill] deliberately omitted to ban discriminatory leases or to provide for right to civil suit or to include as an additional penalty loss of licence. All of these omissions were made on the grounds that they would have been difficult to enforce.

. . . The Martin Committee [set up by the Society of Labour Lawyers] tried to produce the strongest possible Bill to deal with incitement and discrimination in public places. On incitement it proposed that whoever promoted race hatred would be guilty of a new statutory offence regardless of whether he intended to provoke hatred or violence. Discrimination it dealt with in much the same way as Soskice – i.e., criminal penalties, except that it expanded the coverage to public transport and to all places of public resort maintained by a public authority. . . . The Study Group was not very enthusiastic about either Bill and was most worried about the possible infringements to free speech. It did not come to a decision on their respective merits, but later developments rather suggest that the concept of conciliation aroused some spark of interest. The drafts were passed on to the N.E.C. who took no action. It was the July before a certain election in October and the Labour Party was keeping extremely quiet about anything to do with immigrants.

(Keith Hindell, 'The Genesis of the Race Relations Bill', *Political Quarterly*, 36(4), 1965)

In 1964 Labour won the election and Soskice became Home Secretary. Race relations became a major issue in the Smethwick by-election held at the end of that year, which moved an independent group of lawyers led by Anthony Lester to put forward their own proposals.

Early in 1965, after two previous drafts, the group came to the following conclusions:

1 Britain needed a Statutory Commission to deal with discrimination in employment, housing, public facilities, advertising, education including private schools, insurance and credit, Government departments and bodies receiving Government grants.
2 The first aim of the Commission should be to achieve compliance with the law without formal proceedings but it should have full powers of investigation and subpoena and authority to enforce its decisions through the courts.
3 The Commission should also conduct research on problems of discrimination.

These proposals which were sent to the Home Secretary, the law officers, the Prime Minister and selected contacts in Parliament were by far the most comprehensive and strongest put forward in the whole long genesis of the Bill.

[On 7 April 1965] Sir Frank Soskice published his Race Relations Bill. By and large he had not been convinced by the lobbyists. Discrimination in hotels, public-houses, restaurants, theatres, cinemas, public transport and any place maintained by a public authority was to be a criminal offence punishable with fines up to £100. Prosecutions under this section were only to be undertaken with the authority of the Director of Public Prosecutions. Discriminatory restrictions on sub-letting were made unreasonable and therefore unenforceable. Incitement to race hatred in speech or writing was made illegal, with a penalty of up to £1,000 or two years in prison. Lastly, the scope of the Public Order Act was extended so that it would be illegal to publish threatening or insulting material with intent to provoke a breach of the peace.

The publication of the Bill brought forth a wave of Press criticisms and intensified the behind-the-scenes activity. A number of newspapers echoed CARD [the Campaign Against Racial Discrimination, which supported the Lester proposals] in saying that the Bill did not really tackle the main problems, but none of them openly supported a full-scale Statutory Commission. Most of the critics not already immersed in the subject seized upon the simple notion that conciliation was more appropriate to deal with discrimination than the criminal law. Contrary to Soskice's expectations far fewer showed much concern that the incitement provisions might also be used for censorship.

In the month that elapsed between publication and the Second Reading on 3 May, Soskice decided to scrap his proposal to use the criminal law to deal with discrimination in public places. He began his opening speech in the debate by saying that this Bill was merely part of the Government's overall policy for immigrants and that he might reduce the inflow still further. He said that he had already given thought to proposals for conciliation made by the Opposition and by various pressure groups and by the Press and he showed he was about to yield by saying: 'We will take careful note of what is proposed in that regard in argument in this debate.' It is a phrase that Ministers often use but rarely mean. This time was an exception.

Inevitably, one must ask the question, why did the Home Secretary change his mind at such a late stage in full view and change in a direction with which he ought to have been familiar for some months. The Home Office rationalised it this way to the author. Their spokesman said that it was seen from the beginning that there were two possible ways of dealing with discrimination: one by making it a criminal offence and the other by making it only a civil offence and attempting to use conciliation in the first instance. The arguments in favour of each were finely balanced but in the end the Home Secretary decided in favour of using the criminal law on the grounds that it was more in line with our own legal tradition and it dealt with the offence in a quick and exemplary fashion. . . . When, however, it was seen that most people favoured using the other method of conciliation, the Home Secretary said, in effect, all right, it doesn't matter much either way, let us change to suit the popular feeling; after all it is a new area of legislation and we do not want it to be unpopular right from the start.

Many critics of the Home Office do not believe this explanation. In their view the Home Office is ignorant of foreign practice and did not think seriously about using anything but the criminal law until it was forced to. Whether or not this criticism is justified, the Home Office explanation underplays the activity which went on in Cabinet and Whitehall in April. The Government soon realised that it had sponsored a Bill which pleased no one and as it was feeling the strain of governing with a slim majority of three there were good tactical reasons for bending with the winds of criticism. Moreover, it was very short of parliamentary time and did not wish to risk a protracted battle over an issue that certainly would not win any votes from the electorate and might even lose some.

The whole thing is cloaked in Cabinet secrecy, but one person is known to have played a part – Maurice Foley [junior minister at the Department of Economic Affairs] then newly appointed co-ordinator of policy on immigrants. After he had been bombarded by memoranda and button-holed by the interest groups he became completely convinced that criminal penalties for discrimination were wrong. Such evidence as there is suggests that Soskice was persuaded to change his Bill by a Cabinet committee and on that committee Foley was the most ardent advocate of conciliation.

(Hindell, 'The Genesis of the Race Relations Bill')

Certainly in his memoirs Harold Wilson confirmed that such a committee existed, chaired by Herbert Bowden, the Leader of the Commons, and that

Wilson himself was unhappy with Soskice's handling of immigration (Wilson sacked Soskice the following year).

Despite these changes there were further criticisms at second reading stage, and particularly strong support from Labour backbenchers for conciliation and a statutory commission.

In the three weeks between the Second Reading and the opening of the Committee Stage the Home Secretary drafted amendments to his own Bill. From all sides had come support for the principle of conciliation and this was the major change. On the first part of the Bill, dealing with discrimination in places of public resort, the original remedy under criminal law was removed and a civil remedy was substituted. A national Race Relations Board is to be set up which will appoint and supervise the work of local conciliation committees. The local committees will investigate complaints of discrimination and where appropriate bring about the settlement of differences and induce compliance with the law. In the event of conciliation having no effect the local committee can report to the Board which, if it agrees that a pattern of discrimination exists, reports to the Attorney-General. If he agrees with the Board's judgement he can bring an action for injunction against the person discriminating; the ultimate penalty for defiance of such an injunction being imprisonment for contempt of court.

At first sight it seemed that CARD, Lester and company had got most of what they asked. Conciliation had been substituted for the criminal law but not in the areas where in fact they thought it was really important, namely, housing and employment. In fact, like Soskice himself, some of them felt there were very strong arguments in favour of retaining the criminal law to deal with discrimination in places of public resort – for instance, it was quick acting and an unambiguous statement of the public conscience. Consequently they felt that the advantages of the criminal law method had been lost without getting the full benefits of a properly constituted conciliation method. The Race Relations Board is not to be a Statutory Commission with full powers of investigation, subpoena and initiation of civil proceedings.

(Hindell, 'The Genesis of the Race Relations Bill')

The bill passed in this amended form, but in practice proved too weak and had to be amended in 1968 – although still relying mainly on the civil law.

Hindell is no doubt right in pointing to the hidebound legalism of the Home Office (in those days a department with a very conservative – small c – outlook) as the reason for resorting instinctively to the criminal law. But the root of the problem lay in, first, the failure of the Labour Party in opposition to devise intelligent and workable proposals, despite the availability of good advice from an entourage of intelligent sympathisers, and, second, the failure when in office to pay attention to the intelligent and expert criticisms offered by the impromptu policy community that had sprung up around the issue.

2.a.3   Mid-term innovation: the 1985 social security review

Not all policy can be devised in opposition. During a government's term of office new issues emerge, or long-running problems come to the boil. In such cases the government must carry out its own internal review. This becomes particularly necessary when – as happened in the 1980s – a party remains in government for a long spell, and is deprived of the opportunity that opposition affords of rethinking its ideas and recharging its ideological batteries. The advantage of carrying out this kind of review in office is that the government can call on the expert advice and analysis of Whitehall. Therefore in the mid-1980s, when pressure on public spending caused ministers to cast a cold eye over the the social security and health systems, the government staged its own internal policy reviews. The social security exercise was charted in a detailed 'Insight' piece in the *Sunday Times*:

The Fowler review is a tale of two benefits, Serps and child benefit. [Serps – the state earnings-related pension scheme – is a top-up to the state pension related to recipients' earnings during their working lives.] They have some common characteristics. Both are expensive: child benefit costs £4 billion a year while Serps, though in its infancy, might cost £23 billion by the year 2033. They both go to those who qualify, whether or not they are needy. They both affect millions of people – child benefit is paid to the parents of 12m children while up to 11m pensioners would eventually benefit under Serps.

The difference, at the end of the review, is that Serps is doomed while child benefit remains untouched. Yet for most of the period, the likely outcome was precisely the reverse.

Child benefit was to be reviewed by an inquiry into benefits to young people chaired by Rhodes Boyson, a right-wing maverick and minister at social security. Boyson was personally against child benefit and he had powerful allies. Nigel Lawson saw big potential savings here. More important, the prime minister was on principle against a benefit paid regardless of need. She regards it as a prime case of 'churning', a Downing Street term for paying out a benefit with one hand while, with the other hand, collecting the money to pay for it through taxes from most of the same people. As for the poor, 'her view is that, if young people haven't got enough money, they shouldn't have children,' says one of her advisers.

So she detailed two members of her personal policy unit – John Redwood, its head, and David Willetts, a young radical plucked out of the Treasury – to make sure that child benefit did not survive unscathed. Abolition; taxing the benefit; paying it only to the poor – these were the three options under consideration as the review gathered pace last summer.

But last August the *Sunday Times* revealed the Lawson–Boyson plans and public reaction was immediate and hostile, especially from mothers, who can collect the benefit direct; it does not come via a husband's pay packet. Tory MPs returned from their holidays to an undercurrent of revolt.

. . . In the autumn reshuffle Boyson was moved to Northern Ireland. Fowler decided to take over the chairmanship of the young people's review himself. Redwood and Willetts fought to keep the issue alive but in vain. One day that autumn, a discreet message was conveyed to Fowler from No. 10: on this issue, Redwood and Willetts were no longer speaking for Thatcher. The prime minister's political caution had prevailed.

Fowler was relieved: but child benefit's reprieve placed him in a dilemma. The reviews were supposed to be radical. Yet, as he spent his Christmas poring over the rest of the review, it was clear that, shorn of an attack on child benefit, the likely outcome of the hoped-for historic reform looked anything but dramatic. What was to be done?

. . . On January 2 . . . Fowler sat down with 20 of his most trusted friends and advisers for a 10–day summit to debate the review, and try to resolve Fowler's dilemma.

The documentation for the meeting filled two large carrier bags. But even at this stage, it contained nothing which examined the abolition (as opposed to reform) of Serps.

At first blush, this was a surprising omission. Serps, as we have seen, promised to prove very expensive. Moreover, it ran counter to the Tory philosophy that individuals should provide their private savings for their own retirement – a philosophy strongly argued by Nigel Vinson, a private sector member of the pensions inquiry who was present at Steyning.

The reason why abolishing Serps had not been considered is simple: Fowler himself was publicly committed to keeping it. It had been set up in 1975 with an all-party agreement which ended a decade of partisan dog-fighting. Fowler, then opposition spokesman, went along with it.

Then at the Steyning meeting one of Fowler's advisers suddenly ventured: 'Are we really sure that Serps must stay?' A heated debate followed. Most of Fowler's civil servants argued that it should be retained though changes should be made to cut its more expensive features. Most of Fowler's outside advisers argued it should go altogether. Which way would Fowler jump? According to one observer at Steyning there was a sudden and dramatic conversion. 'One night, Fowler went to bed saying he'd decided not to get rid of it. No one knows who got at him – but next morning he came down and said: "Serps is going to go."'

Fowler admits that he was a late convert to abolishing Serps but says there was nothing arbitrary about his decision. During the review new evidence had emerged which proved that Serps was not affordable. When the scheme was launched in 1975 it had been costed only up to the year 2010; by carrying the calculations forward to 2033 Fowler discovered 3m more pensioners than were allowed for in 1975.

. . . On February 4, the cabinet committee chaired by Thatcher to consider Fowler's proposals met. And, for the first time, Nigel Lawson became involved. It was immediately clear that the chancellor and the social services secretary did not see eye to eye. At this stage the difference was not over Serps or any other particular item. It was over the main purpose of the review. Lawson's aim was substantial cuts in the £40 billion social services budget, Fowler's to simplify and rationalise the system.

From Fowler sympathisers reports of a fearsome battle have emerged. 'The Treasury made it clear they were looking for a large chunk of money – £2 billion to £4 billion' – one minister says. 'Norman reacted with horror, and realised he had a political fight on his hands. It developed into a contest to win round the chairman, and the prime minister.' At one stage the argument became so heated that the whole Fowler operation was threatened. Fowler and his deputy, Tony Newton, refused point blank to accept the Lawson demands. For 10 days in February the cabinet committee stopped all work on the proposals.

The Treasury version of events is, naturally, different. 'This £4 billion has been conjured out of the air and attributed to the diabolical Lawson,' says one close to the chancellor. Once the possibility of saving money on child benefit had gone, he says, the Treasury's ambition was no higher than to keep spending under control.

Nevertheless, it was only after a series of meetings, in which Thatcher acted as referee between Lawson and Fowler, that the cabinet committee restarted its work. Despite her own preference for radical change – she was particularly enthused at the time with a feature of the American system whereby those unemployed for more than six months receive no benefits – she took Fowler's side. Eventually the committee agreed on a package that would yield savings of perhaps £750m a year.

But the worst argument between Lawson and Fowler was still to come. The Fowler review was due to be approved by the full cabinet on Thursday, April 25. The Thursday before, at 10.30pm, Lawson dropped a bombshell – a paper to key cabinet members which attacked the plan to abolish Serps. The Treasury argument went thus: under Fowler's plan, those at present not in occupational pensions would be forced to join a private scheme. Their contributions would attract tax relief. There could be 11m such individuals and the tax relief could total as much as £1.5 billion.

Fowler was furious at Lawson's last-minute intervention, which he saw as an attempt to 'bounce' cabinet into rejecting his pensions package by suggesting that his figures did not add up.

Lawson denies any attempt to bounce cabinet. It is true that the Treasury was late to appreciate the full cost of abolishing Serps. But that, it is claimed, was because Fowler himself had switched horses late. Had Lawson not reacted he would, in effect, have been bounced by Fowler. 'All Nigel did,' says one source, 'was to say: "Well, hell: not only has Fowler not come out with any economies, but he's landed us with having to fund tax relief from 7m to 11m people."'

On the Wednesday before cabinet, after Lawson and Fowler had held a frosty meeting, Sir Kenneth Stowe, Fowler's permanent secretary, telephoned the cabinet secretary, Sir Robert Armstrong, to get Fowler's paper taken off the cabinet agenda. Thatcher agreed.

Next day's papers were full of stories of a cabinet shambles.

But Lawson did not give up. In a series of meetings over the next fortnight, the Serps proposal was modified so that abolition would be phased out more gradually, and nobody retiring this century would be affected. Not only does it save Lawson cash: even Fowler concedes that the resulting package, agreed by a relieved cabinet on May 9, is politically superior. It is an apparently radical measure that does not cause any immediate hardship for any voter – although it is hardly the product of cool and measured consideration.

('Whither Welfare?', *Sunday Times*, 9 June 1985)

2.a.4 Mid-term review: the community charge

At more or less the same time a similar exercise was being carried out by Environment Department ministers to devise a new system of paying for local government services. It differed from the social security review in two interesting ways. First, the policy was evolved in a rather unorthodox way, partly outside the civil service framework, making extensive use of outside advisers. Second, it produced a policy that was to fail: the community charge, alias the poll tax.

Late one evening in March 1985 Kenneth Baker sat in a room, alongside William Waldegrave, high in the north tower of the Department of Environment. Around the table were a handful of young civil servants, a member of Margaret Thatcher's policy unit and Mr Baker's special adviser. They were collectively nearing the day when the abolition of domestic rates would become inevitable.

They were, in fact, re-inventing the wheel – in the form of a poll tax. On Sunday 29 March Mrs Thatcher wanted her ministers to present an alternative to the rates at a Chequers seminar. The small group at the DoE had the task of providing not merely a list of options, but a positive proposal.

Two of those present had produced, on a few A4 sheets, after a long winter of deliberations, the essential principles of what they called a 'resident's charge'. They were Tony Meyer, an assistant secretary at the DoE, and Jill Rutter, a principal on loan from the Treasury – two of the very few people in Whitehall who understood the arcane complexities of local government finance.

They had worked closely alongside Oliver Letwin, a philosophy postgraduate from the Downing Street think-tank. Until the group was established he knew nothing of local council finance, but his job was crucial: he had to distil the essence of the problem for the Prime Minister, his boss. And he had to ensure that the group never strayed from a path she would find politically acceptable.

The group's true leader was Mr Waldegrave, then a lowly junior minister, whose sharp intelligence was held in high esteem by Mrs Thatcher. Having decided to recommend the paper, Mr Baker went round the table asking those present to give their views: no one dissented.

In 1974 Mrs Thatcher had pledged to abolish the rates. As ever, the failure to fulfil her commitment had long rankled. The Tories' 1979 election manifesto shied away: 'Cutting income tax must take priority for the time being over abolition of the domestic rating system.' Nonetheless, Michael Heseltine, her first Secretary of State for the Environment, published a Green Paper which looked kindly on the poll tax. It was an idea last tried in the fourteenth century, when it led to the Peasants' Revolt – but a charge that extended to everyone appealed to Mr Heseltine. When it came to the White Paper of 1981, however, the poll tax won hardly a passing reference. Not a single member of the then Cabinet was willing to argue in its favour.

Mr Heseltine succeeded in expunging any reference to rate abolition from the 1983 manifesto. To him the problem seemed not the injustice of the rates, as the Tory grassroots saw it, but the inflation of council expenditure. The manifesto promised rate-capping – and, at Mrs Thatcher's demand, abolition of the metropolitan councils and the GLC.

It seemed enough, until the Conservative annual conference of autumn 1984. Patrick Jenkin, the new Secretary of State for the Environment, was already politically compromised by GLC victories in the Lords. [The House of Lords had imposed many amendments on the government's controversial bill to abolish the Labour-dominated Greater London Council.] He found the motion from the Tory floor unacceptable in its insistence on rate abolition, and was obliged to promise yet another review. The impossibility of inventing a new policy, through the existing Whitehall machine, while in Government, has been a commonplace of constitutional commentary since Dick Crossman's diaries. Mr Waldegrave was to prove that wrong.

The rubric Mrs Thatcher gave Mr Waldegrave was simple. Find something to replace the rates, which also gives voters the power to hold a lid on spending. As usual, her capacity to analyse the policy options was slender; but her intuition told her absolutely that the local government financial grant system was a nightmare that must be swept away.

Yet Mr Waldegrave's group arrived at the poll tax largely by elimination. He deployed a unique tactic, backing up the tiny team of civil servants with four 'external assessors' including Lord Rothschild, former head of the Downing Street think-tank and Professor Alan Walters, who worked on the details of a local sales tax, which was an initial option alongside local income tax. Chris Foster, of Coopers and Lybrand, the chartered accountants and management consultants, and Richard Jackman of the London School of Economics, added expertise.

The Whitehall establishment had long resisted the poll tax as administratively and politically impractical, or wrong in principle. But Terry Heiser, the new Permanent Secretary running the DoE, was one of a new mandarin breed. He had risen from state education in London's East End, through the clerical ranks, to the very top. He knew which way the wind was blowing, and determined to deliver.

But it was politics which wrought the chemical change, with Scottish revaluation as the catalyst. Powerful ingredients topped up the brew: the Town Hall turmoil of Labour councils' fight against rate-capping was at its height, and Liverpool seemed likely to slide into bankruptcy.

Five days before that all-important Chequers presentation Lord Whitelaw, deputy Prime Minister, and Mr Baker met Scottish Tories at their Council. The impending political disaster of rates revaluation north of the border had been bubbling throughout the working party's time: now it blew, with Conservative councillors warning they were an 'endangered species'.

George Younger, then Secretary of State for Scotland, attended Chequers on 29 March, along with Lord Whitelaw, Nick Edwards for Wales, Mr Jenkin, Mr Heiser, and others. At the end of that meeting, the Prime Minister packed off her ministers to concentrate exclusively on the poll tax.

Ever since, it has been suggested that Michael Forsyth, the Scottish Tory, invented the poll tax. Or that it was born from a pamphlet by Donald Mason, published by the right-wing Adam Smith Institute. Neither is true. In the words of one Cabinet minister: 'Scottish revaluation turned the poll tax from the inconceivable into the unavoidable'. The emergent policy entered the Whitehall mainstream for the first time. A team of 50 civil servants was established under Peter Owen, then a high-flying under secretary, now the deputy secretary heading the DoE's housing section.

Those on the inside track had known since February 1985 that it was poll tax or nothing. But not Cabinet Ministers, holed up in their remote departmental outposts. They began skirmishing when the real battle was already lost. In May Leon Brittan, then Home Secretary, put up a brief civil liberties question mark. The Treasury, loath to lose a fiscally efficient property tax, put up more sustained opposition.

But the fundamental objections to the poll tax – that it was unrelated to the ability to pay and potentially difficult to collect – had already been aired with Mrs Thatcher, and she had set them aside in favour of improved financial accountability to voters. By the time the final, crucial meeting arrived – the Cabinet's economic and local government finance committee on 23 September – Mr Jenkin had just been sacked. Ken Baker was the new Secretary of State: he knew what Mrs Thatcher wanted and would not stand in her way.

The Green Paper was completed at the end of 1985, 15 months after the 'sop' to conference. Mr Waldegrave had been appointed Minister for environmental affairs – 'greenery'. . . . Paying for Local Government was published in January 1986. Sadly, no one can remember who thought up the term 'community charge'. For Mr Waldegrave, who had quietly run the

policy-making network in his own unorthodox way, it seemed a triumph of
policy-making while in power.

(Colin Hughes, 'Evolution of the Poll Tax', *Independent*,
2 December 1987)

2.a.5   A change of minister: Prior and Tebbit as Employment Secretaries

A change of secretary of state at a department can herald a major shift of policy,
even if both come from the same party. The most dramatic example of this was
Margaret Thatcher's replacement of James Prior as Employment Secretary by
Norman Tebbit in 1981 – an episode that demonstrates that the Prime Minister's
power to assign a minister to a particular post is as least as important as the
power to include individuals in, or exclude them from, the cabinet. Prior himself
was surprised to be appointed to Employment in 1979, although he had held that
portfolio in opposition.

> Within twenty-four hours of my appointment at the Department of
> Employment I knew exactly what she thought of me from her remark that
> she was determined to have 'someone with backbone' as my junior Minister.
> Neither the Party, the press nor the unions needed a crystal ball to predict that
> I was going to have a rough passage. With Margaret as Prime Minister and
> my views being regarded as well to the left of the Party, there were bound to
> be question marks over my credibility – would I last long on the front bench?
> Was it really worthwhile for the unions to bother to get to know me?
>
> My first great concern on my appointment in May 1979 was to try to
> maintain an effective dialogue with the trade unions. I was haunted by our
> experience towards the end of Ted [Heath]'s Government, when our
> communications with them and their leaders had been quite inadequate.
> . . . I wanted legislation which could work, be seen to work, and would carry
> support, and which would also form the starting point and foundation for
> many years to come. Basically, Margaret recognised that this approach was
> right, although there were times when her instincts and impetuosity would get
> the better of her.
>
> There were, however, advantages in me being seen to hold back the baying
> hordes of the Party's right wing. It was an uncomfortable stance, but made me
> look the reasonable man and therefore difficult for the TUC to attack. It fitted
> in well with my strategy to keep just behind the public's demands for more
> action and to speak quietly but act firmly.

(James Prior, *A Balance of Power*, London: Hamish Hamilton, 1986)

Prior's gradual approach to reform of the law irked right-wingers in the party,
including the Chancellor Sir Geoffrey Howe, but he persuaded the Prime
Minister and cabinet to allow him to introduce a moderately reforming bill in
1979. But in December the House of Lords Judicial Committee, overturning a

judgement of the Court of Appeal, ruled that secondary picketing – that is, picketing by strikers of a workplace not directly affected by a strike – was legal. And in January a strike broke out in the nationalised steel industry, leading to picketing of a private steel company whose management complained to the Prime Minister.

Prior now came under strong right-wing pressure.

The Prime Minister and Mr Prior, Employment Secretary, told leaders of the private steel industry last night that the Government would consider very carefully their call for stronger legislation on strikes.

A six-man delegation from the British Independent Steel Producers' Association expressed considerable concern to Mrs Thatcher and Mr Prior at a Downing Street meeting that the existing law allowed the steel strike to extend into the private sector where managements and unions were not in dispute. The outcome could be more amendments than the Government had planned to the Employment Bill, which is in its committee stage before the Commons.

. . . Mr Prior, whose gradualist approach to trade union reform has been questioned by some ministerial colleagues in the light of the steel strike, defended his policy yesterday, telling the Employment Bill Committee at the Commons: 'We are taking very strong measures on picketing and I do not think the country fully understands how strong these measures are.'

Sir Keith Joseph, Industry Secretary, who is among those in favour of the trade union legislation being as strong as possible, was also present at the hour-long meeting at Downing Street last night. He left most of the talking to Mrs Thatcher and Mr Prior. The Prime Minister told the delegation that the private steel industry's views would be considered very carefully and that she was very anxious and sensitive about the position in which private steel firms found themselves.

Mr Prior, who also expressed willingness to consider the delegation's views very carefully, added a cautious note after the meeting when he said: 'We have to take the whole picture and not look at one individual dispute, however damaging and however wrong that dispute may be. In the case of the individual steel producers it is very wrong.'

(*Daily Telegraph*, 6 February 1980)

On the same day more than fifty Conservative backbenchers tabled a motion complaining of current 'industrial anarchy' and urging the Government 'in accordance with over-whelming popular demand, to introduce legislation to restore industrial equity'. A fortnight later, Prior faced his critics.

Mr Prior, Employment Secretary, last night defended himself against Tory criticism that his trade union reforms are inadequate. He refused to make further changes and described himself as 'a man standing against the stream'.

He told the Commons employment select committee: 'I will not take action to split the country. I will not cause friction and distress.' He also gave a sharp retort to Mr John Gorst, Conservative MP for Barnet, Hendon North, who asked if his proposals did not amount to cowardice and giving in to blackmail for fear of a general strike. 'I don't think there is a question of being afraid, or of blackmail. I am doing what I believe is right.'

He added: 'It might be easier to go for action which would be tougher, but I don't believe it would be right. I sometimes believe there is courage in standing against the stream.'

Although Mr Prior would not admit that the trade union reforms contained in his Employment Bill should be strengthened beyond the changes which he proposed in a consultative document on Tuesday, he did not rule out action on union funds in future. He did not believe there was any necessity for trade union martyrdom in the proposals being put forward.

(*Daily Telegraph*, 21 February 1980)

Prior stood firm against similar pressure from cabinet colleagues despite a hostile speech by Sir Geoffrey Howe, the Chancellor of the Exchequer, complaining that the framework of the law played into the hands of the militants. But the Prime Minister was unhappy.

Margaret was still itching to take immediate steps to crack down on the unions in the steel strike. Patrick Mayhew and I were summoned to see her at ten o'clock on the Monday night before the publication the next day of our consultation document on secondary strikes.

She wanted to rush through Parliament, in a day or two, an immediate, one-clause Bill to outlaw secondary picketing. I have no doubt her advisers were urging her to take a tougher line, and she wished to respond to them. A provision to outlaw secondary picketing was included in the Bill being considered in the Commons, but would not be on the statute book till the summer at the earliest.

I was totally opposed to her suggestion. Rushed legislation almost always turns out to be bad legislation. Plucking one item out of the Bill would look like a panic response, admitting that we should have acted faster from the outset. It would raise the temperature even higher in the steel strike, cause great anger amongst moderate trade unionists and ruin our attempts to continue talks with the unions.

I argued that it would be much wiser to write to Len Murray [General Secretary of the Trades Union Council] reminding him of the TUC's own guidelines issued the winter before, which were being flouted, and also for the Attorney-General, Michael Havers, to make a statement reiterating the existing law which dealt adequately with questions of intimidation and obstruction. In the end Margaret accepted that his would be the more sensible approach.

(Prior, *A Balance of Power*)

Although she accepted Prior's arguments intellectually, Margaret Thatcher's instincts demanded someone more radical in his post. The right wing also kept up the pressure: in April forty-five Conservative backbenchers defied the whip to support an amendment calling for secret ballots before strikes; the government won the vote only because of opposition support. By 1981 Margaret Thatcher felt strong enough to reshuffle the cabinet to promote several right-wingers. Prior was sent off to Northern Ireland, and his place was taken by Norman Tebbit.

> Margaret told me that she wanted me to take over from Jim Prior at Employment – to increase the pace of trades union reform and argue our case on unemployment. . . . The change from Jim Prior to myself was widely seen as significant. To some it was a calculated insult to the unemployed, to others a welcome challenge at last to the abuses of trades union power and the closed shop in particular.
>
> (Norman Tebbit, *Upwardly Mobile*, London: Weidenfeld and Nicolson, 1988)

The press reported the change under such headlines as 'Hardliner Tebbit takes over Employment'. Tebbit's own first pronouncements were guarded, however: in television interviews on the night of his appointment, he told ITN that Margaret Thatcher had not given him a brief to 'get tough with the unions', but perhaps a fresh approach was needed; and he told a BBC interviewer that he was 'a hawk, but not a kamikaze'.

Despite this initial caution, and his great care to ensure that whatever he proposed was workable, Tebbit gave industrial relations policy a firm shove to the right.

> Jim Prior's Green Paper on the next steps in union reform had been published just before I arrived at the Department and it gave me a good basis for my White Paper which I published in late November. I decided it should have three main thrusts – on the closed shop, the tightening of the definition of a 'trades dispute' and the restriction of the unions' immunity from legal actions for damages for unlawful acts.
>
> The first closed shop measures were quite straightforward. I rejected the pressures to 'ban' the closed shop – it simply would not have worked – but I did set out to undermine it. I proposed that compensation for those dismissed as the result of a closed shop should be sharply increased, that the workers concerned could in effect seek compensation from not just their former employer but the union concerned, too, and that unless there had been a recent ballot approving the closed shop any dismissal on grounds of a union non-membership would be construed as unfair. I also decided to make void and unenforceable contracts which specified union-only labour and to remove immunity from those organising industrial action in support of the closed shop.

My solution to the second and third problems was also simple. I decided to bring the immunities of unions into line with those of individuals organising or taking part in industrial action. That would make the unions themselves 'liable in tort' (that is, open to damages) if they committed unlawful acts except in 'pursuit or furtherance' of a 'trades dispute', and for both unlawful secondary picketing and actions to enforce union membership. . . . Together with some other minor provisions it made a much tougher package than I think Jim had in mind.

(Tebbit, *Upwardly Mobile*)

2.b   POLICY INITIATED FROM OUTSIDE

2.b.1   Report of a committee of inquiry: the Annan Committee on Broadcasting

There is a long tradition in British government of setting up inquiries into major problems, usually headed by an eminent impartial outsider. From the government's point of view such inquiries have several advantages. First, they can amass evidence and expertise that the Whitehall machine, staffed mainly by generalists, does not necessarily have the expertise or time to collect. Second, it meets the immediate demands for action: setting up an inquiry is in itself a purposeful act (or at least can be portrayed as such) and demands for further action can be countered with the reasonable answer 'wait for the inquiry to report'. Third, since the government usually finds people of decent calibre to head the inquiry and gives them good administrative support, the quality of inquiry reports is usually high (not all countries can boast the same). Fourth, if the report uncovers an uncomfortable truth or advises unpopular action, such recommendations may be more publicly acceptable coming from an impartial commentator than from a government minister. Fifth, governments can pick and choose which recommendations to adopt and which to turn down.

The traditional vehicle for an inquiry is a committee: either a departmental committee of independent people drawn from 'the great and the good', or a royal commission, which is essentially the same thing but more prestigious and the Chair gets to use a silver inkwell. The report of the Annan Committee is a good example of a study of a subject in which irresistible external forces were compelling politicians to alter their policies. In the mid-1970s it became clear that it would soon become possible for a fourth television channel to start operation in Britain. The BBC had two channels already; the question was whether the fourth channel would, like the third, be openly commercial, or whether it would come under the control of some other independent authority. The Labour government appointed a Committee on the Future of Broadcasting under Lord Annan to review the entire scope of broadcasting policy. It reported in 1977, and most attention focused on the proposals that the fourth channel should come under the aegis of a new 'open broadcasting authority'.

On the recommendations for the running of the fourth TV channel the committee, as reported on Monday, are unanimous. They agree that the best solution is an independent 'Foundation' operating as a publishing outlet for programmes supplied by independent producers, individual ITV companies, and the Open University.

Such a system, they estimate, would cost between £25 million and £40 million annually.

They feel that the greatest temptation in the next 15 years would be simply to leave the BBC and ITV 'duopoly' in possession.

'A great opportunity would be missed if the fourth channel were seen solely in terms of extending the present range of programmes. We see the fourth channel as a challenge to broadcasters.'

(*Daily Telegraph*, 25 March 1977)

The reaction from the broadcasting organisations was predictably self-interested. The BBC welcomed the open broadcasting authority as a rival to the independent companies. The independents did not. The Independent Television Companies' Association (ITCA) said that the open broadcasting scheme appeared to be 'a patchwork, rather than a network' and that the fourth channel recommendation seemed to have been motivated by fears about the effects on programme standards of increased ITV–BBC competition.

There is a tradition of political polarisation on broadcasting issues in Britain. The Labour Party had opposed the Conservatives' introduction of commercial television in the 1950s, preferring to see such a powerful medium confided to a public corporation like the BBC. But amongst Labour ministers in 1977, views were divided.

The Times's Whitehall expert, Peter Hennessy, charted the forward path by which government decision on the report would be made.

The Government is planning to publish a White Paper on the future of broadcasting in December, as a preliminary to legislation early in 1978.

The timetable depends on the Government's survival [by this time it relied on the Liberals for its majority], but whatever happens legislation will be needed before July 31, 1979, when the BBC's charter and the Independent Broadcasting Authority Act both expire.

Mr Rees, Home Secretary, has invited individuals and organisations to submit comments on the Annan report by July 1. The Cabinet's home affairs committee, under his chairmanship, will then consider the shape and content of a White Paper in October and November, and the full Cabinet will decide early in December.

The future of the proposed fourth channel, which Lord Annan recommended should be run by an open broadcasting authority, will be of primary concern to ministers. The independent television companies are expected to mount a powerful lobby for it to be included in their orbit.

(*The Times*, 25 March 1977)

Bernard Donoughue, then head of the Prime Minister's Policy Unit, recalls:

From the beginning the Home Office showed itself (as is often the case with Whitehall departments) to be much closer to the interests of its broadcasting clients than those of central government. Its initial papers . . . rejected the main Annan proposals and stated that the new fourth channel should go to the existing IBA.

(Bernard Donoughue, *Prime Minister*, London:
Jonathan Cape, 1987)

The issue went to a cabinet committee at the start of 1978. Subsequent developments were chronicled in a well-informed *New Statesman* article.

What usually matters about a committee is who is missing from it, rather than who is on it – and the list which the Home Office suggested for the broadcasting committee was exactly a case in point. Certain Cabinet ministers would have to be on such a committee for purely organizational reasons: the Home Secretary himself; the Foreign Secretary, David Owen (because of the BBC's overseas broadcasts); the Secretaries of State for Wales and Scotland (because of regional implications); and the Chief Secretary to the Treasury, Joel Barnett (because of the public-expenditure implications).

Organizationally indispensable they might be. But there was not a minister on the list known to have taken any detailed interest in broadcasting affairs. And the one 'outsider' nominated, Mrs Shirley Williams from Education and Science, was equally innocent of any such connection. Carefully excluded were the names of three ministers known to be interested in broadcasting reform: Tony Benn, Roy Hattersley and William Rodgers.

Had the Prime Minister let this carefully-packed list go through, then the Annan Report would have been effectively sterilized. But on broadcasting – unlike Official Secrets – Mr Callaghan is motivated by something akin to radicalism: specifically, a hearty dislike of the BBC and ITV hierarchies, whom he believes to be guilty of undue arrogance, and cruelty to politicians.

Therefore he rejected the draft White Paper, and, more important, the proposed Cabinet committee list. He brought in Hattersley, Rodgers and Benn to the committee, and put himself in the chair. The committee was now packed in the opposite sense: at its January meeting Mr Rees attempted to defend the conservative paper that his advisers had produced, and in the words of one interested witness 'he got his balls chewed off.'

The membership of the committee now became known – not publicly, but on the grapevine to most broadcasters with an active interest in the fate of the Annan Report. Throughout the spring, its members were energetically lobbied by television producers objecting to the idea that the powers of the

BBC and ITV should be re-established without modification. During March and May the 'radical' side in the committee won most of the arguments. They were better briefed, and they were encouraged by the Prime Minister, who got his personal advisers Bernard Donoughue and David Lipsey to draw up an 'anti-White Paper'.

(*New Statesman*, 21 July 1978)

The upshot – on the fourth channel front, at least – was a decision close to the Annan Committee recommendations, embodied in a white paper in mid-1978.

The Government agrees with the Annan Committee that a different kind of service requires a new authority. Its forthcoming broadcasting legislation will therefore contain proposals for the establishment of an Open Broadcasting Authority (OBA). It will be the new Authority's function to provide and supervise a television service of high quality which informs, educates and entertains, and also fulfils the objectives outlined in the preceding paragraphs – that is, a service in which priority is given to: educational programmes; programmes catering particularly for tastes and interests which are not adequately catered for on the existing three services; and programmes produced outside the existing broadcasting organisations.

(*Financial Times*, 27 July 1978)

The white paper was strongly criticised in the House of Commons by the shadow Home Secretary, William Whitelaw, who when he returned to government reversed the Labour government's intentions in the Broadcasting Act of 1980.

The main feature of the Act was the creation of Channel 4. I suppose there is no decision that I made in my political career that has had more of an impact on the daily life of families in Britain. One of my main reasons for rejecting Lord Annan's proposal for an Open Broadcasting Authority was my feeling that such an authority could never be financially viable. There would have been clear risks in creating an authority directly appointed, and funded to a substantial degree, by Government. I wanted to create a channel that would foster greater, rather than lesser, independence and variety in broadcasting. I was determined to avoid the creation of a new bureaucracy. For that reason we decided to vest responsibility for the channel in the IBA.

This was to be created on a new model. The IBA would have to establish a subsidiary for administering Channel 4 with the duty to obtain programmes and to plan schedules. It would emphatically not, however, become a programme-making organization itself. In order to avoid dominance of the new channel by the ITV companies, I also incorporated in the Act strict safeguards to ensure that significant proportions of Channel 4 programmes would come from independent producers; would appeal to tastes and interests not generally catered for by the existing ITV service; would be experimental and innovative; and would be of an educational nature. These guidelines were important, but I did not want to be too prescriptive. I believed that it must be for the IBA itself to meet effectively the objectives we had set out.

(William Whitelaw, *The Whitelaw Memoirs*,
London: Aurum Press, 1989)

Two subsequent developments are worth noting. The first was that Channel 4 turned out to be much closer to the 'Annan model' than its Conservative creators had intended; an interesting example of implementation quite radically changing the course of a policy. Reading between the lines of Whitelaw's memoirs, you grasp the vehemence of the reproaches he faced.

Channel 4 came into being in November 1982. It soon became evident that producers had taken literally our encouragement of the experimental and the innovative. One of my critics said that I had been responsible for 'letting the loonies on the air'. But all new organizations have to test the bounds of what is open to them and to find their feet in action. In the event, Jeremy Isaacs and his team were seen to have done an outstanding job. The diversity of programmes has, in my view, greatly enriched British broadcasting. Today, there are few who dispute that Channel 4 provides a service of the highest quality and has brought a great deal of new talent into broadcasting.

(Whitelaw, *The Whitelaw Memoirs*)

The second development was that the map of broadcasting was transformed in the early 1980s by the arrival of cable television. This time Margaret Thatcher refused to set up an independent inquiry – she regarded them as prevaricating distractions – but instead set up an advisory panel in the Cabinet Office. It, too, led to a framework for development for the new technological medium enshrined in new legislation, only to be overtaken in a matter of years by the advent of satellite television – a good example of the truth that any government is at the mercy of developments in the society that surrounds it, especially technological change.

2.b.2   The politics of prevarication: the government's response to the Wolfenden Report

When such pressures for change are lacking, however, and an inquiry comes up with controversial or decisive recommendations, its findings may be shelved, or not acted on for many years. The 1970s Bullock Report on Industrial Democracy and Williams Report on Obscenity and Film Censorship have never been implemented; the former because its findings divided industry and trade unions; the latter because of a lack of consensus supporting its largely permissive findings.

The Departmental Committee on Homosexual Offences and Prostitution, which reported under Sir John Wolfenden in 1957, is a good example of a set of controversial recommendations that were implemented only after a long delay, when public opinion had gradually come round to accepting them.

Grouping these two very different subjects under the one heading does, in itself, tell us quite a lot about the lack of understanding of such issues at the time, and the then tendency to condemn any personal behaviour that might be seen as 'irregular'.

Given the Wolfenden Committee's traditional membership – doctors, MPs, clergymen, lawyers and other worthies – it may not be surprising that it advocated heavier penalties for offences arising out of prostitution, but it is astonishing that it made the radical recommendation of changing the law so that homosexual behaviour between consenting adults in private would cease to be a criminal offence. The thinking underlying these findings is to be found in two key paragraphs in the report:

> The function of the criminal law . . . as we see it, is to preserve public order and decency, to protect the citizen from what is offensive and injurious, and to provide sufficient safeguards against exploitation and corruption of others . . . .
> It is not, in our view, the function of the law to intervene in the private lives of citizens or to seek to impose any particular pattern of behaviour further than is necessary to carry out the purposes we have outlined. It follows that we do not believe it to be the function of the law to cover all the fields of sexual behaviour. Certain forms of sexual behaviour are regarded by many as sinful, morally wrong or objectionable for reasons of conscience or religious or cultural tradition. But the criminal law does not cover all such actions at the present time; for instance, adultery and fornication are not offences for which a person can be punished by the criminal law. Nor indeed is prostitution as such.
>
> (*Report of the Committee on Homosexual Offences and Prostitution*, Cmnd 247 (London: HMSO), paras 13 and 14)

As far as homosexual conduct was concerned, this led the Committee to a simple conclusion:

> Unless a deliberate attempt is to be made by society acting through the agency of the law to equate the sphere of crime with that of sin, there must remain a realm of private morality and immorality which is, in brief and crude terms, not the law's business. . . . We accordingly recommend that homosexual behaviour between consenting adults in private should no longer be a criminal offence.
>
> (Paras 61 and 62. The Committee defined 'adulthood' as being over the age of 21.)

The Committee did not take the same liberal view towards prostitution, however, because of the nuisance that soliciting on the streets caused to the public. It made two main recommendations. First, the law in England and Wales required the prosecution to prove that the conduct of a prostitute caused 'annoyance' to inhabitants or passengers.

> In our view, both loitering and importuning for the purpose of prostitution are

so self-evidently public nuisances that . . . the law [should] be reformulated so as to eliminate the requirement to establish annoyance.

(Para. 255)

Secondly, the level of fines – a maximum of two pounds – was derisory, even at 1957 price levels, and provided no deterrent.

We accordingly recommend that the maximum penalty for a first offence should be a fine of £10, for a second offence £25, and for a third and subsequent offence three months' imprisonment.

(Para. 275)

The public reaction was very mixed. As Wolfenden recalled:

It is difficult for me, and it must be nearly impossible for anybody else, to realise the to-do that followed. It entirely filled the front pages of Wednesday's evening papers, with VICE in inch-high capitals as the main headline. And Thursday's dailies, in their different styles, gave it more column-inches than any of us had dreamt of. Naturally some of them concentrated on what they could pick out as 'sensational'; but the striking thing was the balanced and responsible nature of the presentation of the actual contents of the report. It was rather different with the editorial comment, which was extensive. Here there came to light the extreme, indeed sometimes violent, differences of opinion which our recommendations provoked. The *Daily Express* called it 'cumbersome nonsense'; the *Daily Telegraph* said that, 'The Committee's findings, though necessarily controversial, are clear, conscientious and courageous'; the *Evening Standard* said that our recommendations on homosexuality were 'bad, retrograde and utterly to be condemned'; the *Daily Mail* called them 'proposals to legalise degradation in our midst'; and so on. Broadly, though not unanimously, the recommendations about 'cleaning up the streets' were approved; but the recommendations about homosexual offences were harder to swallow.

. . . It went on for weeks. The *Daily Mirror* conducted a poll of its readers. Archbishops supported us, correspondence columns thrived, cartoonists had their fun, street-walkers talked to the Press, obscenities were chalked on the pavement outside our house in Reading.

(Lord Wolfenden, *Turning Points*, London: Bodley Head, 1976)

What this hoo-ha made clear was that the issue was not going to go away. Quite apart from the newspapers' natural delight in an official report dealing largely with sex, there was a genuine debate about personal freedom and moral responsibility under way, even if it was being carried on with different degrees of intellectual rigour at different levels. The government simply could not ignore it.

Gradually the almost hysterical uproar died down, and people began to ask what, if anything, the Government was going to do about it. They were not, understandably enough, in a tearing hurry to do anything. The [anti-reformist] view might well represent the attitude of quite a substantial section of grass-roots opinion in the constituencies; and why should any government go out of its way to lose votes by quixotically championing an unpopular minority? (Friends of mine in the Labour Party did not deny that they would have taken the same line if they had been in office.) The whole business became, in its small way, a political hot potato; it was not surprising that they should take a little time to assess its precise temperature. . . . the sapient Permanent Secretary at the Home Office said to me, when he had read the draft of our report, 'Don't expect legislation quickly. In a thing like this, where deep emotions are likely to be aroused, I would guess fourteen years as the average time-lag between recommendations and legislation.'

(Wolfenden, *Turning Points*)

The liberal-minded Home Secretary Rab Butler favoured reforms along the lines recommended by the report. But it soon became clear that there was stiff opposition within the Conservative Party to reforming the law on homosexuality; indeed his junior minister, David Renton, refused to pilot any liberalising bill through the Commons. Butler was not the sort of man to take a public lead on the issue: reform by stealth was more in his line. So he sat back and waited to see how matters would develop. In late 1957 there was a debate in the House of Lords, which compelled the government to take some stance. Butler put the matter to the Home Affairs Committee of the cabinet.

The Home Secretary said that it was impracticable, in the present state of public opinion, to consider action giving effect to the recommendations of that part of the Wolfenden Report which was concerned with homosexual offences. Parliament could be informed that, while the Government would give attention to any views expressed in debate, they saw no prospect of being able to give legislative effect to the recommendations of the Wolfenden Committee on this subject. A somewhat more forthcoming statement might be made in regard to the recommendations relating to prostitution, although there were certain points of difficulty which would need to be examined before legislation deriving from these recommendations could be introduced. Nonetheless, he hoped that it would practicable to legislate on this part of the Report later in the current session. . . . Discussion showed that the Committee were in general agreement with this view.

(Minutes of the Home Affairs Committee, 29 November 1957, CAB 134 (HA(57)26))

The Lord Chancellor duly stonewalled in the debate. But the Lords' discussion of the issue at least ventilated the arguments and emphasised that it was now respectable to talk about such problems. Indeed, the Archbishop of Canterbury, in an obvious reference to the philosophical views underlying the report, declared it a fundamental right to decide one's own moral code. However, it fell well short of the kind of shift in public attitudes that Butler reckoned necessary.

Ever cautious, for the next year he lay low and waited to see how public opinion moved. In October the following year he went back to the committee to report.

> There was no doubt that public opinion was becoming increasingly critical of Government inactivity on the Report and in his view it had now become desirable to introduce a Street Offences bill which would make it an offence for a common prostitute to loiter or solicit in a public place for the purpose of prostitution.
>
> (Minutes of the Home Affairs Committee, 24 October 1958, CAB 134/1972, Public Records Office)

This was approved and announced, and parliament approved with little opposition the Street Offences Act 1959, which greatly increased the fines for soliciting and for living off the earnings of prostitutes. But even that caused Butler problems.

> My position in clearing up this state of affairs was made peculiarly difficult by the fact that I was related to Josephine Butler, the great social reformer who in 1870 had founded the Association for Moral and Social Hygiene of which I was a vice-president. It had been her cardinal principle that in matters of prostitution the woman is not alone responsible and must not be the target of punitive action; the responsibility of the man must be established. I pointed out to the Association that there were provisions in my Bill against pimps, but could not convince them, as the Commissioner of the Metropolitan Police had convinced me, that whereas the police knew and could trace the women who had regular abodes, they simply could not identify the men, who were unknown, transitory and very often from out of town. Alas, the Association for Moral and Social Hygiene called for my resignation from its ranks. I was sorry to have to comply, for I had a great admiration for the saintly and courageous career of Josephine Butler. But I consoled myself with the knowledge that the Act achieved in a very short period exactly what it set out to do – not, of course, to end vice, but to make it no longer a shameful and open nuisance in the life of a great city. Between 16 August, when the Act came into operation, and 31 December 1959 the number of convictions in the metropolitan district for the offence of loitering and soliciting was less than 10 per cent of what it had been in the same period a year earlier. The streets were in fact cleared.
>
> (Lord Butler, *The Art of the Possible*, London: Hamish Hamilton, 1971)

Having burned his hands on the easier of the two issues, Butler was in no hurry to tackle the more awkward of them. He had carefully engineered matters so that the second meeting of the Home Affairs Committee, while not endorsing reform of the law on homosexual offences, had not ruled it out completely either. But in late 1958 there was a debate in the Commons, in which Labour MPs pressed for implementation of the recommendations on homosexual offences. It revealed deeply divided opinions. Sir Harry Linstead, a Conservative MP who had been a member of the Wolfenden Committee, summarised the rational arguments for reform.

There are two courses open to the community, and the question we have to answer is: by which of those two courses is morality better served? The first course is to make no change. If we make no change, we are acquiescing in convicting a hundred men each year and letting half a million or more go scot-free. We are acquiescing in the continuance of a capriciously enforced Act of Parliament. We are acquiescing in deep divergencies in judicial opinion. We are acquiescing in different treatment before the law for the homosexual as compared with other sexual offenders such as adulterers, fornicators, lesbians and so forth. We are maintaining a law which, judged by the ordinary four standards of good law, fails. The alternative choice is to recognise that this is a moral and not a legal question and to let it be dealt with by the social and moral sanctions of public opinion.

(*House of Commons Debates*, 26 November 1958, col. 44)

In contrast James Dance, Conservative MP for Bromsgrove, spoke for many when he voiced an instinctive revulsion against liberalising the law.

I believe that these homosexual practices are not a potential danger but are a present danger to the youth of our country.

I also feel that it is the sentimental psychiatrists, and people who support their sentiments, who increase this danger. There are far too many people looking into the mind of the murderer and not at the agony of mind of the relations of the murdered person. There are far too many people looking into the minds of the Teddy cosh-boys and not into the minds of the old ladies who have been coshed. In exactly the same way, too many people are looking into the mind of the homosexual rather than considering the repugnance which is caused to millions of decent people all over the country. There can be no question that this practice is a social evil and that it undermines the morals of the country.

One only has to look back into history to find that it was the condoning of this sort of offence which led to the downfall of the Roman Empire. I feel that it was the condoning of these offences which led to the fall of Nazi Germany. [Laughter.] Yes, that is perfectly true. I believe that here at home if these offences are allowed to continue unchecked our moral standards will be lowered.

(*House of Commons Debates*, 26 November 1958, col. 437)

The Home Secretary duly delivered an evasive and neutral speech, the gist of which was that he would follow public opinion, not lead it.

An impression has undoubtedly gained ground – which I do not think is fair to the Wolfenden Committee – that the Committee desired to legalise homosexual conduct. That gives a sort of impression that it wished to make it easier. In fact, what the members of the Committee wished to do was to alter the law, not expressly to encourage or legalise such practices, but to remove them, like adultery and other sins, from the realm of the law. In my opinion, education and time are needed to bring people along to understand this point of view. . . . At any rate, what is clear, after taking this time to think it over and to receive all the impressions and consider the perplexities of this problem, is that there is at present a very large section of the population who strongly repudiate homosexual conduct and whose moral sense would be offended by an alteration of the law which would seem to imply approval or tolerance of what they regard as a great social evil. Therefore, the considerations I have indicated satisfy the Government that they would not be justified at present, on the basis of opinions expressed so far, in proposing legislation to carry out the recommendations of the Committee.

(*House of Commons Debates*, 26 November 1958,
cols 369–71 passim)

When in 1960 a private member's motion called for the Wolfenden recommendations on homosexuality to be implemented, Butler delivered another convoluted and evasive speech which deliberately threw up a host of practical objections, some serious, some spurious.

[N]o one who has to legislate or decide on this subject can deny that there is still a very great difference of opinion, and, in my opinion, a very great deal of work still to be done . . . who will assess the public interest, and how will it be assessed? How are we to decide it in legislation? What does 'consenting' mean? That is a very difficult point, to which I saw no answer in the Wolfenden Report. Why, in the case of a man, should the age of consent be 21, while the age of consent in respect of a girl, in certain Acts, is 16? The Wolfenden Committee excluded the Armed Forces, as my hon. Friend the Member for Ashford (Mr Deedes) said. Are we to accept its recommendations to that extent? It is very difficult to carry through this reform if we make that big omission.

Lastly, can someone help me to say how we should define the words 'in private'? I would remind the House that this is a Private Member's Motion; perhaps that is misunderstood outside. When we are discussing legislation these things will have to be precisely answered, but up to date I do not know the answers, and if I can have some help on that this debate will be of some service. . . .

I do not believe that the full case for a change has yet been made, nor am I convinced that we are yet in a position to take a final decision on what the precise nature of the change should be. We need more information and we are trying to get it. We need more time to discuss the very fundamental issues which arise in this matter of the relationship between law and morals and more time to weigh the possible, and necessarily speculative, consequences of modifying that relationship.

(*House of Commons Debates*, 29 June 1960, cols 1490–8 passim)

Or, in plain English, the government would take the line of least resistance by feigning an open mind, throwing up detailed objections to change, and agreeing to reform only if public opinion had swung round to support it. It is a measure of Butler's contorted approach to the matter that he privately encouraged Conservative backbenchers to vote for reform but himself voted against it. The motion calling for the implementation of the Wolfenden reforms was defeated by 99 votes to 213, and the issue was effectively killed for the remainder of the parliament, which lasted until 1964.

Slowly, however, opinion swung round. In 1965 the Earl of Arran persuaded the House of Lords to support reform. Eighteen months later the MP Leo Abse persuaded the Commons to follow suit with the support of the famously liberal Home Secretary Roy Jenkins, but even then the bill that became the Sexual Offences Act 1967 went through as a private member's bill, given debating time in the Commons by the government.

Wolfenden accepted this ten-year delay philosophically.

There can be plenty of argument about whether the law should lead or follow public opinion. It may well be that in matters of international relationships or national economic policy the government of the day should give a lead and bring the public along behind it. But it may also well be that in sensitive matters of private behaviour any government should wait until public opinion is ready for any steps any government might take. Far better to wait a year or two and act with public opinion behind you than to leap in and find yourself out of tune with it. Certainly public opinion, as reflected in Parliament, changed very considerably over those ten years.

(Wolfenden, *Turning Points*)

Even so, it took another twenty-seven years before the law was further amended. Even then after furious public debate, the House of Commons, in a free vote in 1994, agreed to lower the age of consent only to 18 and not, as some wished, to 16.

2.b.3 Incremental tinkering: the motor car in London

Most policies usually unfold over time, developing gradually, impinging by degrees on the mind of a government department until it has to decide what, if anything, to do about it. Although this type of incremental policy evolution is the staple diet of Whitehall, it lacks glamour and there are few studies of such tortoise-paced development. One rare example is William Plowden's story of the impact of the motor car on public policy. As private car ownership grew, traffic congestion worsened. In these extracts Plowden traces the government's gradual introduction of parking meters in the 1950s: a good example of incremental policy development and of the working of a policy community.

The motor car continued to create problems. The most obvious was London traffic congestion, the city's perennial problem in the ages of the motor and the horse alike. . . .

Several central streets were already saturated at rush hours. The Ministry of Transport's London and Home Counties Traffic Advisory Committee [LHCTAC], concerned at what might happen when both cars and petrol were freely available [i.e. when wartime restrictions and rationing were phased out], set up an inquiry of its own in early 1950 to consider what might be done. Although at this period only 5 per cent of those working in London came in by private car or motor cycle, cars already made up nearly a third of traffic in the centre. The Committee made no suggestions at all for trying to limit this proportion, or the total amount of traffic. All its proposals were in fact aimed at making it possible for the largest possible number of people to use their cars in central London. Trying to keep anybody out would be too difficult; it was also questionable 'whether it would be desirable at the present time, after so many years of severely restrictive private motoring, to impose new restrictions on the freedom of movement of private cars in Inner London'.

The Committee's main proposal was for better parking arrangements. Car parks should be built under some squares, while others should be built on land bought partly out of central funds. The charges for using these car parks should be 'nominal', so as to encourage motorists to use them. Once more or less adequate provision had been made for the long-term parker, an experimental scheme of parking-meters should be tried; any profits from these meters should go to the local authority, to be spent on paying for off-street parking accommodation.

Two years later, the Committee's parking proposals were broadly approved by a special working party set up by the Ministry of Transport. This was a classic 'representative' body, including members from the commercial vehicle and bus operators, the motor trade, the motoring organizations, the police, the LCC [London County Council], the Ministry of Housing and other departments. By now the London traffic situation, like road safety and the roads programme, was becoming a subject of Parliamentary discussion. The kerb space in certain West End streets, 50 per cent full of parked cars in 1951, was 75 per cent full in 1953. There were questions in the House, and occasional adjournment debates.

. . . In a minority report, the representative of the Ministry of Housing, Colin Buchanan, [questioned] the whole principle of subsidizing the long-term parker. Might the answer not be to keep him off the streets? If motorists were unwilling to pay the economic costs of parking, they could use public transport. Local authorities would do better to provide for the short-term parker; private enterprise could meet the long-term demand by putting car parks in new buildings.

But in the early 1950s such views were, as the Traffic Advisory Committee had recognized, politically unacceptable. Governments anxious to take the credit for finally ending the era of austerity could not afford to shackle the motor car, now becoming one of the prime symbols of 'normal' times. Labour Governments wanted to show that they were not the implacable enemy of the middle-class; Tory ones were determined to prove that there was more room for self-expression under the Conservatives. They were encouraged by commentators like the Economist, which in October 1953 urged the Government to stimulate the motor industry by deliberately encouraging motoring and by taxing the motorist only as much as was necessary to help finance a liberal road-building policy; the prospect of owning a car would greatly stimulate productivity.

In 1954 the Department of Transport brought forward a road traffic bill, a hotch-potch of measures on road safety and road spending. This bill proposed

to give the Minister of Transport powers to introduce an 'experimental' scheme of parking meters, the revenue from which was to go towards providing off-street parking.

This last provision was the outcome of a bargain struck between the Ministry of Transport and the motoring organizations. The AA and RAC were basically opposed to meters, and had protested against proposals to introduce an experimental scheme in Manchester. But they had said little on the subject in public recently, and so when their views were sought by the Ministry of Transport in 1954 there was room for manoeuvre. The Minister, Boyd-Carpenter, personally discussed his proposals with them and persuaded them to accept meters in principle on condition that the revenue was used only to provide additional parking space (the arrangement suggested by the LHCTAC committee in 1951) . . . it was to remain an albatross round the necks of Ministers of Transport and local authorities for years to come.

[But in 1955] the motoring organizations – apparently regretting their earlier acquiescence in a proposal which many of their members were likely to resent – had changed their tactics and in October had opened a full-scale publicity campaign against meters. This was not wholly effective, being sharply criticized in the press, for instance by the *Daily Telegraph* and the Manchester *Guardian* (which commented that the campaign discredited the motorists' case). It also roused some hostile reactions among MPs; in the Commons committee discussions, Mr George Strauss declared it 'monstrous' of the organizations to put forward such views on behalf of their members, and Mr David Renton, himself a member of the AA's governing committee, attacked the whole SJC campaign as inaccurate and misleading. [The Standing Joint Committee was a lobbying group representing the main motoring organisations.] The Ministry of Transport invited the organizations to confidential discussions on the proposals, in which Watkinson [Minister for Transport] himself took part. The SJC, in return, promised to drop the campaign, although feeling bound to continue to oppose meters in Parliament.

By the spring of 1956 the organizations were once again wooing the press. In March the Ministry of Transport set up a working party to discuss the details of introducing meters. This was at first intended to be a 'representative' body, and the SJC were invited to nominate a member. But soon after, the Ministry of Transport – realistically, given the organizations' current views about meters – withdrew the invitation and set up the working party as a purely official body, including Ministry of Transport, local government and police representatives.

. . . The working party, proposing parking-meters in central London, went out of their way to emphasize the importance of not turning motorists against the police. They recalled two episodes which, they said, had threatened to endanger the public's customarily high esteem for the police: the enforcement of the original 20-mph limit, and the attempts to keep the streets clear of waiting vehicles during the later 1920s and 1930s. If meters were introduced

> the motorist's feelings against the enforcing authorities are likely to be roused again. We cannot emphasize too strongly the importance of reducing any tendency towards such resentment to a minimum and above all of maintaining the good relations which now exist between the motoring section of the general public and the enforcing authorities, particularly the police.

. . . The SJC continued their opposition, producing an illustrated pamphlet called 'The case against parking meters'. In April, another press conference launched a three-week campaign leading up to the Bill's committee stage in the Lords; the SJC argued that traffic problems were mainly caused not by indiscriminate parking, but by inadequate roads. The meter proposals were passed without difficulty. The following year the SJC let it be known that although they still objected to meters, they were calling off their active opposition.

The Bill as a whole went through without trouble. It was indeed, as the critics had protested and the Government modestly admitted, a far from comprehensive measure, dealing at the margins with a few specific aspects of the road safety problem. The parking-meter provisions were probably the most important part of the Bill; by at last legalizing charging for parking on the public highway, they opened the way to the first systematic attempts to regulate the use of cars in city centres.

(William Plowden, *The Motor Car and Politics*, London: Bodley Head, 1971)

2.b.4 A policy of inertia: the law on blasphemy

Occasionally government policy consists of a 'policy not to have a policy': that is, when all the available options seem unworkable, to stick to the status quo, even when that is unsatisfactory. A well-publicised instance of this was the decision by the government in 1989 not to reform the law of blasphemous libel. This antique law had been invoked in 1979, for the first time since the 1920s, by Christians who prosecuted *Gay News* for publication of an allegedly blasphemous poem – and that prosecution was withdrawn in mid-trial. Subsequently the Law Commission, a body which advises the government on desirable reforms to the law, split on whether the offence should be abolished outright, as a majority of its members urged, or should be extended to cover other religions as well.

In 1988 the British-based Salman Rushdie published *The Satanic Verses*, a novel which many Muslims found offensive and blasphemous. In many Muslim countries it was banned, and in February the Ayatollah Khomeini, spiritual leader of Iran's Shia Muslims, declared a sentence of death on Rushdie and his publishers. While the great majority of British Muslims rejected Khomeini's call, many called for the book to be withdrawn by the publishers or banned by the government, and for a prosecution to be brought for blasphemy. The publishers refused to withdraw, and the government would not – indeed, had no power to – ban the book. But the demands of Muslims that their faith should, like Christianity, receive the protection of the law of blasphemous libel acutely embarrassed a government professing dedication to a peaceful multi-cultural society.

In the early months of the crisis, Muslims found difficulty in obtaining press coverage for their complaints, but in February 1989 a *Sunday Times* article summarised the first five months of their campaign, tracing its start to Dr Syed Pasha, secretary of the Union of Muslim Organisations in Britain.

Pasha, sensing a serious problem for Britain's Muslim community, summoned the union's 19 council members to a crisis meeting on October 15 [1988]. One of those present was Sher Azam, a representative from Bradford, whose 50,000 Muslims have since become the centre of protest in Britain against the book.

It was decided to start a campaign to get the novel banned. Pasha wrote to Penguin on October 20 but got no reply. At the same time he asked Margaret Thatcher to prosecute Rushdie and Penguin under the Public Order Act (1986) and the Race Relations Act (1976).

Pasha's letter to the Prime Minister set the tone for the Muslim assault on Rushdie: 'Never have we encountered such a ferocious and savage attack on our Holy Prophet, using abominably foul language,' he wrote. He added that 'the Muslim community is shocked and seething with indignation.'

The response from the Prime Minister on November 11 was detailed. Thatcher made it clear that 'there are no grounds in which the government would consider banning' the book. 'It is an essential part of our democratic system that people who act within the law should be able to express their opinions freely.'

Thatcher's only concession was to refer the matter to Sir Patrick Mayhew, the attorney-general, who decided the book constituted no criminal offence. But Pasha was not prepared to give up. He wrote to Lord Mackay, the Lord Chancellor, and the Home Office, demanding a ban. The responses were all negative. The Home Office said no change in the law of blasphemy was contemplated. Last week a frustrated Pasha commented: 'People are looking at this issue through Christian eyes. You must look at it through Muslim eyes.'

Meanwhile a parallel campaign was being run from the Regent's Park mosque in London, which houses the Islamic Cultural Centre. The mosque's leaders met at the end of November to discuss the book and chose three Muslim ambassadors to convey their doubts to the Home Office. The government promised to give 'careful attention to their views'.

By this time Bradford's Muslim community, too, was lobbying actively. As long as two months ago a meeting about the book attracted 500 protesters. It was decided then to make a gesture of burning the book publicly.

The highly evocative photograph of *The Satanic Verses* in flames went round the world on January 14 and an uncomprehending Britain woke up to a crisis that had been simmering for months.

(*Sunday Times*, 19 February 1989)

The protestors followed two parallel courses. Despite the discouraging legal advice, they applied for summonses against Rushdie and his publishers for blasphemous libel. This led to a prolonged legal battle that eventually reached the High Court.

Moves by Muslims to have Salman Rushdie, author of *The Satanic Verses*, and Viking Penguin, the book's publishers, punished for blasphemy failed in the High Court yesterday as three judges ruled that the law protected only the Christian religion. . . . In the first case of its kind, three Divisional Court judges refused to quash the decision of Sir David Hopkin, Chief Metropolitan Magistrate, not to issue trial summonses against Mr Rushdie and the publishers for the common law crime of blasphemous libel, ruling that there were 'no doubt' the law covered only Christianity.

Giving the court's judgement in a judicial review brought by Abdal Choudhury, convenor of the British Muslim Action Front, Lord Justice Watkins said the court had no power to extend the law to protect Islam. If the law was clear, only Parliament had the power to change it, even though it might be anomalous or even unjust.

(*Independent*, 10 April 1990)

At the same time, anticipating defeat in the courts, Muslims continued to press for a change in the law.

A group of eminent Muslims campaigning against Mr Salman Rushdie's novel, *The Satanic Verses*, left the Home Office empty-handed last night as Foreign Office officials prepared for today's near-certain break in diplomatic relations with Iran.

Mr Iqbal Sacranie, chairman of the Balham Mosque, south London, described a 45-minute meeting between Muslim representatives and Home Office minister Mr John Patten as 'constructive and positive'.

But a Home Office spokeswoman said Mr Patten did not move from the Government's position that expanding the blasphemy law to embrace Islam would not be the right way to tackle the affair.

Both sides agreed to meet again. Mr Sacranie said the Muslim community wanted legal redress against books such as Mr Rushdie's, but the delegation did not suggest 'any particular form of legislation.'

(*Guardian*, 28 February 1989)

It is not difficult to deduce the arguments being put forward for and against a change in the law within the Home Office, since the first reaction of ministers and officials would have been to turn to the report of the Law Commission, which set out the pros and cons. For complete abolition of the blasphemy law it could be argued that the statute was hardly even used, and that existing public order law would be adequate to deal with any incitement to hatred. On the other hand, traditionalist Christian opinion would probably make the parliamentary passage of any abolitionist legislation problematic. In favour of the extension of the blasphemy law to cover all religions could be argued the plain fact that as it stood the law extended favouritism to one religion in a multi-faith Britain, and that the Public Order Act of 1986 made illegal only incitement to *racial* (as opposed to religious) hatred, which protected ethnic groups like Jews and Sikhs, but not religious groups like Muslims. Against the extension of the law could be argued the extremely practical point that defining a religion was difficult, and an extension of the law could be exploited by any crackpot sect. Furthermore, a new law might lead to a rush of cases which would actively harm religious and ethnic relations.

With all causes of action problematic, ministers could hardly be blamed for choosing inaction. After all, religious leaders from other faiths seemed in two minds about what should be done about the law of blasphemy as well.

The Archbishop of Canterbury, Dr Robert Runcie, said yesterday that he no longer wanted the Government to introduce legislation making blasphemy an offence against all religions and not just Christianity. He said his thinking had changed since he wrote to the Lord Chancellor, Lord Mackay, in March, 1988, urging an extension of the blasphemy laws.

He now believed that existing blasphemy laws were 'unworkable' and that consideration should be given to replacing them. This, he said, could be achieved with an extension to mainland Britain of Northern Ireland's law against incitement to religious hatred.

(*Daily Telegraph*, 24 March 1990)

The Chief Rabbi, in a letter to *The Times*, also fudged the question of where the line was to be drawn.

> In my view Jews should not seek an extension of the blasphemy laws. In any event, the Jewish definition of blasphemy is confined to 'cursing God' and does not include an affront to any prophet (not even Moses, in our case). Living in a predominantly Christian society, with an established Church, we should be quite content to leave the legislation on blasphemy as it stands, enshrining the national respect for the majority faith.
>
> What should concern us are not religious offences but socially intolerable conduct calculated or likely to incite revulsion or violence, by holding up religious beliefs to scurrilous contempt, or by encouraging murder.
>
> Both Mr Rushdie and the Ayatollah have abused freedom of speech, the one by provocatively offending the genuine faith of many millions of devout believers and the other by a public call to murder, compounded by offering a rich material reward for an ostensibly spiritual deed. It should be illegal to allow either provocation to be published or broadcast.
>
> We already have legislation proscribing by common consent many excesses in the freedom of expression, precious as this is. There are laws not only on blasphemy, but on pornography, libel, incitement of race hatred, subversion, and breaches of national security. There may be arguments on the precise definition of these offences, but the principle is universally accepted.
>
> Likewise there should be widespread agreement on prohibiting the publication of anything likely to inflame, through obscene defamation, the feelings or beliefs of any section of society, or liable to provoke public disorder and violence. It must obviously be left to public and parliamentary debate to determine where the lines of what is illegal are to be drawn.
>
> (Lord Jakobovits, from a letter to *The Times*, 9 March 1989)

Muslims continued their pressure, organising a huge march through London in May 1989.

> The largest ever demonstration of British Muslims, under a three-line whip from the mosques, will march on Downing Street today to petition for the extension of the blasphemy law to include an offence against Islam.
>
> This latest manifestation of Muslim anger at Salman Rushdie's book, *The Satanic Verses*, is an unprecedented coalition of Britain's diverse Muslim community and suggests that the controversy, six months after the Bradford book burning, will continue to rage unabated.
>
> A spokesman for Penguin, the publishers, said yesterday that not a week passes without several death threats against the directors from Muslims in Britain following the Ayatollah Khomeini's edict in February for Mr Rushdie and his publishers to be killed as apostates.
>
> A turn-out of 50,000 is expected at the demonstration, but the size will

depend on how persuasive the mosques have been. There have been reports of heavy pressure being put on Muslims to participate.

(*Guardian*, 27 May 1989)

The government's response came in a lengthy letter from the Minister of State at the Home Office, John Patten, to a number of leading British Muslims. After stressing the importance that the government attached to the integration of Muslims and other ethnic minority groups into 'the mainstream of British life' while respecting their traditional faith and customs, he restated the government's policy of inaction.

> Many Muslims have argued that the law of blasphemy should be amended to take books such as this outside the boundary of what is legally acceptable. We have considered their arguments carefully and reached the conclusion that it would be unwise for a variety of reasons to amend the law of blasphemy, not least the clear lack of agreement over whether the law should be reformed or repealed.
>
> Firstly, the difficulties in redefining what should or should not be blasphemous would be immense. People hold with great passion diametrically opposing views on the subject. For example, should protection be extended to all faiths, including the very minor or very obscure? Should it extend only to faiths believing in one God? Or to 'major' or 'mainstream' faiths only? I believe there is no right answer.
>
> Secondly, an alteration in the law could lead to a rush of litigation which would damage relation between faiths. I hope you can appreciate how divisive and how damaging such litigation might be, and how inappropriate our legal mechanisms are for dealing with matters of faith and individual belief.
>
> Indeed, the Christian faith no longer relies on it, preferring to recognize that the strength of their own belief is the best armour against mockers and blasphemers. The important principle, and the only one which Government and the law can realistically protect, is that individuals should be free to choose their own faith and to worship without interference, in an atmosphere of mutual respect and toleration.
>
> At the heart of our thinking is a Britain where Christians, Muslims, Jews, Hindus, Sikhs and others can all work and live together, each retaining proudly their own faith and identity, but each sharing in common the bond of being, by birth or choice, British.
>
> I very much hope this is a message you will be able to share with members of your community.

John Patten (4 July 1989)

Muslims were not satisfied. But the government would not budge, and there the matter rested.

2.b.5   A private member's bill: Margaret Thatcher as advocate of open government

Virtually all legislative change is initiated by the government, which monopolises time for the discussion of bills in parliament. Backbench MPs' influence on policy mainly takes the form of debating and amending proposals initiated by the government, an influence examined in Chapter 6. But there are procedures through which backbench MPs can initiate legislation themselves, although the only way in which they can realistically hope to steer a bill through into law is the 'balloted' private member's bill.

At the start of each session a ballot is held of all interested MPs, and twenty or so names are drawn. The bills they bring forward are given priority, although in practice only the first six are assured of a second reading debate, and these six are entitled to drafting assistance from Parliamentary Counsel. There is a shortage of parliamentary time for private members' bills; most lapse after little debate. Steering such a bill through into law depends on luck, mustering support amongst other members, and not proposing something the government will oppose.

For that reason, the successful bills are usually those which propose minor, unexceptional reforms, and even then the backbencher may have to work quite hard to persuade the government to let the bill through. An unusual insight into how a department reacts to a private member's bill has been provided by the Campaign for Freedom of Information, a pressure group arguing for greater openness in government, which has documented from public records the history of a private member's bill in the late 1950s seeking to compel councils to open their meetings to the public. It was promoted by a newly elected backbencher by the name of Margaret Thatcher.

In November 1959, Mrs Margaret Thatcher – who had been elected to parliament only a few months earlier – drew top place in the ballot for private member's bills and introduced a bill to entitle the press to attend local authority meetings. Mrs Thatcher was partly influenced by a recent print industry dispute. In sympathy with the print unions, some Labour councils had barred journalists from their meetings. However Mrs Thatcher's bill – the eighth on the subject in recent years – also had significant Labour support.

Mrs Thatcher's decision put the government on the spot. Its election manifesto had promised to improve press access to council meetings. But it had been planning a voluntary code of practice not legislation.

Dame Evelyn Sharp, permanent secretary in the Ministry of Housing and Local Government, tried to anticipate what Mrs Thatcher might be planning. Did she intend 'the full rigour of Mr Simon's bill' which applied even to sub-committees? If so, she reminded the minister: 'You have always recognised that . . . (this) would be quite unworkable, and I cannot see any variant of the above which would be workable.'

On the other hand, the government would not find it easy to oppose the bill. As the Minister of Housing acknowledged in a memorandum to the Cabinet Home Affairs Committee: 'Mrs Thatcher's bill, coming at this moment, presents us with something of a problem. In our election manifesto we declared our intention of making quite sure that the press should have proper facilities for reporting the proceedings of local authorities. I drafted those words myself, and it is a pledge which we must honour.'

'Our Minister's general attitude is that he would not be averse to a modest bill,' an official noted.

The government decided to offer Mrs Thatcher a deal. If she agreed to a minimal measure, they would draft it for her. If she refused, they would oppose her bill.

The minutes of the Home Affairs Committee recorded: 'the appropriate course seemed to be to prepare and hand to Mrs Thatcher a bill which the government could accept' but 'only on the clear understanding that she would reject amendments which had not been agreed with the government'.

Mrs Thatcher was not easily tempted. After meeting her in December 1959, Dame Evelyn reported: 'I am not confident that she will accept the only sort of bill that I think we can reasonably offer; she is likely anyway to have trouble with some of her supporters. She may yet take Mr Simon's bill and try to touch that up. I warned her flatly that if she did I thought the Government would be bound to advise the House to vote against it and that the local authorities would secure sufficient opposition to it to ensure that it did not get second reading. She may yet decide to go for the tougher bill even though she knows it will fail.'

The two sides then discussed the terms of the bill. One crucial issue was under what circumstances the press could be excluded from meetings. Mrs Thatcher wanted the circumstances to be tightly defined. The government wanted councils to have a broad discretion to close their meetings 'in the public interest'. It did not want to define this phrase, the Minister told Mrs Thatcher, as 'we doubt whether a satisfactory definition can be devised'.

At a meeting with the parliamentary draftsman in January 1960, Mrs Thatcher complained about this vague term. It would allow the press to be excluded 'for reasons of mere expediency or to cloak the ineptitude of the council' the minute of the meeting recorded. 'Mrs Thatcher regards this whole sub-section as far too weak'.

The officials told her that it wasn't possible to be more precise. But privately, they recognised that it could be done.

Mr C. J. Pearce, an assistant secretary, recorded: 'I repeated the warning given by the Minister . . . about the difficulty of defining the nature of the public interest which warrants exclusion of the press . . . Mr Fiennes (parliamentary draftsman) indicated afterwards that there would be no great technical difficulty in re-drafting clause 1(2), either strengthening it or not according to our instruction.'

The files show how Mrs Thatcher was frustrated by the government's reluctance to impose even the most modest requirements against local authorities' wishes.

Mrs Thatcher wanted the press to have the right to see reports being discussed at meetings. Mr Pearce recorded 'I said I thought we should have to resist this . . . local authorities would certainly fight any move which obliged them to make available the reports of committees or officials even though they related to matters which were to be discussed in public'.

Mrs Thatcher wanted the bill to apply to a wide range of bodies other than local authorities, and 'expressed general disappointment' at the narrow scope offered. She wanted criminal penalties for officers who obstructed access and regarded as 'quite useless' the government's suggestion that the press could get injunctions under civil law to enforce their rights.

Privately, officials agreed with her. A brief to the minister acknowledged that: 'The absence of any express reference to means of enforcement is generally considered a weakness in the (previous legislation) . . . and has probably encouraged local authorities in the pursuit of practices which run counter to the spirit if not to the letter of the law.' However, the Attorney General expressed outright opposition to criminal penalties, not least because of the precedent this might create. 'I am emphatically of the view that the bill should be silent about sanctions,' he told the Housing Minister. Sanctions were dropped.

Mrs Thatcher accepted the deal offered, but with such reluctance that officials questioned whether she would keep her side of the bargain: 'Mrs Thatcher wanted the bill strengthened in ways which seemed to indicate that she was expecting a much more drastic bill than we have had in mind. Some of her remarks suggested, moreover, that she would not put much conviction into opposing amendments which in her view would strengthen the bill.'

In a January 1960 note Dame Evelyn Sharp referred to the 'extremely unsatisfactory discussion with Mrs Thatcher' who, she said, 'seems to be going back on the clear understanding which I thought I had reached with her, and on the undertaking which she gave to the Minister in response to his letter'.

Dame Evelyn had been blunt about how little was on offer. 'At my talk with her I thought I was quite clear. I said the bill would have to be one through which an ill-disposed local authority could drive a coach and horses. She said that provided the bill made some advance – which I said it would – she would be content.

'I also said that if she did not like the outline which the Minister would give her that would be her opportunity to reject it. She could then introduce the Simon Bill or any variant of it – and the government would fight it. She indicated that she did not want that; she would be most grateful for a Government drafted bill in the lines I had outlined.

'I was specific about the schedule (bodies to which the bill would apply). I said it would be very much shorter than that attached to the Simon Bill. She entirely agreed that was right.

'If she writes to me I would propose to remind her in no uncertain terms of what passed between us.'

After seeing Dame Evelyn's note the Minister, Henry Brooke, noted: 'Her technique is to say she must have much more than she really expects to get! . . . We have got to hold to what she agreed. . . . I will see her again if necessary. Meanwhile the sooner we can get a draft of this bill to the (Cabinet) Legislation Committee the better. Then we can enlist the Chief Whip's help.'

Mrs Thatcher later accepted and published the government drafted bill.

The Government now displayed a remarkable degree of opportunism. Having forced Mrs Thatcher to introduce their bill and drop many of her essential demands, ministers still refused to back her. The Housing Minister told the Cabinet Legislation Committee that 'it had been made clear to her that the Government were not committed to supporting it on Second Reading'.

Mr Brooke added: 'now that a bill was before the House it appeared desirable that the Government should support it. On the other hand, it would be inadvisable for the Government openly to support the bill unless there were a reasonable assurance that it would not be defeated on Second Reading, and it was difficult at present to estimate how much support the bill would receive. Opposition to it was growing in local authority circles and Government supporters were known to be divided in their attitude'.

The Lord Chancellor, Viscount Kilmuir, proposed that the government should wait to see which side was winning before deciding its position: 'the Minister of Housing must be given discretion to decide his tactics in the Second Reading debate. . . . It would be necessary to judge from the course of the debate itself the extent to which the Government could safely indicate approval and support for the bill'.

Mrs Thatcher, however, had made an embarrassing request: she wanted to know if she could say that the government had drafted the bill during her Commons speech. As officials pointed out, the minister could hardly dissociate himself from the bill if it was known that it had been drafted to his instructions. Sir Keith Joseph, then a junior housing minister, accordingly wrote to Mrs Thatcher: 'I am afraid that it would be contrary to protocol for you to say that.'

None the less, matters had now gone too far for the bill to be stopped. Mrs Thatcher pressed ahead; the bill attracted cross-party support; and the government prudently avoided opposing it. It passed into law.

(The article extracted in this section was prepared by researchers for the Campaign for Freedom of Information for a forthcoming issue of the Campaign's journal *Secrets*.)

2.b.6   Select Committees: the repeal of the 'sus' law

Another way in which parliament can take the initiative in making policy, rather than just responding to government proposals, is through its select committees. The present system of select committees of the House of Commons dates from 1979. In the previous decade reform-minded leaders of the House had initiated the piecemeal creation of a number of committees, with powers to investigate issues, summon witnesses and issue reports. A few of these – notably the committees on nationalised industries and on race relations and immigration – made an impact, but others cut little ice. In 1979 Margaret Thatcher's newly elected government proposed the creation of a systematic network of select committees, each shadowing the work of a government department.

Early on the Select Committee on Home Affairs gave proof of its independence. Its race relations sub-committee carried out a critical examination of the 'sus' law, and its report, recommending the law's outright abolition, was adopted by the full committee and reported to the House.

Immediate repeal of the highly controversial 'suspected person' provisions of the 1824 Vagrancy Act was forcefully recommended yesterday by the House of Commons Home Affairs Committee.

After an inquiry into the 'sus' law and its effect on race relations, the committee, made up of six Conservative and five Labour MPs, said it was 'totally committed' to recommending immediate repeal. It did not believe that the powers of the police to prevent crime would be in any way diminished as a result. 'Most importantly the repeal of "sus" signifies the removal of a piece of law which is contrary to the freedom and liberty of the individual'.

The committee, whose chairman was Sir Graham Page (C., Crosby) said 'sus' had acquired a symbolic significance out of all proportion to its significance as a criminal charge. Its recent transformation into a symbol of the fraught relationship between the police and young blacks had had the ironic effect of obscuring the fundamentally objectionable nature of the offence, long familiar to libertarians and lawyers. While they hoped its repeal would marginally improve relations between the black community and the police, they did not see it as a miracle cure or instant solution.

Section 4 of the Vagrancy Act makes it an offence to be a suspected person loitering with intent to commit an arrestable offence. It is only triable summarily before magistrates and carries a maximum penalty of a £200 fine or three months' imprisonment on first conviction.

. . . The case for the retention of 'sus' was most strongly put by the Metropolitan Police which argued that it was essential in the public interest to arrest suspected persons loitering with intent.

The Committee said some of the evidence they had received suggested that there was some confusion among the public and particularly the black community as to the meaning of 'sus' and a range of powers used by the police were wrongly seen as being forms of it. They included general police powers to arrest without a warrant, to caution, and powers to stop and search conferred by local acts.

Examining the use made of the law by the police, the committee said the number charged had not only fallen far behind the general rise in crime but had scarcely changed since the 1930s. In recent years the numbers proceeded against for 'sus' had fluctuated between 2,579 in 1973 to 3,791 in 1978. More than 70 per cent of the charges were in the Metropolitan Police District, Greater Manchester and Merseyside.

In the Metropolitan Police District, there was an unexplained variation both in the number of 'sus' arrests in each division and in the number of black arrests as a proportion of that sum. It was undesirable that a law of general application should be so selectively enforced that behaviour in one street in London bore with it a serious risk of criminal prosecution while identical behaviour a mile away carried no such risk.

(*Daily Telegraph*, 21 May 1980)

Much police opinion was opposed to the repeal of 'sus': not only the Police Federation but, more significantly, various chief constables who, in evidence to the sub-committee and later representations to the Home Office, feared that it would leave them with inadequate powers. Home Office ministers accepted that the law was unsatisfactory, but took the police reservations seriously.

A clear indication that the Government will not repeal the controversial 'sus' law until the law dealing with attempts to commit criminal attempts has been strengthened was given last night by a Home Office Minister.

Mr Raison, Minister of State, said the Government was committed to ending the present 'sus' law, whose immediate repeal was urged last month by the Commons Home Affairs Committee. But the Government felt the Committee had understated the practical difficulties which would accompany its repeal and that there were some areas where it would leave a vacuum.

Mr Raison, addressing the Northamptonshire Asian Advisory Panel at Weston Favell, Northampton, said the Government was concerned there was some risk the police would be left with insufficient powers to protect the public. . . . The Government believed the matter needed to be looked at carefully in the light of a Law Commission report on the law of attempt, which was to be published soon.

(*Daily Telegraph*, 14 June 1980)

The Commons debated a call for the Select Committee's recommendations to be implemented immediately. The Home Secretary, William Whitelaw, sought to delay matters: he wished to wait for the Law Commission's review of this area of the law, and therefore immediate repeal was impossible. He proposed a Government amendment to make the motion read:

That this House welcomes the important contribution made by the Report of the

Home Affairs Committee relating to section 4 of the Vagrancy Act 1824, accepts the need for a change in the law, and looks forward to the imminent publication of the Law Commission's Report on Attempt and to the public response to these reports, as providing the basis for an early decision as to the best way of reforming the law while ensuring adequate protection for the public.

Members of the committee were not happy to delay, aware that the Home Office was under heavy pressure from the police not to make any change to 'sus' at all. Mr Whitelaw's position was made all the more embarrassing by the fact that the Chairman of the Select Committee and its sub-committee, the Conservatives Sir Graham Page and John Wheeler, opposed him.

MR WHITELAW　The Government are grateful for the analysis made by the Committee of the principles underlying the offence and of the arguments which were advanced in evidence for and against its retention. It is helpful to point out, as the Committee did, that the offence is one for which, over the country as a whole, comparatively few prosecutions are brought. It is true that, as the Committee acknowledges, abolition of the offence could be only one factor in the efforts to develop trust between the police and the black community. Yet I fully recognise and will take into account the strong feeling among ethnic minority group leaders that positive action on the 'sus' law would be of considerable help.

　. . . I have to say that I cannot advise the House to accept the recommendation which the Select Committee has made for the immediate and total repeal of the 'sus' law without provision to fill any of the gaps in the criminal law which would be left as a result. What kind of gap would simple repeal open up? How, for example, should the police deal with a case when they see somebody try car door handles, or when they find somebody attempting to steal from someone else's handbag, which turns out to have been empty?

SIR GRAHAM PAGE　This so-called weapon in the hands of the police for the prevention of crime is a boomerang. The resentment which its use generates causes it to cut down the co-operation and the good will of the public – I mean the public, not the criminal – on whom the police must rely in carrying out their duties.

　I wish that my right hon. Friend the Home Secretary had noted with approval the report of the Select Committee. I do not object to the words at the end of the amendment:

> the basis for an early decision as to the best way of reforming the law while ensuring adequate protection for the public

provided that means only the form and trimmings of the repeal. My right hon. Friend asks a lot of me, as the Chairman who is presenting the Committee's report to the House, when he asks me to do nothing more than look on this as a contribution relating to 'sus'. He is asking a lot when he asks me to accept it as nothing more than showing a need for a change in the law without a commitment to what that change may be, and when he asks me to pledge myself to do no more than look forward to the Law Commission report, and to public response. How does one ascertain public response, except at a general election? I hope he does not mean that we will have to wait that long to accept the recommendations of the report. I hope that the House will approve the report today.

(*House of Commons Debates*, 5 June 1980, cols 1767, 1768, 1777–8)

The Commons accepted the government amendment, but several Conservative members of the Select Committee, including Page and Wheeler, joined opposition MPs in voting against it. However, the Law Commission's report, published at the end of June, offered a way forward.

Gaps in the criminal law which would follow outright abolition of the present controversial 'sus' laws would be partially filled by legal reforms proposed by the Law Commission yesterday.

In its latest report to Parliament, the commission said the law should be changed and clarified so that a person would be guilty of attempting to commit a crime even if it was impossible to complete the crime. For example, a would-be pickpocket could be convicted of attempted theft even though the pocket he was trying to pick was empty.

While the Government has committed itself to repeal the 'sus' law, it has made it clear it is not prepared to do so until the present law of attempt has been strengthened. It will now study the Law Commission's proposals to see whether, in themselves, they go far enough to fill gaps in the armoury of the law that police and many lawyers fear would follow the abolition of 'sus'.

Mr Justice Kerr, the Law Commission's chairman, stressed yesterday that its report was not concerned with the controversy over the repeal of the offence of being a suspected person under the 1824 Vagrancy Act. It was directed to reform the general law of impossibility in relation to attempt, conspiracy and incitement. 'Whether the Government see any solution to the problem of "sus" in the light of what we say is a matter for them. We are not expressing any views on that'.

The commission reported that there was uncertainty in the present law as to how far along the line towards committing a crime a person had to go before he could be said to have 'attempted' it. The law should be simplified and put into statutory form so that a person was guilty of attempt to commit a crime if with intent to commit that crime, he did any act which went so far towards its commission as to be more than merely a preparatory act.

(*Daily Telegraph*, 27 June 1980)

While this report offered a way round the 'criminal attempt' issue, the police still resisted erosion of their powers. The Select Committee kept up the pressure in the opposite direction by issuing a further report in August criticising the Home Secretary for delaying the repeal of 'sus'.

The Select Committee won. At the turn of the year Whitelaw brought forward a bill to codify the law of criminal attempt and repeal the 'sus' law. Moving the second reading, he said:

> I should like to acknowledge the debt that the Bill owes to the work of two bodies – the Select Committee on Home Affairs and the Law Commission. As the House will recall, the Select Committee produced a report in May last year recommending the immediate repeal of 'sus'. It produced a second report in August criticising me for delaying the implementation of that recommendation. The inclusion in the Bill of a provision to repeal the offence obviously owes a great deal to the Committee's report.
>
> (*House of Commons Debates*, 19 January 1981, col. 21)

2.b.7   Select Committees: the law on football hooliganism

By the early 1990s the select committees had grown quite expert and very industrious. In the 1992–3 session, they published seventy-four reports and these were usually of a high standard, despite the fact that the committees have only slender resources: usually one clerk and a part-time adviser (usually an academic). Their major difficulty was persuading the government to act on their reports. If they were quick-footed and investigated a topical issue, they could inform the debate and perhaps influence ministers, as witness the Social Security Committee's report on the Child Support Agency (5.a.4). Even if the government agrees with the recommendations, it may not act on them: it may want to tackle the subject in a wider framework (like 'sus') or in a different way; it may not accord the issue great priority; or it may simply not have the necessary time available in the parliamentary timetable.

In 1991 the Home Affairs Committee (whose chairman was Sir John Wheeler) got round this problem by the simple expedient of promoting its own bill. As part of its report *Policing Football Hooliganism*, it raised the issue of criminal sanctions against hooligans. In particular it took up recommendations made by Lord Justice Taylor in his report on the Hillsborough stadium disaster.

> [Taylor] recommended three new specific offences at designated sports grounds of
>
> (i)   throwing a missile
> (ii) chanting obscene or racialist abuse
> (iii) going on to a pitch without reasonable excuse
>
> He also recommended the creation of a further offence of selling tickets for and on the day of a football match without authority from the home club to do so. According to Lord Ferrers [Minister of State at the Home Office] Taylor

preferred specific offences because 'it would act as more of a deterrent if people knew exactly what was outlawed'. The then Home Secretary announced in the debate on the Queen's Speech that the government accepted Taylor's recommendations and proposed to 'bring proposals before the House as soon as parliamentary time allows'.

Our witnesses were largely supportive of the Taylor recommendations. . . . This Committee is not anxious to create unnecessary new crimes or to clog up the courts any further. It does not wish to stymie young men's futures with criminal records, and certainly has no desire to increase the prison population. Nevertheless, we cannot ignore the evidence from Scotland that the policy of arrest rather than ejection has improved the behaviour of Scottish fans, and the widespread view that there is an important deterrence factor through the existence of criminal offences. We support the introduction of the four Taylor offences. We pay particular regard to the advice of Assistant Chief Constable Malcolm George that 'if we have specific criminal law under which the police could operate at the turnstile, on the concourse and on the terraces, that would be of great value to the policeman operating in the execution of his duty'.

Lord Ferrers suggested on three occasions that a Private Member's Bill might be a suitable vehicle for giving the Taylor proposals legislative effect. Since there is no immediate possibility of government legislation, we believe that we should be letting down the witnesses who gave evidence to us if we did not ourselves bring forward a Bill. Members of the Committee will therefore seek to present the Football (Offences) Bill on the day of publication of this Report. We are confident that the Bill will be uncontroversial and that it will receive government support. We recommend that the House pass the Bill without delay.

(*Second Report of the Home Affairs Committee*, session 1990–1)

This time the Committee had forearmed itself against Home Office prevarication. Wheeler, on behalf of the Committee, presented the football (offences) bill as a private member's bill to the House and asked it to enact it 'without delay'. This put the Home Office very neatly on the spot. Since it was committed to creating these offences, and to enacting them through a private member's bill, it could not without great embarrassment oppose the bill or allow it to fail for lack of parliamentary time. Discreet discussions took place behind the scenes; ministers agreed to provide parliamentary time, and Sir John was helped to redraft his bill to make it legally watertight. The bill passed into law.

3   Inside the 'black box'

3.a   MINISTERS AND CIVIL SERVANTS

The constitutional theory underlying civil servants' role is familiar. They present ministers with the data, the options and covering advice. Ministers weigh the considerations, often throwing in a few more political thoughts of their own, and reach a decision. Officials then do what ministers say. The practice is, of course, messier; on occasion, civil servants argue the toss. Why?

Officials do not press their views on ministers out of political partiality (although more zealously partisan ministers will see it that way). Their views will be moulded by a variety of professional pressures. Firstly, they are cautious by instinct and experience; the litmus test of a policy is: will it work in practice? Ministers come and go but officials remain, and in the history of Whitehall there have been quite a few policies launched with great panache by a minister, only to crash three fields beyond the end of the runway. Secondly, there is often a 'departmental view' on a policy issue – the term was given currency in a book on the Treasury by a former Head of the Home Civil Service, Edward Bridges – a compound of ethos, experience and outlook. So, for example, the Board of Trade was traditionally opposed to economic intervention, until it was merged into a Department of Trade and Industry; for historical reasons, the Ministry of Agriculture takes a rather interventionist attitude towards farming; and the Home Office was notably reactionary in the 1950s, although today it is often criticised for being too liberal.

Thirdly, as Sir Edward Playfair writes in 1.a.2, civil servants who work for months on a policy come to their own conclusions about the best way forward: it is a bit much to ask of any group of intelligent people to devote their minds to an issue for a long time without coming to some personal conclusion about it. This is not so much a matter of imposing their own political beliefs as drawing the conclusions to which they think the evidence points. If they say to ministers 'Policy x will not work' it will not be because they believe it to be morally wrong but because, having worked through all the details, they think it will achieve results A, B and C, of which A and B are undesirable. Occasionally a civil servant may overstep the mark and become over-committed to, or against, a policy.

William Armstrong, Head of the Home Civil Service under Heath, became disastrously over-committed to his prime minister's counter-inflation policy and was saved from ignominy only by the collapse of his health. There is very little evidence of other such lapses in recent times, and indeed most of the evidence emerging from the plethora of ministerial diaries and memoirs is of cordial relations and trust between ministers and officials, tempered by the highly desirable culture gap between partisan politicians and impartial administrators.

All this should not be taken as meaning that ministers and officials spend their lives in conflict. In the majority of cases there is little argument over policy, and where there is argument it rarely develops into open warfare. The two most important requirements are for a minister to recognise a good practical argument from his officials when he sees it and to demonstrate sufficient political weight and judgement for officials not to waste time arguing with him when he says 'It shall be so.'

3.a.1   Tony Benn and the betrayal theory

When trust and respect do not exist between the two sides, however, relations between the two sides can deteriorate sharply and give rise to the sort of 'betrayal theory' which Tony Benn, first Industry Secretary and later Energy Secretary in the 1974–9 Labour governments, expounded within a year of leaving office. He complained bitterly that civil servants had gone out of their way to block the government in general and his own radical initiatives in particular, a criticism that he set out in detail in a public lecture reproduced in the *Guardian*.

> How do the permanent secretaries view the process of party policy making? It would be a mistake to suppose – as some Socialists have suggested – that the senior ranks of the Civil Service are active Conservatives posing as impartial administrators. The issue is not their personal political views, nor their preferences for particular government. The problem arises from the fact that the Civil Service sees itself as being above the party battle with a political position of its own to defend.
>
> Civil Service policy – and there is no other way to describe it – is an amalgam of views that have been developed over a long period of time. It draws some of its force from a deep commitment to the benefits of continuity and a fear that adversary politics may lead to sharp reversals by incoming governments of policies devised by their predecessors, which the Civil Service played a great part in developing.
>
> To that extent, the permanent secretaries could be held to prefer consensus policies and hope they would remain the basis for all policy and administration. As the word implies, consensus politics draw their inspiration from many sources in all political parties.
>
> When the senior civil servants see a new government come into power with

a policy that goes outside that consensus, there is an anxiety at the possible effect upon their policy and plans are laid that would have the effect of containing this new surge of political power and diverting ministerial energies into safer channels that do not disturb the even flow of established Whitehall policy.

I have seen this process of Civil Service containment successfully practised against both Conservative and Labour governments over the last 30 years. It will be interesting to see how long it is before the same pressures are successful in guiding Mrs Thatcher back to the well-trodden paths followed on the advice of the Civil Service by Macmillan, Wilson, Heath and Wilson.

It would, of course, be quite wrong to attribute all these policy changes to Civil Service pressures alone. All ministers must take responsibility for what they do and all are subject to a wide range of other pressures besides those which come from Whitehall. But it is not a coincidence that governments of both parties appear to end up with policies very similar to each other; and which are in every case a great deal more acceptable to Whitehall than were the manifestos upon which they were originally elected.

It is also true that the central theme of consensus, or Whitehall, policies which have been pursued by governments of all parties for the last 20 years or more have been accompanied by a steady decline in Britain's fortunes, which has now accelerated into a near catastrophic collapse of our industrial base.

The governments which followed these policies – especially 1964, 1970, 1974 and 1979 – have paid a heavy price in electoral terms, whilst those who furnished the briefing for the ministers concerned have continued in power, subject only to the normal wastage occasioned by retirement at 60.

Whatever the future may hold for this Government, a new centre party is being promised which, it appears, will be dedicated to the pursuit of those same failed policies. Where Whitehall agrees with what ministers wish to do it can give formidable and effective assistance in the execution of policy. But how does it get its own way when it disagrees? It is necessary to list explicitly the techniques that are used by Whitehall. Let me therefore list these methods broadly.

- *By briefing ministers* – the document prepared by officials for presentation to incoming ministers after a general election comes in two versions, one for each major party. A similar document is produced after a reshuffle.

  It is a very important document that has attracted no public interest, and it is presented to a minister at the busiest moment of his life – when he enters his Department and is at once bombarded by decisions to be made, the significance of which he cannot at that moment appreciate.

  The brief may thus be rapidly scanned and put aside for a proper reading when the pressure eases, which it rarely does. It may be dressed up to look like a range of options for implementing his manifesto, but beneath that presentational language it reveals the departmental view. For example the

172 page Department of Energy brief for in-coming Labour ministers in 1974, several of the 35 sections of which were marked 'Secret' or 'Confidential', included one sentence I want to quote: 'In principle it is desirable that all new orders for base load power stations should be nuclear.'

In fact this policy was not followed by the Labour Government which ordered the DRAX B coal-fired station, but the brief correctly forecast both the sustained Civil Service opposition to the ordering of DRAX B, and also forecast the recent policy announcement of the present Government on nuclear power made late last year [1979].

That is only one example, and there are many others. In October 1974 after the second General Election I was reappointed to the Department of Industry and one of the briefing sheets in the package was headed 'For an in-coming Labour Minister – if not Mr Benn' – which indicated a premature hope of the reshuffle that occurred nine months later.

It however gave me a useful insight into the policy which the Department hoped my successor would follow – as indeed he did. I believe that academic research on the full set of briefs, prepared by the Civil Service for ministers in all departments in all governments when they enter office and throughout their term since the war would offer a more accurate explanation of policies followed and why, than a similar study of the manifestos upon which each government was elected.

- *By setting the framework of policy* – the key to Civil Service influence lies in its power to set the framework of policy. Lord Armstrong wrote very frankly about this power as quoted in The Times: 'Obviously I had a great deal of influence. The biggest and most pervasive influence is in setting the framework within which questions of policy are raised.'

Thus ministers are continually guided to reach their decisions within that framework. Those ministers who seek to open up options beyond that framework are usually unable to get their proposals seriously considered.

- *By the control of information* – the flow of necessary information to a minister on a certain subject can be made selective, in other ways restricted, delayed until it is too late or stopped altogether.

One example comes to mind over defence. The first draft of the Defence White Paper that came to one Cabinet I attended showed such a large gap in the military balance between East and West as to arouse questioning. It turned out that in calculating the military strength of the West, the Ministry of Defence had left out the French armed forces.

When questioned the reason given was that NATO did not exercise the same operational control over the French forces as applied to the rest of the alliance. In fact, of course, this crude misinformation was designed to win public support for a bigger defence budget by suggesting a more serious imbalance than existed.

The Ministry of Defence was instructed to put the French back into the

White Paper charts, and it did. But, it was fortunate that someone had spotted it in time.

- *By the mobilisation of Whitehall* – it is also easy for the Civil Service to stop a minister by mobilising a whole range of internal forces against his policy.

The normal method is for officials to telephone their colleagues in other departments to report what a minister is proposing to do; thus stimulating a flow of letters from other ministers (drafted for them by their officials) asking to be consulted, calling for inter-departmental committees to be set up, all in the hope that an unwelcome initiative can be nipped in the bud.

The techniques used include the preparation of statistics upon undisclosed assumptions – such as an exaggeration of costs, used to delay the implementation of the health and safety legislation. There may be a warning that 'the lawyers advise that it would require legislation,' followed by a second warning that 'the legislative timetable is so crowded that the measure is unlikely to get into the Queen's Speech in the foreseeable future'.

Ministers can be briefed against each other. In October 1977 a senior official at the Department of Industry minuted his Secretary of State to alert him to an initiative I was taking about the restructuring of the turbine generator industry.

This minute was shown to me. It recommended a way of blocking my initiative and a draft that would do it, and went on: 'if, however, you feel that you need to take a more active line in order to avoid being upstaged by Mr Benn then the letter at E5 would be appropriate.'

One of the most amusing examples occurred when my own permanent secretary in one department was violently opposed to a course of action I had decided to adopt. He knew that the matter would come up at a Cabinet committee attended both by me and a junior minister in may own department whom he rightly thought was more sympathetic to his view.

He therefore briefed this junior minister against my view. Unfortunately the junior minister concerned actually read out what he had been given, and said that he ought to tell his colleagues that the permanent secretary did not agree with what the Secretary of State was advocating. Everyone looked rather embarrassed at this tactless revelation of what was going on.

- *By the mobilisation of external pressure* – a telegram from an embassy abroad can be elicited to give a warning of the consequences that would flow from the pursuit of a certain course of action. NATO, the EEC or even the views of multinational companies or international bankers may be cited in support of a line of policy. The IMF may actually have been informally encouraged to put pressure for public expenditure cuts upon the last Labour Cabinet. And these techniques can easily be reinforced by domestic pressures through the press.

- *By the use of expertise* – most of my life has been in the departments which have a high technical content: Post Office, Technology, Power, Industry and Energy. It is the task of ministers in such departments to interrogate their officials and the experts responsible until the political issues can be disentangled from the technical ones.

Any lay minister will start at a disadvantage in dealing with such matters. It would be a mistake to suppose that senior officials are any more expert than an experienced minister. They may, however, seek to persuade a minister that the experts must be right and that such technical decisions are non-political.

I recall receiving a long minute in my Friday box in July 1966, advocating the expenditure of many tens of millions of pounds on two new scientific projects – the high flux beam reactor (HFBR) and the High Magnetic Field Laboratory (HMFL). My permanent secretary had written 'I agree,' and had put his initials below.

I laboured over the paper all weekend, and in the end decided to ask him to give me the reasons why this huge sum of money should be spent on these projects. Not having received a satisfactory answer, I vetoed them. It was just a bounce and it had failed.

Nine years later a similar incident occurred. A paper was put before me to put before the Cabinet committee recommending one or two courses of action on the fast breeder reactor. Option 1 was to build the fast breeder at a cost of about £2 billion. Option 2 was to pay about £1.5 billion for a watching brief which would allow us to be ready to build one later.

Colleagues rejected both options, and the Cabinet Office, which had masterminded the operation, realised that it had over-egged the pudding.

Sir William Hayter in his recent letter to *The Times* argued that: 'There can be no question of a manifesto commitment as between alternative nuclear reactors. And if expert opinion in this field is unanimous in favour of a particular course, is it likely that a minister, and one without any scientific qualifications, would be right and all the experts wrong?'

This argument amounts to a declaration that democratic control cannot extend to technical matters and is only tolerable in the shrinking areas of policy that laymen can comprehend. It is a recipe for technocracy and the transfer of power to non-elected laymen in the persons of the mandarins.

- *By the use of the Think Tank* – though the idea of a Think Tank has certain superficial attractions, it has in the event turned out to be a very different body. It has in practice become a powerful lobby for the Cabinet Secretary himself to whom it is responsible. It should be put under a minister or disbanded altogether.
- *By the use of patronage* – one extra source of power available to the Civil Service lies in its strategic command of patronage. Most public attention is focused upon the mere handful of appointments that are specifically in ministerial control.

But thousands of run of the mill appointments to nationalised industries and quangos of one kind or another come from Civil Service lists and reflect Civil Service preferences even if only because ministers are too busy to concern themselves with such appointments. Thus the Civil Service exercises an influence far beyond the confines of Whitehall, and can call upon the resources of its own appointees when it is necessary to do so.

• *By the use of national security* – another power available to the Civil Service is the use of security arguments. MI5 reports to the Home Secretary and MI6 to the Foreign Secretary, and the Prime Minister exercises supreme responsibilities. How close the control of these services by the ministers responsible really is only those who hold those offices will know. But published information suggests that it may not be very effective.

Sir George Young, former head of MI6, recently said on BBC Radio 4: 'The higher reaches of the Civil Service undoubtedly make most of the decisions for ministers and put them in front of them and say "minister, do you agree?"'

Britain's membership of the Common Market has had the most profound influence upon our whole constitution and method of government. Whitehall is now busy adapting itself to these new arrangements and doing so with real zest. The Common Market is a mandarin's paradise.

The permanent secretaries who masterminded the preparatory work for all these activities through the Cabinet Office and the Foreign Office have now got a legitimate excuse to bypass and override departmental ministers in the interests of co-ordination and the need to be good Europeans.

Unless this process is stopped in its tracks, Britain could be governed by a commission of permanent secretaries reducing ministers to ciphers only able to accept or reject what is put before them and the House of Commons will be a consultative assembly which can express its opinions but do little more.

Over all that I have described an official curtain of secrecy is supposed to be maintained. Why?

It is in the interests both of weak ministers and strong civil servants, both of whom prefer to keep the public in the dark. Weak ministers because they dare not invite challenges to their policy which they fear they could not answer; strong civil servants because their strength lies in that they cannot be challenged if they can remain anonymous.

I have reached the solemn conclusion that what we have constructed in Britain is the embryo of a corporate state that more resembles feudalism than the democracy of which we often boast.

If we are to reopen the campaign for democracy, certain things must be considered urgently: Freedom of Information Act; stronger Parliamentary control; a constitutional premiership; more ministerial control over the Civil Service; the abolition of patronage; the amendment of section 2 of the European Communities Act – to restore full law making and tax gathering powers to the elected House of Commons.

In considering these issues, we do not want to find new scapegoats or pile the blame upon ministers or civil servants who have let the system grow into what it is. What matters now is that we should examine what has happened to our system of government with fresh eyes and resolve to reintroduce constitutional democracy to Britain.

(Tony Benn, 'The Mandarins in Modern Britain',
Guardian, 4 February 1980)

3.a.2 The counter-thesis: a Labour version

Shortly after Benn's critique appeared, David Lipsey, a Labour Party supporter who had served in Whitehall under the Labour government as a political adviser at Environment, the Foreign Office and Number Ten, published his disagreement.

Now, truth may come from error; and every democrat should be delighted that Benn has put these issues on the political agenda. Yet it is a frightful dog's breakfast of an analysis: misleading in fact, misguided in interpretation. Most seriously it deflects attention from the reforms we really need.

It helps to understand the political context of the theory. The Fulton report in 1968 contained no suggestion that the civil service was too powerful. Its emphasis was entirely on making it more professional, brighter, more planning-oriented – in short, on all those changes that would enhance its effective power.

But from 1964–70, and again in 1974, Labour governments came to power with bright hopes and earnest ambitions to change the world. In the event, their performance fell short of their expectations. To this reality, there were two reactions. One set of ex-ministers – the Labour pragmatists – have adjusted their expectations to fit the reality. They conclude that the world, especially post-OPEC, is a difficult place, on which even the brightest and most committed minister can make only a limited mark.

Another set condemned the performance, not the hopes. For them, the programme on which they were elected remained the shining ideal. Those failures which could not be ascribed to the weakness of individual politicians, or the cussed conservatism of the electorate, should be attributed to an obstructive civil service opposition.

Seen in this way, much of the debate boils down to whether it is the job of governments to implement the policies their parties evolve in opposition. On the one hand, politicians without policies resemble fish out of water; they flap around, then expire. Manifestos give ministers a sense of direction. Moreover, if politicians have no programme, there is a vacuum of accountability, not to the electorate, who can vote them out if they don't like what they do when they're in, but to their party and its active members.

On the other hand, the idea that the manifesto on which a government is elected encapsulates the policies for which the electorate has voted is a myth. In the Labour Party (I don't suppose that the others are much different) manifestos are compilations of the policy suggestions of a myriad of subcommittees and study groups, with a high ratio of pressure group representatives to a low ratio of representatives of the general interest. Policies are frequently nodded through the party's national executive committee and conference. They pay far too little attention to overall costs, strategy, priorities and objectives; and they cannot by their nature respond to fast-moving events.

These documents, the electorate itself sensibly declines to read. You would expect that to apply also to the civil servants. Most of them believe, after all, that greater damage has been done by ill-conceived attempts at change than by an unwillingness to change.

But it is not so at all. When I arrived at the DOE I was astonished by the word-perfect way in which senior officials could recite our programme. I spent happy hours instructing them on the correct exegesis of some of its less pellucid passages. Fortunately for me, the housing section of the manifesto was a rather good document, thanks to a close and productive relationship in opposition between Tony Crosland, as environment spokesman, and the party machine. We proposed (in brief) a rent freeze; public ownership of development land; security of tenure for furnished tenants; abolition of the agricultural tied cottage; and a shift from mass demolition to mass improvement of housing.

Most of these policies were ones the department's officials had traditionally opposed. Their arguments were not just administrative convenience (which is not to decry such arguments; many policies come to grief because they are unworkable). They were arguments of substance. Security for furnished tenants? Yes, Minister, but what about the danger to the supply of relets? Abolish agricultural tied cottages? But how are the cowmen to tend a stricken beast in the middle of the night when the buses aren't running? Public ownership of land? But what do the private builders build on while they are having to wait for the compulsory purchase orders to go through?

In each case, we decided that the benefits outweighed the costs and the policies went ahead – whether in every case to the benefit of the general good, history alone will judge. I, at any rate, did not hold it against civil servants when they argued the contrary case. Their views have their legitimacy, too. They, like the country, will have to live with the perhaps irreversible consequences of such decisions long after the ministers who made them are no more than a footnote in British Political Facts. Moreover, change itself is costly, as the Heath–Walker Osymandian reorganisation of local government tragically proved.

So there is a continuous dialectic between politicians committed to rapid change and a more evolutionary Whitehall approach (though there is another kind of politician who is committed to nothing very much: and there the civil servants, who abhor a vacuum, do take over).

An example of the dialectic at its best – no villains again – was the Labour government's policy towards a fourth TV channel, the subject of a well-documented row in 1978. Predictably, party pressures were for the public service Open Broadcasting Authority, recommended by the Annan committee on broadcasting. But equally predictably the Tories were committed to a commercial channel, ITV2. The parliament was drawing towards its end. What were Home Office officials to recommend? Give Labour its OBA – and risk having to tear the whole system up by the roots at the whim of the incoming Tory administration? Understandably, they looked for a middle way that they could sell to everyone: in this case, a second commercial channel, but one designed to be protected from the ratings war, and with a special emphasis on giving scope for independent programme makers.

The Prime Minister was able, after a battle, to get their proposals thrown out. We in No. 10 were much less willing to contemplate the likely mortality of the government than were the denizens of the Home Office. But they had a right to try. At the end of the day, they have had their reward on earth as well as heaven: Willie Whitelaw's broadcasting proposals bear more than a passing resemblance to the Home Office's original draft, long since destroyed in the shredding machine of Downing Street.

In this case, it was outside the Home Office that the civil servants were defeated. But according to the Benn thesis, it usually happens differently, with departmental civil servants briefing other civil servants to brief their ministers to get the policy they didn't like defeated.

It may sometimes happen, but it isn't necessarily evil. Any government will have to have an interdepartmental machine, since departmental policies have implications for other ministers, and indeed for the government as a whole. Take the DOE policies I have already discussed. The Treasury had to pay for our rent freeze. Industry would suffer if it couldn't find homes for mobile workers. The agriculture minister would get the hammer if food production fell. Now, civil servants owe a dual loyalty – to their own minister, yes, but also to the government as a whole. It is a tightrope they have always to walk. I remember it at its sharpest and funniest during our interminable discussions with the Treasury on one controversial bill. It so happened that the official responsible at DOE was married to the Treasury's man. But the loyalties of their happy marriage came second. In our meetings, they fought like tigers for their departmental positions.

No selling us down the river there. It might have been a different matter, of course, had the Prime Minister been an opponent, rather than a passionate supporter, of our land policy, and that accounts for 99 per cent of the inter-departmental difficulties against which Benn had to battle, both at Industry and at Energy. But then, making an overall judgement when departments fall out is precisely what Prime Ministers are for.

Take next the charge of bureaucratic manipulation. Ministers, it is said, are given papers too late or not at all. They are swamped or information is withheld from them. Their diaries are filled up with trivia and their nights with boxes. I can understand why ministers come to feel that way. Tony Crosland was a slow, meticulous worker. He fought a constant battle against the third box; we used sometimes to tease him by sending it round with just the *Evening Standard* inside. Other ministers – Harold Wilson was an example – consume paper by the trunkload.

But until we breed ministers with an infinite capacity for work, they just can't know everything that is going on. There is no need to attribute malice or manipulation to see that the decisions to what to show them are constant, and often tricky.

Of course, occasionally a minister is not shown something he should have seen. Crosland once learnt that he had granted planning permission for another frightful London office block from the pages of the *Evening Standard*. Civil servants are human, too. It would be naive in the extreme to expect intelligent men with views of their own not to seek to maximise their chances of getting their way. But if it goes too far, a minister need only manipulate back. Senior civil servants can be fearfully hurt by exclusion from a minister's meeting, which cruelly diminishes their standing in the eyes of their colleagues. With such aces up his sleeve if it comes to poker, a good minister will always scoop the pot. Unfortunately, too many ministers are not good.

. . . Although I reject the charge of manslaughter brought against the civil service, it does not mean I want it to walk from the court scot-free. First, while I respect its skills of analysis, I get worried when it gets carried away by a desire to out-politic the politicians. An example was the Foreign Office and Europe. From being rational individuals who could soberly assess where Britain's interest lay (not a penny Britain would lose from being beastly to racist South Africa escaped their tallyman) the most senior officials displayed the blind devotion of a convert when it came to Europe.

In 1976, Tony Crosland asked his senior officials at the FO what assessment they had made of the economic gains and losses to Britain as a result of entry. The shocked pause that followed was reminiscent of one of Bateman's 'The man who . . .' cartoons. A paper was eventually commissioned from the senior official in charge of our European policy. It arrived a few days later; a spirited little essay on the benefits of free trade, whose content, though not style, would have been well within the reach of any competent second-year under-graduate.

It began, I recall: 'The Secretary of State's question on the benefits of entry reminds me of the man who jumped off the Empire State Building who, passing the 58th floor, remarked: "Not much seems to have happened yet".' In my reply, I pointed out that the skyscraper jumper had presumably ended up in a mess. The official concerned now works with the Brussels Commission.

Secondly, we pay a real cost for the narrow social background of our mandarins. We had no council tenants, but plenty of beneficiaries from higher rate tax relief advising us on the housing finance review (to be fair, it was the cabinet, not DOE officials, who funked abolishing higher relief). There can be no really satisfactory solution to this problem while the British class system persists. Top mandarins are not noticeably worse than top judges, or doctors, or even Tory cabinet ministers come to that.

A number of piecemeal reforms could be considered. The hardy perennial is greater interchange with industry (though when a civil servant does join industry, the politicians stop complaining about narrowness, and start complaining about corruption). Interchange with local government, hospital administration, even journalism, might help.

Bill Rodgers, the former Transport Minister, suggests that young civil servants should be seconded to MPs. And many more outsiders should be taken on temporary contracts into government: not just political advisers, but experts broadly committed to the government of the day.

Thirdly, we need better central policy planning so that, for example, we don't get the tax system pulling one way while the social security system is pulling the other. With better policy planning should also go better monitoring of existing policies, so we see the next crisis before, not after, it hits us.

Interviewed on Granada's 'World in Action' in January, Tony Benn opened thus: 'When I was reappointed to the Department of Industry in October 1974, I got a document which was extremely amusing. One of the briefs I got said For a Labour Minister, open brackets, if not Mr Benn. So they had actually prepared three briefs, one for a Conservative victory, one for the Labour Minister of Industry they might have hoped for, and one for Mr Benn. So I got an idea of what my successor would have been advised to do to bypass the Mr Benn who had been Secretary of State for Industry. You couldn't have a clearer example of Whitehall manipulation.'

You could, actually. No self-respecting department would give the same brief to a new minister as to an existing one – who presumably already knew what he was doing and why. Different options would have to be given to a new minister, particularly if by removing the old one, the Prime Minister had indicated that he didn't like the way the policy was going. Finally, that new minister would, of course, have been free to accept or reject the different policy options before him if he wanted.

The lot of radicals in government is a hard enough one, heaven knows, without inventing imagined phantoms to haunt the way forward.

(David Lipsey, 'Who's in Charge in Whitehall?',
New Society, 24 April 1980)

3.a.3   The counter-thesis: a Conservative version

At the same time as this exchange between Benn and Lipsey was taking place, George Cardona was serving as a special adviser at the Treasury. It is interesting to compare his conclusions with the more hostile findings of John Hoskyns (in 1.a.4) who was serving in Number Ten during these same years.

> I arrived at the Treasury as a special adviser in May, 1979, clutching an armful of files which contained the policies we had worked on in the years of Conservative Opposition.
>
> I had read, and heard, about the obstructions the Civil Service would place in the way of a new Government. Books and articles by Labour ministers and special advisers (particularly in the Bennite wing of the party) warned me of what to expect. I was ready to defend our policies against the most dirty tricks.
>
> I soon realized that the Treasury civil servants had also absorbed the 'Yes, Minister' myth that officials obstruct ministers and advisers. An important part of the myth is that an adviser must be given an office near the minister, and that the Civil Service will do its best to prevent this happening. I realized how powerful the myth was on my first contact with the Treasury.
>
> I was telephoned by the Establishment Officer who said: 'A room is ready for you. It is very near the Chancellor'. The security guard who met me at the door, and the messenger who took me to my room, expressed their delight that I had been given office near the Chancellor. So did the women who brought me tea several times a day. Then I called on Sir Douglas Wass, the Permanent Secretary.
>
> The first thing he said was: 'I hope you have been given a room very near the Chancellor'. (There are actually seven Permanent Secretaries of various kinds at the Treasury, if one includes the heads of the Inland Revenue and Customs and Excise. Sir Douglas is their supremo.)
>
> For the next few weeks each member of the new team of ministers and advisers was treated by officials with a nervousness that suggested we were unstable fireworks that might explode at any time.
>
> They worried and fretted about what was said at 'Morning Prayers', the meetings of ministers and advisers held at nine o'clock most mornings, from which officials were excluded. The fears of both sides proved unfounded. Treasury officials could not have been more kind, helpful and cooperative.
>
> Of course, individuals vary: the few officials with whom my relations were anything less than extremely good were, without exception, also the officials who had poor relationships with their Civil Service colleagues.
>
> Another strand of the 'Yes, Minister' myth is that officials deliberately do not copy papers to political advisers. This is nonsense. It is true that officials frequently forgot to copy papers out of simple negligence; but by snooping in ministerial intrays, one could soon discover what important papers had been

missed. If I asked for them they would usually plop on one's desk in less than an hour. I never encountered a single case of a deliberate attempt to exclude a political adviser.

The helpfulness and cooperation I found could, of course, be explained in several ways. Maybe I was too stupid to notice that officials were subtly obstructing ministers and advisers. Labour ex-political advisers tell me that, of course, the Treasury would not obstruct a Conservative Government: it is a right-wing department. (However, the Treasury is usually disliked by most members of a government, regardless of which party is in power.)

To the advisers, the officials were merely helpful and kind. To ministers they were fiercely loyal, in an impressive and consistent display of hard work and dedication. Arguments over policy were conducted frankly, quite often with some ministers and officials arguing on each side of the question. Once a decision was taken by the Chancellor, the argument stopped.

An example was the Medium-Term Financial Strategy. Some officials thought it too great a hostage to fortune. There was a straightforward discussion; the Chancellor decided to publish; and officials have loyally defended it ever since.

All this does not mean of course that a weak minister will not be dominated by his officials. But a weak superior will be dominated by his underlings in any walk of life.

There is, however, one serious shortcoming in the way the Treasury treats ministers and advisers. It is reluctant to let them become involved in issues at an early stage. It likes to present ministers with a fully worked-out set of options that have been exhaustively discussed at official level. By the time this process is completed, there can be too little time left for ministerial consideration of the options: ministers have to take a decision, and advisers have to advise, without having had the opportunity to watch the argument develop.

Most major policy papers are processed through a committee, consisting of all the Permanent Secretaries and Deputy Secretaries, called the Policy Co-ordinating Committee. I think it is rather a pity that political advisers did not attend any of its meetings.

On the few occasions when a minister tried to intervene in policy formulation at an early stage, the official reaction was rather like what would happen if a diner in a smart restaurant were to get up to serve himself: no one would actually stop him, but six waiters would rush forward to do it for him.

In the past, some ministers have criticized another aspect of the official reluctance to let ministers become involved at an early stage. They have complained that officials are made to follow the line laid down by the Permanent Secretary, but this is by no means universal practice.

It was quite normal at meetings for Sir Douglas Wass to ask different officials to put different sides of the argument; and it was also quite normal for them to do so without being asked. However, I can think of at least one occasion on which a Permanent Secretary told his subordinates to argue a case contrary to the main thrust of the Government's privatization policy, even though those subordinates were in sympathy with the Government's strategy.

It is a great pity that the myth of conflict between ministers and advisers on the one hand and the Civil Service on the other has been allowed to grow.

Perhaps, more important, the myth would make it easier for a Bennite Government to introduce a political Civil Service, in which perhaps 3,000 top posts might change at an election, as part of a campaign to remove any constraints – such as the House of Lords, the EEC and, possibly, the five-year parliamentary term – on a government's freedom of action.

But if the Treasury is any guide to the Civil Service as a whole, the Bennites need have no fear that the Civil Service is biased against them. A highly able Treasury Assistant Secretary, who will go far, said to me on my last day in the Treasury: 'If Mr Benn becomes Prime Minister, I and my colleagues will serve him faithfully.'

I am sure he was right, and from my political position, I find it frightening that if there were a Bennite government – with a majority in the Commons – it would be under no effective constitutional constraints, and it would have at its disposal in the Civil Service a machine of great efficiency prepared to serve its political masters with loyalty and dedication.

(George Cardona, 'One Step Ahead of "Yes Minister"', *The Times*, 11 November 1981)

3.b   CO-ORDINATION AND CONFLICT BETWEEN MINISTERS

3.b.1   The cabinet committee on aerospace policy

Just as conflict between officials and ministers is exceptional rather than the norm, so conflict between ministers is, although not unusual, certainly confined to a minority of cases. Most policy developments require some co-ordination between departments: for example any initiative on juvenile crime prevention requires co-ordination between the Departments for Health (responsible for social services), Education and the Home Office, and an export promotion drive will require collaboration between Trade and Industry, the Treasury and the Foreign Office. Most of this can be sorted out at official level. If things get difficult, letters may pass between ministers; there may even be a meeting between two ministers to clear the lines between their two departments. But if issues cannot be resolved that way, a cabinet committee will meet.

The extract from *Questions of Procedure for Ministers* in 1.d.1 sets out the official definition of the purpose of such committees. Quite a good, if relatively routine, example of the machinery for interdepartmental co-ordination resolving differences between ministers was the debate within Whitehall in 1978 on aerospace policy.

By the mid-1970s decisions were looming about the next generation of long-haul aircraft. In Britain, there was a major user interest in the form of British Airways. In this case as in others, British Airways wanted to buy from Boeing. There was a major producer interest in the form of British Aerospace and Rolls-Royce (who constructed the engines) but whose interests diverged sharply in that British Aerospace naturally wanted to sell their airframes to British users, while Rolls-Royce seemed to see more secure long-term prospects in collaboration with Boeing so as to produce American airframes for British engines. There was a powerful US competitor in the form of Boeing itself, but a beguiling alternative in the prospect of collaboration with European manufacturers, with whom British Aerospace felt more nearly on equal terms. This diversity of interest was reflected by a diversity of views among Whitehall departments. The Department of Trade was the 'sponsor' for British Airways, the Department of Industry for the airframe and aero-engine manufacturers. The Foreign and Commonwealth Office was alternately swayed by the economic arguments in favour of collaboration with Boeing and the EEC arguments in favour of the European connection. The Treasury had a close interest in the outcome, even if uncertain as to what it wanted this to be.

> (Tessa Blackstone and William Plowden, *Inside the Think Tank:
> Advising the Cabinet 1971–83*, London: Heinemann, 1988)

Whitehall resorted to the traditional machinery: a committee of ministers, in this case chaired by the Prime Minister, which marked out aerospace as an issue of perceived importance; and, shadowing this, carrying out the more detailed technical work, a committee of officials representing the departments involved, chaired by Sir Kenneth Berrill, director of the government's 'think tank', the Central Policy Review Staff (CPRS).

> Berrill was at the time chairing an interdepartmental group of officials advising the Prime Minister, James Callaghan, on economic matters. The aerospace issue came up in the group and was, in effect, taken over by Berrill and the CPRS. Berrill himself had good contacts with Rolls-Royce and with British Aerospace, less good with British Airways. He saw the CPRS role in this matter not as advocating a particular outcome but as helping the Prime Minister to elicit an outcome which made reasonable sense from all points of view. Berrill himself, in his role as Prime Ministerial adviser rather than chairman of an official Cabinet committee, accompanied Callaghan to the United States to talk to Boeing.

> (Blackstone and Plowden, *Inside the Think Tank*)

By mid-May 1978 accounts of the Whitehall discussions were filtering into the newspapers.

> A cabinet committee of senior ministers chaired by the Prime Minister is expected to meet this Tuesday to discuss a report suggesting McDonnell-

Douglas as a potentially more suitable partner for co-operation with the British industry than Boeing.

The report, drawn up by senior civil servants following meetings last week between ministers, officials and senior executives from McDonnell and Boeing is also likely to recommend that British Airways be asked to buy four British built BAC 111 jets.

Any proposals to buy four 111s and cut back BA's intended purchase of Boeing 737s from 19 to 14 is bound to cause considerable irritation among the management and particularly with the chairman, Sir Frank McFadzean, who has been pressing very hard for the airline to be allowed to buy what it wants. But it is hoped that pitching the number of 111s at four will placate unions without pushing McFadzean into resignation.

Boeing's widely publicised offer of a partnership in building a 160-seat twin-engine jet, the 757, which could have its wings and engines built in this country had attracted support from civil servants and ministers, and particularly from Rolls-Royce chairman, Sir Kenneth Keith. British Airways, which has just announced it wants to spend £1,600m on new aircraft, most of them from Boeing, also favours the partnership.

In recent weeks, British Aerospace, which wants to explore fully the possibilities of collaboration with European firms, had seemed increasingly isolated as opinions swung in Boeing's favour. But even before the civil servants had completed their report last week, senior ministers were developing reservations about Boeing's offer.

Though they recognise that co-operating with the world's most successful civil jet maker has its attractions, there are risks. A deal with Boeing would certainly mean British Aerospace (BAe) turning its back on Europe, leaving it entirely dependent on the American company. Equally they have come to accept that while the offer from F. H. 'Tex' Boullioun, head of Boeing's commercial aircraft company, looks generous, it may be a price Boeing is willing to pay now to weaken the European competition in the longer term. . . .

Within the Cabinet, there is a recognition that the interests of British Aerospace and Rolls-Royce are not necessarily identical. The debate now revolves around whether it is possible to define an aerospace policy that will protect the futures of both companies. The key question may well prove to be whether Rolls-Royce can get its engines into Boeing's programmes even if British Aerospace does not participate in a deal with the American company.

(*Sunday Times*, 14 May 1978)

British Airways is likely to be allowed by the Government to buy the bulk of the American Boeing 737 airlines which it wants to replace its aging Trident 1 fleet.

The state airline has said that it wants to order 19 Boeings at a cost of about £140m. Opinion among ministers is that although the bulk of the request should be acceded to, four of the new aircraft should be British-built BAC 1–11s.

Such a split decision would give the British Airways board most of what it wants, keep the British Aerospace production line for 1–11s moving and partly placate the trade unions.

The subcommittee of the Cabinet responsible for a decision met yesterday under the chairmanship of the Prime Minister. The Chancellor of the Exchequer, the Foreign Secretary, and ministers with responsibilities for industry, trade and employment were present.

Another aerospace subject discussed by the subcommittee was whether Britain should collaborate in developing the next generation of subsonic airliners with American or European aircraft companies.

An important factor that the meeting took into consideration was the effect on the future of Rolls-Royce of such a decision. The JET airliner proposed by the Europeans would have American–French engines, while that proposed by both Boeing and McDonnell Douglas, of the United States, might employ the Rolls RB 211–535.

Several more meetings of the subcommittee are expected before a decision is made in several weeks' time.

(*The Times*, 17 May 1978)

In the words of Edmund Dell, who as Trade Secretary served on the ministerial committee:

The upshot of this exercise was that the three nationalised Aerospace Corporations achieved their principal requirements but not all their subsidiary requirements. British Airways, by far the largest of the three and the one most likely to make a profit on its activities, won its commercial freedom to buy the aircraft it preferred. Rolls Royce obtained an entry to Boeing for its engines on the back of a British Airways order. British Aerospace rejoined Airbus Industry and obtained participation at a price in the new airbus; and in addition was permitted to proceed with the HS 146. One may think that this was exactly the kind of compromise that one would expect to arise out of a confrontation between Departmental Ministers committed to their Departmental briefs, and that therefore nothing was in fact gained either by the intervention of the CPRS or by the existence of the Cabinet Committee or by the Prime Minister's invitation to Ministers to think nationally rather than Departmentally.

Such a view would under-estimate the significance of the decision to permit British Airways its commercial freedom, a decision taken against the well-publicised opposition of powerful sections of the Trade Union Movement, of European aircraft manufacturers, and of certain friendly European Governments.

(Edmund Dell, 'Some Reflections on Cabinet Government by a Former Practitioner', *Public Administration Bulletin*, 32, April 1980)

3.b.2   The cabinet in conflict: child benefit

The aerospace decision was essentially a matter of reconciling the different concerns of Whitehall departments and their 'client' interest groups. The 1976 child benefit decision, on the other hand, was a fight by the Social Services Secretary both against the Treasury – on cost grounds – and against the rest of the cabinet on wider issues connected with incomes policy. In 1974 the Labour Party returned to government pledged to replace income tax allowances for children and family allowances with a single cash benefit. In May 1976 the government announced deferral of the plan until 1978. The following month Frank Field, director of the Child Poverty Action Group and later a Labour MP, published an article in *New Society* detailing how the commitment came to be abandoned. It caused such a stir that it was reprinted the following week. Field's account has since been confirmed by the memoirs of the Chancellor Denis Healey, the Chief Secretary Joel Barnett and – in detail – the diaries of Tony Benn.

> Within the space of two cabinet meetings in May, ministers decided to go against strong arguments that had been developed for a decade in favour of reforming financial support for children. In the mid-1960s, Richard Titmuss called attention to the haphazard nature of child support in this country. Second and subsequent children only received family allowances. Differing rates of benefit were paid for children whose parents were drawing supplementary benefit and national insurance benefits. Parents in work could claim tax allowances for all children. But many parents on a low income did not earn enough to set the child tax allowances against tax. So poverty groups began calling for a merging of the family allowance and child tax allowance system in the payment of a single uniform benefit.
>
> This argument was reflected in the thinking of the Tory party. Miss Mervyn Pike (now Baroness Pike) advocated a simple form of negative income tax. Under this, parents who did not earn enough to claim their child tax allowances would gain the value of the allowances as a cash payment.
>
> The debate on how best to give financial support for children got a Great Leap Forward with the publication of the Heath government's green paper on tax credits. As part of the scheme, family allowances and child tax allowances were to be replaced by the payment of a uniform tax credit for children. . . . As part of an alternative package deal, the Labour Party proposed a new 'child endowment' scheme. This was later renamed 'child benefits'. The scheme was in essence exactly the same as the tax credit proposals as they applied to children.
>
> A child benefit bill duly reached the statute book on 7 August 1975. Some MPs moved an amendment to write into the bill the starting date for the full scheme. But the government said this was unnecessary because it had given a number of binding commitments.

There were indeed difficulties of the most down-to-earth kind. There were delays over the building intended to house the staff administering the benefits and problems with the ordering of a computer, and with the recruitment and training of staff. Nevertheless, ministers gave a categorical assurance that the scheme would begin in April 1977. Privately ministers have admitted that the scheme could have started a year earlier if the money had been available to pay a generous rate of benefit. Instead, the 'child interim benefit' was brought in in April 1976. The first child of single-parent families became eligible for a benefit of £1.50 a week.

The one remaining issue on which the cabinet had to decide was the rate at which full child benefit would be paid from April 1977. On 8 April this year, three days after Callaghan's election as prime minister, the reshuffled cabinet received a memorandum from the new secretary of state for social services, David Ennals, who had that day taken over from Barbara Castle. This spelt out that families with children were now getting substantially less support than the Tories provided in 1970, 1971 and 1972, and less than the Labour government provided in the late 1960s. Further, the increase in child tax allowances announced in Denis Healey's 6 April budget had done little more than restore family support to its 1974 level, which was still substantially below the provision in 1971. Ennals' memo concluded with the words: 'If we continue to let child support be eroded by inflation, the whole scheme would be condemned as a trick to give children less, not more.'

The secretary of state's memorandum informed the cabinet that a child benefit of £2.90 was required to restore the support for a three-child family to the level it had been under the Tories in 1971. Healey, as Chancellor of the Exchequer, countered this proposal in a note of his own. The Treasury was thinking in terms of a child benefit of £2.50 a week plus 50p premium payments. These were to go to the children of single-parent families, and to those families with larger numbers of children.

The Treasury position was attacked in a further memorandum by the new secretary of state which was issued for the cabinet meeting of 4 May. A £2.50 child benefit plus 50p premium would mean that almost all two-parent families with more than one child would be worse off in real terms by April 1977 than they are now.

The cabinet minutes for 29 April record the secretary of state as saying that failure to increase the real level of support for families would add to the difficulties in negotiating pay policy with the TUC, and would be likely to harden their resistance to the phasing out of food subsidies. It was at this cabinet meeting that members began to discuss the effects of withdrawing child tax allowances on the negotiations for stage three of incomes policy. The cabinet concluded that it might be best to postpone child benefit if the funds were not available to pay an acceptable rate.

Sensing the danger, Ennals outlined the obstacles to a postponement of the scheme at the following cabinet meeting, on 4 May. Some of the objections were administrative. For example, what would happen to the building and the staff who were now in post to administer the new scheme? Further, the government would be rightly accused of bad faith. The DHSS itself argued that £2.70 child benefit remained the lowest desirable rate, and £2.65 the lowest flat rate that would ensure that no family was made worse off in cash terms. The cost of a £2.65 child benefit was put at £160 million a year, plus £45 million for dependent children overseas.

At this 4 May meeting the cabinet also received a further note from the chancellor and a memo from Joel Barnett, the chief secretary to the Treasury. These reiterated the point that a basic rate of £2.45 plus 50p premium payment would give cash gains to all families and a real gain to families with one child and to one-parent families.

Healey added that there was no commitment to maintain the child benefits in line with inflation as had been assumed by the previous submission by Ennals. Furthermore, as the chancellor believed that only 7 per cent of families drawing family allowances were poor or hard-pressed, the use of premium payments was a more cost-effective way of tackling poverty.

After the 4 May cabinet meeting, the new prime minister began working behind the scenes. At the cabinet meeting of 6 May, he reported receiving an 'excellent report' from the Whips Office that had created fresh doubts in his own mind about the political implications of introducing child benefit. The new chief whip, Michael Cocks, reported to the cabinet that, after surveying opinion, the introduction in April 1977 of child benefit would have grave political consequences that had not been foreseen when the bill went through the Commons. In the ensuing discussions, cabinet ministers expressed the belief that the distribution effects of child benefit could not be 'sold' to the public before this scheme was brought in in April 1977. In summing up, the prime minister commented that to defer the scheme would also require careful public presentation. The two cabinet meetings of 4 and 6 May had scuttled the child benefit policy.

Under the guise of how best to present publicly the immediate abandonment of introducing child benefits, DHSS officials later put forward a number of policy alternatives. Shirley Williams as paymaster-general and secretary of state for prices and consumer protection, and David Ennals argued in an attached memorandum for those proposals that were aimed at salvaging something for families. Their view was that the government would gain respect for introducing the child benefits scheme in a modest form, rather than by making a U-turn on a major commitment on which the government had fought two general elections and which it had enshrined in subsequent legislation.

The cabinet discussed this on 20 May. But it was now having to make its decision on child benefit in the knowledge that much of the cabinet discussion was being leaked to two national newspapers. As a result of these leaks, those trade union leaders committed to child benefit insisted on inserting a crucial phrase into the statement agreed by the TUC/Labour Party Liaison Committee at their meeting on the 24 May. The statement read: 'It is of the utmost importance that the new child benefit scheme, to be introduced next year, provides benefit generous enough to represent a determined and concerted attack on the problem [of poverty].'

The full trade union delegation at that meeting did not know that a small group of union leaders had arranged to see the chancellor and other senior ministers later in the day. At the cabinet meeting on the following day (25 May), the prime minister asked the chancellor to report on this meeting with TUC chiefs to discuss the proposals put forward at the cabinet meeting on 6 May. The TUC were asked to agree to a postponement of the child benefit scheme for three years because of the effect the loss of child tax allowances would have on take-home pay. The cabinet minutes record: 'On being informed of the reduction in take-home pay, which the child benefits scheme would involve, the TUC representatives had reacted immediately and violently against its implementation, irrespective of the level of benefits which would accompany the reduction in take-home pay.' Both TUC and cabinet ministers were agreed in opposing any cut in child tax allowances, on the ground that this would appear to reverse part of the budget strategy underlying stage two of the incomes policy.

In order to prevent any further leaks to the national press, the cabinet then proposed that the announcement on the effective postponement of child benefits scheme should be made in the Commons that afternoon. On 25 May, Ennals therefore rose and made the best he could of the government's abandonment of its plan to tackle family poverty.

(Frank Field, 'Cabinet v. Children', *New Society*, 24 June 1976)

3.b.3   The cabinet in conflict: deferring the raising of the school-leaving age

In late 1967 and early 1968 Harold Wilson's Labour government agreed a package of severe public spending cuts, at the behest of the Chancellor Roy Jenkins, including cancellation of the F111 military aircraft, reintroducing prescription charges, withdrawal of the British military presence east of Suez, and delaying by two years the raising of the school-leaving age from 15 to 16. Any package of spending cuts causes great conflict between Treasury ministers and their colleagues, but the school-leaving-age decision caused particular heart-searching within the cabinet: Jenkins admitted that it was the element of the package that he found most worrying, and Wilson described it to the Commons as 'difficult, not to say repugnant'.

One of the more peculiar features of the cabinet debate was that the Education Secretary, Patrick Gordon Walker, had supported the postponement of the raising of the school-leaving age before being moved to Education in 1967, and now saw no reason to change his mind, as he told Jenkins:

On Friday December 22 had lunch at his club with Roy (Jenkins). He told me that . . . 'A surprising number of Ministers' were against putting off raising – Stewart, Geo. Brown and Callaghan (who first proposed it as Chancellor!). There is a preference for reducing University Expenditure and loans (instead of grants) for undergraduates – all impossible things.

I told Roy that if there had to be cuts I preferred RSLA being put off rather than cuts on Universities. This would bring a most powerful interest upon us – we would have to cut science as well. It would hold back increase in students.

Roy and I agreed that if we, who were the two who would have to bear the brunt, preferred school leaving age to Universities, then it would be ludicrous to force us the other way.

We were agreed it should not be over 2 years. Roy offered £3 million or so back first year and £10 million second year – for EPAs (Educational Priority Areas) and Comprehensive reorganisation.

> (Patrick Gordon Walker, *Political Diaries 1932–71*, London:
> Historians' Press, 1991)

The following accounts of the cabinet discussion, by Barbara Castle, Richard Crossman and Tony Benn, show us the unusual spectacle of a departmental minister refusing to fight his corner, and other ministers making the case for him. They also show how three different eye-witness accounts of a cabinet meeting can give different perspectives on what happened, even though, reassuringly for those who use the diaries for historical purposes, they tally in their basic account of what happened.

The first item was education, where Roy [Jenkins] is demanding a three-year delay in raising the school leaving age. Patrick Gordon Walker's reaction was very equivocal; it was hard to say at the end of the pros and cons where he stood, but I suspect he secretly favours postponement. His normal allies, however, took a very different line. The group which had been fighting for F-111 [a fighter aircraft reprieved at an earlier meeting] now united to resist postponement with equal ferocity, backed this time by Crosland who is gunning hard for my roads programme. George [Brown] said he would rather accept any cut at all from the Chancellor than this. None of the rest of us, he said, knew what it was like to be denied a proper education – not only at University but also at school. It rankled one's life. ('No one would notice any deprivation in you, Foreign Secretary,' soothed Harold [Wilson].) Jim [Callaghan] and Ray Gunter argued on exactly the same lines, while Longford hinted that he might have to 'consider his position' if this went through.

I thought no one would dare to speak out against this barrage and that the whole thing would go by default. But I reckoned without Dick [Crossman]. Tentatively but courageously he argued that postponement might do as much educational good as harm but agreed that it would be wrong to concentrate our education cuts on schools and that we ought to cut back the Universities, particularly on the post-graduate side, where we were developing a generation of perpetual students utterly divorced from the needs of industry. We shouldn't forget, too . . . the need to put first the education priority areas which might suffer if we raised the age. This rallied the rest of us. The PM, also accepting it, then asked Patrick where he stood and he mumbled acquiescence.

(Barbara Castle, *The Castle Diaries 1964–70*, London: Weidenfeld and Nicolson, 1984)

Next came education and George Brown, who'd obviously hotted himself up a bit at lunch time, came out with an attack before the feeble Gordon Walker could say anything. It was an unpleasantly class-conscious speech, strongly implying that no one except the middle-class socialist who had never felt the pinch or never had a child at a state school could dare to suggest postponement of the raising of the school-leaving age. Ray Gunter and Jim Callaghan followed much the same working-class line while Tony Crosland and Gerald Gardiner spoke as socialist ideologists. Fred Peart and George Thomson provided the professional trade-union case as represented by the N.U.T. Gordon Walker sat through this debate speechless and obviously trembling. He had been off the day before to a great meeting in Newcastle where he had talked about heartbreak decisions. Damn him! What an idiotic thing to say – heartbreak decisions! Either you take the decision and don't resign or you resign with heartbreak, but you don't stay put with heartbreak. Roy Jenkins put our case very moderately. He pointed out that no one had suggested another way of getting £40 million out of education without irreparable damage. Then he quietly added that there were really quite a number of teachers and parents of children at comprehensive schools who would welcome postponement. Denis Healey then bashed in saying that if he was going to have cuts of far more than £40 million he wanted to see adequate cuts in home policy. Dick Marsh, the youngest member of the Cabinet and also a trade-unionist, clearly didn't feel a crisis of conscience any more than Peter Shore. They both sided with Roy. Barbara, of course, was in a difficulty. Her left-wingism would make her naturally opposed to postponement but on the other hand she wanted to preserve her road programme and to support Harold. It was obvious that we were getting terribly close in numbers and that if there was a majority on Roy's side it was very small. At this point Harold said that Gordon Walker should tell Cabinet what his view was. 'It's an agonising decision,' he replied, 'but in the last resort I must accept two years' postponement.' I don't know which I disliked more – the pathetic weakness of Gordon Walker or the outrageous cynicism of Callaghan, who as Chancellor of the Exchequer had urged the postponement and was now joining the working-class battle against it.

(Richard Crossman, *The Diaries of a Cabinet Minister, Volume II: Lord President of the Council and Leader of the House of Commons, 1966–68*, London: Hamish Hamilton and Jonathan Cape, 1976)

On education the big debate centred about the proposal made by Roy Jenkins, with which Pat Gordon Walker agreed, that the school leaving age should not be raised to sixteen on the date planned. Roy wanted it deferred by three years. This led to an extremely tense discussion. Pat Gordon Walker introduced it by more or less agreeing to what Roy had asked for and said, 'I am suggesting this in place of the cuts in university expenditure because the universities represent such an influential body of opinion.'

George Brown exploded, 'May God forgive you. You send your children to university and you would put the interests of the school kids below that of the universities.' It took some time to restore order. George then continued his attack, in which he said that education was the basis of class in Britain and if we denied these kids the opportunity of staying in school for an extra year, we would be perpetuating class distinctions.

Michael Stewart made a really excellent speech also in favour of raising the school leaving age, as did Ray Gunter who said that we were critically short of technicians in exactly the group that would benefit by an extra year at school. Fred Peart and Frank Longford supported it, as did Jim Callaghan, on the grounds of his own experience, and George Thomson and Tony Crosland who said the date had been fixed to meet a specific demographic situation and could not be altered easily.

In favour of postponement were Roy, of course, Pat Gordon Walker, whose arguments were quite disgraceful, Dick Marsh, who didn't see it mattered, Denis Healey, who was obviously trying to get his own back for the cuts in the F-111, Cledwyn Hughes, for no very clear reason, Gerald Gardiner, which was really rather surprising and Willie Ross, who gave no particularly strong argument. Tony Greenwood was in favour of postponing too and Dick Crossman, Barbara Castle and Peter Shore were so vague in their comments as to suggest that they didn't give much priority to this. Harold Wilson indicated that he was in favour of postponement for two years.

I said that I had a direct departmental interest because, of course, my industries were customers of the universities and the school system, and that there were too few science and technology candidates, too many of them staying at university doing soft and pure research and too few going into industry. I also pointed to the danger of the brain drain which was taking 40 to 50 per cent of our annual output and said that these considerations had led me to believe that there should be economies in the university sector. . . . But the argument went against and the raising of the school leaving age is to be postponed by two years.

(Tony Benn, *Office without Power: Diaries 1968–72*, London:
Hutchinson, 1988)

In fact, the only minister to resign was Frank Longford, an old Etonian. Gordon Walker was dropped from the cabinet a few months later.

3.c THE PRIME MINISTER AND POLICY CONFLICT

What of the Prime Minister in these conflicts? In the cases described above it is clear that Callaghan's views swayed the child benefit decision, and that Wilson's semi-covert support for postponing the raising of the school-leaving age was a help to his Chancellor in getting that decision through. But while having the Prime Minister on your side helps, it is not a guarantee of victory in cabinet.

3.c.1 Harold Wilson and overseas aid

In July 1965, during the public spending allocation round, Barbara Castle – then Minister for Overseas Development – had her budget cut, but persuaded Harold Wilson to allow her to re-open the issue in cabinet. Although she received support from some colleagues who had a marginal interest in seeing her succeed – Anthony Greenwood at the Colonial Office, and Arthur Bottomley at Commonwealth Relations – her attempt foundered on the opposition of the Chancellor, Jim Callaghan, and George Brown who then headed the Department of Economic Affairs.

> Got up at 4.30am to mug up my briefs in preparation for my trial in Cabinet. We plunged into overseas aid right away. I spelt out in detail the consequences of keeping me to my 'basic' of £216m in 1966–67 and £230m in 1969–70. Arthur wasn't very effective in backing me up, though Tony Greenwood and Longford did their best. Jim Callaghan said it was all very sad but where was the money coming from: which domestic Minister would take a cut? Michael [Stewart, Foreign Secretary] was feeble in the extreme. Harold then jumped in to try to save the day. He asked me if I could manage within an increase of £10m of foreign exchange, and when I said yes Jim Callaghan and George Brown nearly hit the roof. There could be no increase in foreign exchange, they insisted. When Harold said that, as he understood it, the basic was merely the acceptance of Tory policy and we had always held ourselves free to rearrange their priorities, they accused him of undermining the work of the Public Expenditure Committee. A nasty ten minutes followed in which Jim and George scarcely bothered to hide their defiance of him. Harold fought back doggedly, but not very effectively. . . . At the end all Harold succeeded in doing was to avoid Cabinet reaching a conclusion, saying we had got to wait for the outcome of the social services review.
>
> (Barbara Castle, *The Castle Diaries 1964–70*, London: Weidenfeld and Nicolson, 1984)

Richard Crossman's version of events suggests that the cabinet had detected the behind-the-scenes agreement between Wilson and Castle, resented it, and inflicted a sharper rebuff than Castle admits.

> It had been clear at the previous meeting that both Harold and the Foreign

Secretary felt the cut in overseas aid was greater than we could defend as a Party or as a country. Something had to be restored to Barbara. On the other hand, the system under which PESC had been working guaranteed that if one Minister were to get more money another would get that amount less.

. . . Nevertheless, this Cabinet was in a mood to finish the job off and had no inclination to give anything away to Barbara. Their attitude was strengthened when she spoke for thirty-five minutes. The sensible thing would have been to speak for five minutes and then to ask Michael Stewart, Arthur Bottomley and Anthony Greenwood to plead her case for her. When she had finished Callaghan simply said, 'I'm sorry about this but I can't believe there is any special case here, and anyway, if there is, what other Ministry is to be cut back?'

At this point Harold Wilson intervened. 'We mustn't be absolutely rigid about these programmes,' he said. 'After all, they are not our own – we only inherited them. I suggest we set up a working party to see whether we can't give Barbara at least some increase in areas where the dollar spending is not too severe.' At this point Cabinet suddenly moved into a major row. Callaghan refused to serve on a working party of this kind. 'All these points have been argued out,' he said, 'and at the end of July it is far too late to go back on the basic programmes which we've assumed for the last eight months. You can't challenge them now.' On this he was strongly supported by George Brown, who reminded us that he had to have the final figures by the end of the week for inclusion in his National Plan. After this there came an altercation which took nearly an hour and a half and which most of us sat through looking pretty embarrassed. The First Secretary and the Chancellor, clearly in some sense working together, leapt on Harold like wolfhounds in at the kill. That sounds a bit exalted for Harold, but that's what it was. They tore him from both sides. They insulted him, tried to pull him down in the most violent way, obviously both feeling that Harold was evading his responsibilities as Prime Minister and trying to do an unseemly fix. And of course that is what he was doing. He was trying to help Barbara without openly saying so and planning to get her allocated another £20 million or so and then later to save the money by cutting the road programme of Tom Fraser, who was sitting just beside me. . . . It was the worst Cabinet we have had, and the worst for Harold Wilson.

(Richard Crossman, *The Diaries of a Cabinet Minister, Volume I: Minister of Housing 1964–66*, London: Hamish Hamilton and Jonathan Cape, 1975)

3.c.2   Wilson versus Benn: industrial policy

One of the more curious episodes of conflict occurred in 1974 over the white paper on industry produced by Tony Benn, who managed to end up in conflict simultaneously with the Prime Minister, his ministerial colleagues and his departmental officials. This episode provided the basis for Benn's later thesis that civil servants set out to sap the radicalism of any new minister, set out in 3.a.1.

Labour won the February 1974 election on a manifesto that included a commitment to create a National Enterprise Board to extend state involvement in industry, and to reach planning agreements with key companies, although the exact practical meaning of these commitments were not clear. The key mover behind this policy was Tony Benn (formerly Anthony Wedgwood Benn), who had undergone a conversion to left-wing socialism in opposition, and whose following within the party made it impossible for Wilson to refuse Benn appointment as Industry Secretary.

From the outset Benn faced problems on three fronts. Firstly, within the department, there was friction between him and his permanent secretary, Antony Part. This exchange between them, taken from Benn's diary, is fairly typical.

> At 12.15 Sir Antony Part came to see me. He hummed and hawed a bit then said, 'Minister, do you really intend to go ahead with your National Enterprise Board, public ownership and planning agreements?'
>
> 'Of course.'
>
> 'Are you serious?' he asked.
>
> 'Of course. Not just because it is the policy but because I was deeply associated with the development of that policy.'
>
> He said, 'Well, I must warn you, in that case, that if you do it, you will be heading for as big a confrontation with industrial management as the last Government had with the trade unions over the Industrial Relations Act.'
>
> 'I am not going to jail any industrialists. I am not going to fine them. We have just got to move forward.'
>
> 'I know,' he said, 'and I will try to lubricate things, if that's really what you mean.'
>
> 'Well, of course it is. I know I can't do it now but we have got to move in that direction.'
>
> (Tony Benn, *Against the Tide: Diaries 1973–76*,
> London: Hutchinson, 1989 (11 April 1974))

On his side, Part found the relationship equally uneasy. Unusually for a civil servant, he wrote his autobiography, which records his view of Benn.

> He took an immediate personal dislike to me and arrived with a strong but completely false conviction that the department was the unquestioning ally of industrial management and had an ignorant bias against the trades unions and the 'workers' generally . . . the seating arrangements for his tête-à-tête several times a week with his Permanent Secretary emphasised his approach. Usually for such informal talks the Secretary of State and his Permanent Secretary would sit in armchairs in a corner of the office. Mr Benn wished us

to face each other across the long narrow conference table next to his desk. As he did at meetings with deputations, he put a block of paper in front of him and drew a line down the middle. As the conversation proceeded, he noted my remarks to the left of the line and any comment or counter-argument of his to the right of the line. This did not make for a relaxed atmosphere and occasionally it was as though he were pointing a pistol at my head. Metaphorically, I would watch his finger tightening on the trigger and when I judged that he was about to fire I moved my head to one side. With any luck, I heard the bullet smack harmlessly into the woodwork behind me.

(Antony Part, *The Making of a Mandarin*, London: André Deutsch, 1990)

Secondly, Benn was the object of vehement, sometimes absurd vilification in the press, much of which in the view of Benn was fanned by briefings by Wilson. This extract from a commentary by Anthony Shrimsley in the *Daily Mail* is one of the more lurid examples:

The true menace of Citizen Benn is that he has far greater ambitions than merely to take over everything that contributes to the industrial and commercial strength of these islands.

Mr Benn's objective is to obliterate democracy as we know it and replace it with something else under the same name.

It is a cause in which he never tires.

Speeches pour from his lips. Ceaselessly he crops up on radio and television – from the current affairs programmes to an extraordinary appearance in a late night TV slot extolling the activities of a workers' control group in the South East.

When he fails to carry his ideas in the Cabinet he switches the pressure to the Labour Party National Executive, using his advocacy of 'open Government' to force his plans into Labour policy statements and then into grudging acquiescence by colleagues too scared of the Left to make a public counter-attack.

. . . Mr Benn, who is always talking about the democratic struggle, the rights of man and Magna Carta, has even more fascinating plans for Parliament.

His idea of a Labour Government is one responsible neither to the voters of the whole country nor even those who voted Labour.

He wants it to take its orders from the Labour Party conference, which, in turn, is dominated by the block votes of unions cast by delegations chosen, usually, on a minuscule minority vote of the membership and often Left-Wing dominated.

(*Daily Mail*, 18 July 1974)

Benn's third problem was his poor relationship with the Prime Minister. Harold Wilson had been irked and embarrassed by the left-wing industrial policy that

Benn had been instrumental in creating. The strength of the left in the party had left him little option but to make Benn Industry Secretary, but he carefully limited his power by splitting the Department of Trade and Industry in two, and made sure that responsibility for the newspaper industry went to Trade and responsibility for broadcasting went to the Home Office. As time passed it became clear that he was not happy with the industrial policy taking shape in Benn's department and would sooner just ditch the manifesto commitments. In mid-June he instructed Benn to make no more speeches on industrial policy until they had discussed the matter. At that discussion, Wilson was angry and hostile.

'What is your strategy?' he asked gruffly.

So I described it to him. I said I didn't disagree with his view on industrial policy.

'Why are you having this "debate"? You are only helping the Tories. Why haven't you produced a bill? Anyway, who said there should be a Green Paper? We don't want a prolonged debate about it. We want legislation. You have been lazy, you haven't got on with it, you have just been making all these speeches. We are in Government now. Why don't you get on with the policy?'

(Benn, *Against the Tide* (17 June 1974))

The election of February 1974 had left Wilson's government well short of a working majority. A further election was clearly necessary within the year – it eventually came in October – and the country lived in a state of suppressed election fever. Wilson pressed Benn for a statement of policy.

Work had been proceeding in the Department of Industry on the manifesto commitments referring to the NEB and 'planning agreements'. Since there was no possibility of getting legislation through in the Short Parliament I had been pressing for a White Paper setting out exactly what we proposed to do, and, no less important, what we were not going to do. It was vital that no vague statements or half-veiled threats should be left around for use as a scare by the Opposition in the autumn election on which I had decided.

(Harold Wilson, *Final Term: The Labour Government 1974–76*, London: Weidenfeld and Nicolson and Michael Joseph)

Within the department the first draft of the green paper was to be drafted by a working group chaired by the minister of state, Eric Heffer. (Why Benn delegated this job to Heffer instead of leading the group himself is a mystery; virtually any other secretary of state would have taken direct charge himself.) Although Benn and Heffer were both left-wingers – in the 1980s they were to join forces against Neil Kinnock's leadership – their working relationship at Industry was uneasy. Heffer recalled:

Tony was a great one for consultation. I noticed, however, that it was his view which usually prevailed. If he failed to carry you at first he would raise the same thing again under different circumstances. He generally won in the end. We had many arguments and he could be naive. But he was honest and he passionately wanted what was best for working people. . . .

Tony Benn asked me to chair the committee to draft the White Paper on the new Industry Act covering planning agreements and the establishment of the NEB. The committee comprised two senior civil servants, Alan Lord and Ron Dearing, Tony Benn's political advisers, Frances Morrell and Francis Cripps, and Michael Meacher (another Industry Minister) and Stuart Holland, who played such a constructive part on the party committee. Meetings were held sometimes three or four times a week, and the work made slow but real progress . . . the White Paper contained all the policies in the manifesto. Even though it was couched in civil service language, I was not bothered. What was important was that it contained the policy. Cripps, Morrell and Meacher said very little in committee but when the paper was completed they told Tony that it was not radical enough in language and was changed. I was furious. Why had they not spoken up at the time or come to see me personally?

(Eric Heffer, *Never a Yes Man*, London: Verso, 1991)

Heffer apparently told another left-wing member of the government, John Silkin, that 'the experience had been hell'.

In late June the document – now changed by Benn to a green paper, and as such more of a discussion document – was circulated within Whitehall. Wilson's immediate reaction was to take over himself the chairmanship of the cabinet committee that was to discuss the white paper – a decision which, not surprisingly, leaked to the press. The *Daily Telegraph* reported

disclosures that Mr Wilson had taken over the chair of the Cabinet Committee on Industrial Policy.

It seems that he decided last April that it was time that he took personal command of the Government's strategy in this sensitive field.

The move is being seen as an attempt to curb the enthusiasm of Mr Benn, who, in his own words, has embarked on 'a great debate' aimed at convincing the public that there must be more nationalisation and a direct say by Government in the running of the largest manufacturing firms.

Some Cabinet Ministers are believed to be alarmed at Mr Benn's public statements, as they are afraid that they could cost Labour votes in the election.

(*Daily Telegraph*, 13 June 1974)

This seemed to confirm Benn's and Heffer's fears that the Prime Minister was leaking against them.

Barbara Castle records having had copied to her a hostile minute from the Chancellor.

Denis [Healey] begins: 'I am strongly in favour of a substantial extension of public ownership and a more dynamic industrial policy.' He also supports the idea of the NEB and agrees the functions Wedgie [Tony Benn] outlined for it. But he stresses that 'a further important objective must be to ensure that the manufacturing sector which remains in private hands must be enabled to operate vigorously and competitively'. Therefore we must remove uncertainty as quickly as possible. Nor does he oppose the nationalization of the aircraft industry and shipbuilding. But compensation would have implications for the government's borrowing requirement and he does not think he should be asked to sign a blank cheque. So programmes should be defined as closely and as soon as possible. On planning agreements he welcomes the intention to introduce these on a limited scale in the first place. He is sure we should not be thinking in terms of the biggest hundred firms, but rather in terms of the sectors most urgently requiring attention – e.g. engineering rather than food or tobacco. We should also go for co-operation rather than sanctions. I must say I find all this common sense.

> (Barbara Castle, *The Castle Diaries 1974–76* (15 July 1974). Castle records that the minute had been circulating for some days before this date.)

Clearly Benn was going to run into trouble at cabinet level; if a fellow left-winger like Castle would not support him, who would? When the green paper finally reached cabinet committee, the answer proved to be: nobody much.

To the Industrial Development Committee of the Cabinet at Number 10, with Harold [Wilson] in the chair. I opened, saying that my Green Paper was a major policy initiative and should be seen against a background of industrial decline and a forecast of further decline. Our policy was well known, I wouldn't deal with it in detail – it was to introduce a National Enterprise Board and planning agreements: the object was to argue and explain the policy, and to discuss the transition.

I said the old policy hadn't worked and what we had to go for was better value for money. As to the problem of whether firms would go abroad, they were doing that anyway: for example, Ford, under the Tory Government, decided to use the profits at Dagenham to invest in Spain.

Denis Healey favoured a mixed economy which must be profitable. We had had lower productivity and he thought there might be a case for planning agreements in the NEB. His worry was that this policy would not provide an adequate return on capital and would be a way of propping up lame ducks like Concorde. The main purpose, which was to make profit, had to be made clear. Workers' control was no good and he wanted that to be understood. As to private industry, confidence was important, and vague threats had led to a blight on investment. We must make clear what we wanted.

Jim [Callaghan, Foreign Secretary] agreed entirely with Denis. He said that the uncertainty argument that I had used was ingenious but in fact this was causing an investment blight; Para 58 had to be rewritten completely. 'I am not agreeing to this policy – it will tear the Party in two, and we won't accept it.'

Harold spoke. 'I accept fully the Manifesto and the planning agreements and the NEB. I cannot however support an NEB outside the control of Ministers regardless of Government policy, and I resent other Ministers saying they are custodians of parts of the Manifesto.' . . .

[Tony Crosland, Environment Secretary, said] Denis Healey was right about the need to increase profits, and the NEB had not been properly thought out.

Shirley Williams [Prices Secretary] thought that unclear proposals were very dangerous and might precipitate a collapse or recession. 'Tony has alarmed industry. We must carry industrialists with us, they are on the edge of total non-cooperation.'

Harold Lever [Chancellor of the Duchy of Lancaster] agreed with all the criticisms, but Peter Shore [Trade] defended me. 'Labour can't build up confidence while it is re-distributing wealth and power,' and there was a new abrasiveness as compared with 1964 when there had been consensus. 'We have to establish a new consensus; we can't retreat.' The weaknesses of the paper, however, were that people couldn't manufacture without a new structure, without planning agreements which didn't seem to frighten ICI at all.

Willie Ross [Scottish Secretary] wanted to tell the Committee that on the previous day a thousand people in the carpet factory in Ayr had lost their jobs and people had withdrawn their confidence from the system. Planning agreements were absolutely essential. 'As for the attacks on Tony Benn, if it had been my job to produce this policy, the attacks would have been on me.' That was warm support.

Although Benn made a strong plea for his paper, Wilson's summing-up was clearly a sign that he was taking charge.

Harold declared, 'I have decided what I will do. I will circulate a paper and it will come back to Ministers in a week's time for discussion. Then it will go to an official committee who will report back to a small group of Ministers. Then it will come to this committee again and back to Cabinet.'

(Tony Benn, *Against the Tide* (28 June 1974))

This was the crucial meeting which proved that Benn did not have the support of his colleagues. Surprisingly, he recorded in his diary that it had been a successful meeting because his colleagues had got their anger off their chests. But Healey (according to his Treasury colleague Edmund Dell) was very happy, and said that Benn had been slaughtered. Healey was right. Wilson had spoken circumspectly at committee, but in his memoir of the 1974–6 government recorded:

It was not until later July that the Department of Industry's draft White Paper emerged. As I had feared, it proved to be a sloppy and half-baked document, polemical, indeed menacing, in tone, redolent more of an NEC Home Policy

Committee document than a Command Paper. One basic weakness was that it appeared to place more emphasis on the somewhat amorphous proposals for planning agreements than on the NEB.

A special committee of senior ministers was set up under my chairmanship to mastermind its re-drafting, which quickly decided that the document should be re-written.

(Harold Wilson, *Final Term*)

According to Wilson much of the re-drafting was by the left-wing Employment Secretary Michael Foot, although the head of Wilson's policy unit claimed a major hand in the re-writing. On 9 July Benn recorded his dismay at receiving

a new paper on industrial policy that has been put in by Harold Wilson under the names of the Secretaries. It really was a disastrous paper. I'd only got it at 10 last night and I'd stayed up late reading it. It was completely different in character from the policy on which the Party had fought the Election. I did get my Private Secretary to ring Number 10 to see if they would agree to postpone it, but they wouldn't.

Under this paper, the National Enterprise Board would control all the nationalised industries and the planning agreements would be the responsibility of the little Neddies. Absolutely crazy.

(Benn, *Against the Tide* (9 July 1974))

There followed a series of cabinet committee meetings at which Wilson systematically diluted Benn's proposals. Other ministers would not back Benn. On 31 July the cabinet overruled Benn's last-ditch attempt to salvage the radical manifesto policy; again other left-wingers failed to support him. Wilson made sure that the following day's press was full of Benn's defeat.

With the coming General Election in mind, the Prime Minister appeared yesterday to endorse suggestions that Labour's proposals for extending State ownership and control of industry have been watered down by the Cabinet and that the White Paper containing them will come as a relief to apprehensive businessmen.

'Above all, it meets my demand that it is clear, and removes a great deal of the uncertainty for business which has been created by the public debate,' he said, in what sounded like a dose of soothing syrup.

. . . The Prime Minister was presumably thinking of Mr Benn when he said in an interview on BBC radio: 'I think there has been too much of a public debate carried on from the election about what should be in the programme. In fact the Cabinet have now agreed on the programme. I took charge of this operation several weeks ago and chaired all the meetings.

'The Cabinet quite happily on Friday accepted the draft which a small group of us under my chairmanship put before it. I believe the country will think that it is relevant, sensible and designed to deal with our economic and industrial problems, some of which have been very grave.'

> . . . According to Whitehall sources, it will be at least a fortnight before the White Paper on industry is published, even if the Stationery Office printing strike is quickly settled. Mr Wilson, who rather fancies himself as a copywriter, revealed in an aside that he was still putting some finishing touches on the draft during his weekend at Chequers.
>
> *(Daily Telegraph*, 3 August 1974)

Heffer, according to his memoirs, considered resigning at this point, but decided to hang on. Benn remained in office and, despite being in a minority within the cabinet for the next five years, seemed never seriously to contemplate resignation.

Benn's fundamental problem was that, although he had captured control of his party's industrial policy in opposition, two-thirds of his colleagues heartily disliked it and the others gave it at best only tepid support. Wilson was clearly determined to ditch as much of the manifesto policy as he could get away with, and that seems to have been made clear to DTI officials who, quite independently, had their own reservations about the practicability of Benn's plans. Benn then played into Wilson's hands by taking over-long to produce his green paper, a product of the fact that he was a more gifted communicator than administrator. And while a gift for speech-making and writing will suffice in opposition, a minister in government needs sufficient administrative drive to generate a coherent policy and sufficient gifts of political organisation to mobilise support amongst his colleagues.

3.c.3   The Prime Minister defeated: Margaret Thatcher and Northern Ireland

Despite the Benn episode, a departmental minister is strongest on his or her departmental ground, and a prime minister will hesitate to challenge him or her on it. If they do clash, much turns on the support that the departmental minister can muster from colleagues. It was Benn's isolation in the cabinet that allowed Wilson to outgun him. But the opposite happened when, in 1982, James Prior, then Northern Ireland Secretary, determined to attempt a further experiment in the devolution of power to local politicians through a local assembly. Margaret Thatcher was against the idea. Prior's memoirs probably play down the virulence of the argument:

> I drafted a White Paper, based on the proposed framework for devolution which I had developed. My draft went first to a small Cabinet Committee, which was not enthusiastic.
>
> The Prime Minister, a natural sympathiser with the Unionists, was very much against the whole idea. . . . She was worried about any form of, or even any suggestion of, devolution, for fear that this would give an opportunity once more to the advocates of devolution in Scotland and Wales to revive their campaigns. And, although the suggestions which I had made for greater

co-operation with the Republic of Ireland fell well short of the arrangements which had been agreed at Sunningdale between the British and Irish Governments in 1973, they were too much for her. She insisted that the separate chapter on Anglo-Irish relation in my draft should be scrapped, and a less positive version incorporated at the end of the chapter on 'The Two Identities' in Northern Ireland.

However [at cabinet committee], I had good support from Willie Whitelaw, Francis Pym, and Humphrey Atkins, the Cabinet's three former Northern Ireland Secretaries, and from Leon Brittan, Quintin Hailsham and of course Peter Carrington; but no support at that stage from Geoffrey Howe, who was still at the Treasury, and not much from other colleagues. . . . When I came back to Cabinet with a revised White Paper I was able to get it through.

The revised White Paper was less supportive of the Irish dimension. I knew that it was therefore unlikely to be as well received by the Nationalists in the North or by the Irish Government as I had hoped. This was probably our great mistake. But I could not push either Margaret or Quintin Hailsham into a better position, and the others felt that I had got as much as I was going to achieve.

. . . The Bill was comparatively short, but we made little progress with it. Before long we faced the inevitable question of whether to introduce the guillotine procedure to limit the amount of time to be spent on the remainder of the Bill. This had to be discussed by the Cabinet. The vast majority of colleagues backed me wholeheartedly. The Prime Minister, however, was opposed. She made her views abundantly clear, saying that she thought it was a rotten Bill, and that in any case she herself would not be voting for it because she was off to the USA. But the guillotine went through and the Bill then completed its passage.

(James Prior, *A Balance of Power*, London: Hamish Hamilton, 1986)

3.c.4 Margaret Thatcher defeated: public spending

This was only one of many occasions on which Margaret Thatcher's colleagues overruled her. Another case occured in the summer of 1982. As the annual public spending allocation round progressed, the Treasury became alarmed at what it saw as the mismatch between demand and resources projected over the rest of the decade. Treasury ministers turned to the Central Policy Review Staff, a free-standing 'think tank' within the Cabinet Office, whose remit was to advise the cabinet on strategic and cross-departmental issues. A swift review led to a paper outlining various radical options for cutting public spending, which went to the cabinet in early September. What happened next was described in an article in *The Economist*.

The special meeting of Mrs Thatcher's cabinet on September 9th was devoted to a long discussion on the problems of controlling public spending. Far more intriguing, however, is what was not discussed: a paper from the Central Policy Review Staff, the government's think-tank, outlining options for radical cuts in public spending, many involving the dismantling of huge chunks of the welfare state. Cabinet wets were so appalled at the think-tank's suggestions that they argued successfully that it would be wrong for the cabinet to give it serious and instant consideration. But that will not be the end of the matter.

The think-tank's paper was circulated along with other cabinet papers on September 7th. It came with the seal of approval of the treasury, which recommended that it form the basis of a six-month study of a public spending strategy for the rest of the decade. This means that its ideas were not pulled out of the ether and that it has more significance than most think-tank papers. Here are details of its contents.

The paper begins by saying that, on present plans and assuming low annual economic growth, public spending will continue to gobble up at least its present 45% of gross domestic product for the foreseeable future. That is only 1% less than its peak under the last Labour government. If the Thatcher government is serious about cutting public expenditure, argues the paper, then it must consider some radical alternatives in the four areas that account for the lion's share of public expenditure: education, social security, health and defence.

The think-tank then deals with each one in turn:

- *Education*   Its controversial suggestion is to end state funding for all institutions of higher education. Instead, fees would be set at market rates, at present around £12,000 for the average three-year course. About 300,000 state scholarships could be made available, along with student loans for those with the entry qualifications but without scholarships. The paper also says that there could be great savings if the state no longer had to provide for primary and secondary school education, but it acknowledges the political difficulties of abolishing state schooling. It considers moving to a system of educational vouchers for parents, which they could cash at schools of their choice to pay for their children's education. The idea has long been popular with free-market Tories and its supporters include Sir Keith Joseph (the education secretary) and Mr Ferdinand Mount (who recently became the head of the prime minister's policy unit in Downing Street). But the think-tank points out that vouchers would not cut spending and might even increase it, since parents at present footing the bill for their children's private education would qualify for state vouchers too. There are, however, some savings to be made in the school system by allowing the teacher–pupil ratio to rise. It has been falling, argues the paper, without any rise in the quality of state education.

- *Social security*   Big savings can be made, says the paper, if all social security payments – from pensions to supplementary benefits – no longer rise in line with inflation. There are echoes here of the Reagan administration's budget battles in the United States. The task of cutting federal spending in Washington has been made harder because of the political difficulties of abolishing the indexation of pensions.

- *Health* The paper suggests replacing the National Health Service with private health insurance: this could save £3 billion–4 billion a year from a 1982–83 health budget of £10 billion. The problem is that the less well-off might underinsure, so the paper suggests that there might have to be a compulsory minimum of private insurance for everyone. In the meantime savings could be made by charging for visits to the doctor and more for drugs.
- *Defence* The think-tank is short of bright ideas on how to curb the £14 billion now spent annually on the armed forces. It recognises that Mrs Thatcher does not want to budge from Britain's commitment to Nato to raise defence spending by 3% a year in real terms until 1986. It suggests, however, that beyond the mid-1980s defence's share of the nation's resources should be frozen. It points out that Britain spends a higher proportion of its GDP on defence than its European allies and says that, in the long run, it would be to the country's advantage if defence was funded from the budget of the European Community.

The think-tank's paper was circulated by Mr John Sparrow, the CPRS director and former merchant banker who is now widely regarded in Whitehall as a stalking horse for the Treasury. A key drafter was Mr Alan Bailey (a Treasury deputy secretary on loan to the CPRS, an expert on public spending and Mr Sparrow's deputy). In his own paper to the same cabinet meeting, Sir Geoffrey Howe, the chancellor of the exchequer said that a failure to shift social spending from its present trend would have severe consequences for the government's fiscal strategy. On the worst economic growth assumptions, and present welfare-state policies, the state's share of GDP could rise to almost 60% before 1990.

Treasury ministers were furious when the wets lined up en masse to block discussion of a paper which owed its inspiration to them. So was Mrs Thatcher. There is to be no record of the matter in cabinet minutes. The September 9th cabinet meeting produced the first wet–dry clash for over a year. It could be a harbinger of cabinet meetings to come. Mrs Thatcher sympathises with the think-tank's drift. But she is now in no doubt that to pursue such a radical course risks splitting her party wide open. Many of the think-tank's suggestions for health and education would be as unpopular with middle-class Tories as with Labour voters. But Tory wets expect that the think-tank's ideas will soon resurface in another guise.

('Thatcher's Think-tank Takes Aim at the Welfare State', *The Economist*, 18 September 1982)

Nigel Lawson, then Energy Secretary, described what happened at cabinet rather more tersely.

The result was the nearest thing to a Cabinet riot in the history of the Thatcher administration. . . . The episode played into the hands of the 'wets'. They not only managed to get the CPRS report shelved at the meeting; but made sure that its contents were leaked to *The Economist*. . . . Margaret, who in those pre-Poll Tax days knew how to beat a necessary retreat, was forced to state publicly that the Government had no intention of pursuing any of the options in the CPRS paper.

(Nigel Lawson, *The View from No. 11: Memoirs of a Tory Radical*, London: Bantam Press, 1992)

The Economist's story appeared in the run-up to the Conservative Party conference, and caused an uproar in the press. On the weekend of 2–3 October, newspapers carried front-page lead stories that Margaret Thatcher had disowned the report. But a week later, *The Economist* disclosed more.

The think-tank report, which suggested dismantling chunks of the welfare state, hung over the Tory conference like a dark cloud. In the run-up to Brighton, the prime minister's press office attempted what is known in Washington as a 'damage-limitation exercise'. The official line emerged that when Mrs Thatcher returned from her trip to the Far East she was so appalled by the reports that her government was seriously considering the think-tank's ideas that she immediately issued instructions for the report to be thrown into the rubbish bin. Since this involves a rewrite of recent history, it is worth reconstructing what really happened.

The think-tank report was circulated to ministers along with the rest of the cabinet papers on the evening of September 7th. . . .

When Mrs Thatcher and Sir Robert Armstrong, the cabinet secretary, discussed the agenda for the special cabinet of September 9th, they decided to devote the morning to the more pressing problems of public spending for 1983–84 and discuss the think-tank report in the afternoon.

The day before that cabinet meeting, senior civil servants in each department briefed their ministers on what they might say about the paper. One minister said there were 18 civil servants at his briefing. On the eve of September 9th, several cabinet 'wets' plotted how to kill the paper at the next day's cabinet.

Mrs Thatcher's first shock came before lunch during the cabinet meeting. She was surprised to discover that the think-tank paper had come with the usual cabinet papers. It should have been distributed separately to ministers only. It was feared that, as a result of its wide distribution within Whitehall, there was a strong chance of a leak. At least four cabinet ministers (all wets) said they did not want a formal cabinet discussion about its contents anyway.

When the cabinet broke for lunch, there was much intrigue. At one stage, Mrs Thatcher was closeted downstairs with Treasury ministers, while upstairs the rest of the cabinet sat round the lunch table deciding how to kill the paper. When the cabinet reassembled, Mrs Thatcher was faced with a clear majority in favour of ditching the paper without further ado. Sir Geoffrey Howe and his chief secretary, Mr Leon Brittan, attempted a rearguard action to save the paper they had inspired. They were backed by Lord Cockfield, the trade minister, and Mr John Biffen, the leader of the house. Almost every other cabinet minister registered his disapproval. The prime minister expected the usual wets, such as Mr Jim Prior and Mr Peter Walker, to take fright. But more centrist figures (such as Mr Francis Pym) and respected veterans (like Lord Hailsham) were also opposed to considering it.

Mrs Thatcher argued that the cabinet should not shirk any paper that came before it. She was told by several of her colleagues that the think-tank exercise should have been done by the Tory party's own research department, so that there was less chance of it being branded as a indication of government policy. At this stage, Mr Cecil Parkinson, the party chairman, agreed that that might be the best way to proceed. In the end, an angry Mrs Thatcher bowed to the majority and ended the meeting without there being any discussion of the substance of the document. Next day the newspapers carried Downing Street lobby reports that the cabinet had simply considered public spending.

On September 17th, details of the think-tank paper appeared in *The Economist*. At Brighton, Mrs Thatcher was saying bitterly that it had been passed to us 'within hours'. In fact it took several days to leak out and was pieced together from a variety of sources.

Tory party managers were afraid that a think-tank controversy might overshadow a party conference which was supposed to celebrate the Falklands victory and the Tories' lead over Labour in the polls. Mrs Thatcher was aware of the troubles brewing at home while she was in Hongkong. On her return, she was told bluntly by Mr Parkinson that drastic steps had to be taken to dissociate the government from the think-tank's thoughts.

On Friday, October 1st, Downing Street briefed Sunday newspaper correspondents on Mrs Thatcher's supposed reaction to the think-tank. She was said to be against its report and had shelved it. Several Sunday and Monday papers carried a story along these lines, though some added their own caveats. In reality, Mrs Thatcher had shelved a report because she had met a cabinet brick wall.

('Mountains out of Molehills?', *The Economist*, 9 October 1982)

4   External influences on policy

4.a   THE EUROPEAN UNION

Section 1.e gave some idea of the impact that EU membership has had on Whitehall. As the member states of the EU have moved gradually towards closer integration, the commission's role in harmonisation and regulation of economic and social activity has expanded, and the EU's influence has spread steadily into new areas of activity in which member states previously ran their own show. However, co-ordinating the interests of fifteen states in any area is technically a highly complicated business, and getting their ministers to reconcile their different viewpoints involves a lot of haggling, brinkmanship and compromise.

4.a.1   The Council of Ministers: the single market in bananas

An example of the difficulty of devising commercial policies that will suit all EU countries, and one which became notorious for its complexity in the early 1990s, was the single European market in bananas. Despite the irresistibly comic nature of the subject – plenty of newspaper headlines about banana splits, and the like – the implications of the price at which bananas were sold in Europe were immense for the mainly poor countries that grew them. The key problem was that most European countries imposed limits on imports of cheaper bananas from South America to safeguard trade from places like the Windward Islands whose bananas were more expensive but with whom EU countries had historic ties. A common policy towards imports became necessary once trade barriers within the EU were lifted, and in the second half of 1992, when the British held the presidency of the Council of Ministers, they made a determined attempt to break the impasse.

> Until this month, bananas have been the bane of Brussels bureaucrats, as officials struggled to produce a compromise plan for a single European market in bananas after 1992.
> At stake is the future of many small overseas EC territories, such as Belize, Guadeloupe, and the Windward Islands, whose fragile economies depend on bananas even though they are inefficient, high-cost producers.

The fear is that if these countries stopped producing bananas the profitable drugs industry, already a threat, could take hold.

A proposal to solve the banana controversy was painstakingly forged by the European Commission in late July – after nearly five years of debate – and the English version has just been published.

. . . Most EC members except Germany restrict imports of inexpensive Latin American bananas and give preferential treatment to their overseas territories – anathema to the principles of the General Agreement on Tariffs and Trade and the objectives of the single European market.

These different policies cause significant variations in national prices, so that consumers in Britain pay about 50p for a pound of bananas while Germans pay only 40p. Americans, who eat 'dollar' bananas from South America, pay an average 28p.

The European Commission has proposed a two million ton annual quota on banana imports from 1 January 1993, plus an additional 'autonomous quota' to be decided later at the commission's discretion. Europeans eat 3.5 million tons of bananas a year.

In addition, imports will face a 20 per cent duty when they enter each EC state. This 20 per cent levy now applies to all EC countries except Germany, which imports dollar bananas duty-free.

Under the proposal, EC number-crunchers say national prices should converge, with German bananas becoming more expensive and British banana prices falling.

(*Independent*, 21 December 1992)

Unanimity proved impossible to obtain. However, the introduction of 'weighted majority voting' in the Council of Ministers made a decision inevitable, albeit after a certain amount of (fairly typical) manoeuvring. Under weighted majority voting, each member state has a fixed number of votes, according to its size. A weighted majority was required to carry a proposal. In 1992, this effectively meant that a coalition of countries if they formed an alliance on an issue could exercise a veto.

EC agriculture ministers were yesterday facing the prospect of another long night debating a deal that everyone believed had been concluded in December. Disagreements over monetary union, social dumping and competitive devaluations are but nothing to the banana battle.

On one side are the free-traders, led by Germany, who argue that the single market should open Community markets to unlimited imports of cheap so-called dollar bananas from the Caribbean plantations. Against them are France and Britain – an unusual trade alliance – Spain and Greece, who argue that the EC has commitments to back producers in territories such as the Canary Islands or former European colonies such as the Windward Islands. The result: deadlock.

December brought a breakthrough compromise: dollar banana imports into the Community would be limited to 2 million tons a year and a 20 per cent import levy charged; beyond that the tariff would rise steeply. Any rise in market demand and the levy would be readjusted according to a special mechanism. To agree on this alone required big concessions from France and Britain.

Germany and Denmark continued to resist, but all a decision requires is a 'yes' from a weighted majority of the other member states. All that stood between the compromise and its adoption was the legal text. But when EC agriculture ministers gathered this week to sign the historic deal, prompted by the creation of the single market in January, Belgium and the Netherlands brought up unexpected objections.

Ministers were last night pinning their hopes on a change of heart by Belgium or the Netherlands. European banana-eaters also have a vested interest in seeing the deal go through, because if it does, bananas will be cheaper.

(Independent, 13 February 1993)

Eventually the Danes, who in January 1993 had taken over the presidency from the UK, took it upon themselves to break the deadlock.

After a long night of debate during which allegations of unfair play were traded, the EC finally, early on Saturday morning, agreed to accept rules governing the import of bananas. The deadlock began when Belgium and the Netherlands, on taking a second look at a compromise deal agreed last year, had decided it was unacceptable. Denmark, which with Germany had originally opposed the deal, now found itself as current holder of the EC presidency with a responsibility to find a way through the impasse. So Copenhagen changed position to create the weighted majority in favour needed to break the stalemate.

. . . Germans in Hamburg woke up yesterday to blink at the full-size, colour banana picture across the front page of a city newspaper to illustrate the headline 'Germany loses the banana war'.

(Independent, 16 February 1993)

4.a.2   The Council of Ministers: harmonising alcohol duties

The Council of Ministers meets in private, and comparatively little has been written about its workings. However, Jock Bruce-Gardyne, who served as a junior minister at the Treasury in the early years of Margaret Thatcher's government, has left an account of his appearance at the Council which – although allowance must be made for the author's light-hearted cynicism – offers some insights into its internal workings.

For some time the European Commission had been campaigning for the harmonisation of national duties on alcohol. There were many cross-currents of interest at stake. The French, and still more the Italians, had for long been accused by the Scotch whisky industry of practising discrimination against Scotch by rigging their duty structure in favour of home-produced brandy and grappa. The Germans were similarly charged with artificially sustaining their home wine production vis-à-vis imported wines from France and Italy; while the French had from time to time brazenly flouted Community rules to keep out Italian wine. We were in the dock for perpetuation of an excessive – by Community standards – disparity between duties on beer (low) and duties on wine (high).

In the second half of 1981 Britain held the chair in the Community (a position which rotates between the member countries every six months). This meant that for major meetings of the Council of Ministers of the Community we had to field two Ministers: one to take the chair, and one to represent HMG. At lesser meetings one Minister was deemed to suffice, to take the chair: HMG was represented by a senior civil servant.

It thus came as a rude shock to me to find that almost my first assignment after entering the Treasury in the autumn of 1981 was to preside over a meeting of the Community's Customs Council consisting of the national Ministers responsible for Customs and Excise Duties, called in that most inaccessible of Europe's several headquarter-cities, Strasbourg, to consider the awkward topic of alcohol duty harmonisation.

First I had to be briefed by the Chairman of Customs and Excise, Sir Douglas Lovelock. Sir Douglas was – is – a gallant Christian gentleman to whom I fear I caused a certain amount of trouble and disappointment. My task in Strasbourg, Sir Douglas explained to me, was to preside over the meeting in such a manner as to ensure that it would fail.

I suppose I looked slightly fazed by this explanation. 'Yes, Minister,' Sir Douglas assured me with a cheerful mixture of metaphors which seemed entirely appropriate, 'we're throwing you in at the deep end. From now on it'll be downhill all the way.' The point was that harmonisation of beer and wine duties would not suit HMG one little bit. It would involve either a large cut in our taxes on wines, which the Chancellor would not appreciate, or else a substantial increase in beer duties, which would bump up the retail price index and, even more serious, be highly politically contentious.

I mentioned frivolously that personally I never touched beer, and had a strong addiction to wine. Harmonisation sounded like a splendid wheeze to me. Sir Douglas patiently explained that, be that as it might, I would not win friends and influence people if I went down that road. I hastily conceded his point.

Fortunately, Sir Douglas added, nobody else really wanted harmonisation either. But there was a snag. The Commission was running out of patience with the Council of Ministers. A number of suits before the European Court were pending, against a number of member Governments, including HMG, on this particular issue, and it was therefore vital to 'keep the ball in play'. So long as the Council continued to pretend that it was vigorously pursuing harmonisation, the Commission, which was the plaintiff in the pending suits before the Court, would have to hold its hand.

So my task was to make sure that the Council failed to reach agreement; but to avoid an admission of failure; and – above all – to ensure that the blame for our failure to agree rested on the shoulders of some other participant, and not – repeat not – on the shoulders of HMG. 'You see, Minister, as president, you've got somehow to contrive to give the impression that you want us to reach an accord even though, as I say, you don't.'

Eager to enter into the spirit of these interesting diplomatic manoeuvres, I enquired who was to be the fall-guy. The French, I suggested, knowing the pleasure which our civil service takes in scoring off the wicked froggies? 'Well, no, Minister,' the worldly wise Sir Douglas advised, 'I don't think that would be a good idea on the whole. I think I'd go for the Greeks if you can. Nobody likes the Greeks.' Since the Greeks seemed to be a little peripheral to the argument I was worried about this. But I promised to do my best.

. . . So we arrived in Strasbourg. The following morning my first appointment was with Sir Kenneth Christofas, a senior British diplomat on the staff of my erstwhile Westminster colleague, Christopher Tugendhat, who had been unexpectedly elevated to the position of second British Commissioner in Brussels by Jim Callaghan (legend had it that his most important qualification for the post had been an inability to speak French, since Callaghan's first Commissioner, Roy Jenkins, was not proficient in that language, and had not wished to be upstaged by his team mate). With innocent but misplaced frankness I told Sir Kenneth that, as I understood it, our purpose was to abort the meeting as swiftly as could decently be achieved. Sir Kenneth was aghast.

Naturally, he conceded, Her Majesty's Government might have views about the harmonisation of taxes on wine and beer about which he, as a servant of the Commission, could know nothing. But it was a matter of life and death, certainly for the good name of the Community, but also – he ventured to suggest – for the reputation of the British Government, that I, as President ad interim of that afternoon's Council, should be, and be seen to be, dedicated to the discovery of a generally acceptable compromise outcome. It would not be easy, that he acknowledged. But we must bust a gut if need be.

We proceeded to a gargantuan meal at one of Strasbourg's better restaurants (where the risk of busting guts appeared to me considerable), during which a fair amount of preliminary sparring was conducted. As President I found myself subjected to bizarre courtship rituals, being advised by Sir Kenneth Christofas, who had now emerged as my principal minder, entirely displacing Sir Douglas Lovelock, hovering anxiously in the background, to take pudding with the Italian Minister, and coffee with the French. Then there was a second round of coffee, tête-à-tête with Christopher Tugendhat, his mandarins, and the ubiquitous Sir Kenneth. I naively assumed that Christopher and I, as old backbench (and even before that *Financial Times*) contemporaries could dispense with the diplomatic niceties. There was, I pointed out, a 5pm plane from Strasbourg back to London, and I was keen to catch it. Since it was obvious from our lunchtime conversations that nobody was remotely interested in a settlement, I suggested that we cut the cackle, agree to disagree, and disperse.

Once again, dismay. 'I think', Sir Kenneth hastily intervened, 'the Minister is understandably disappointed by the conversations over lunch. But I am sure, Commissioner, you would agree with me that appearances can be deceptive. The Minister will, I am sure, wish to impress upon his Ministerial colleagues the gravity of the situation which would arise in the absence of agreement this afternoon.' The Commissioner agreed emphatically.

OK, I said, so we'll give it a whirl. We would conduct the time-hallowed ritual known in Community circles as a 'tour de table'. This is a stately minuet in which the Chairman invites each of the Ministers seated round the table to read out his brief. But if, as looked to be self-evident, these briefs displayed a gulf of conflict, then we would call it a day. That seemed to be acceptable. Or so I thought.

We all assembled. After a suitable and apparently indispensable exchange of politesses, we launched upon our tour de table. Sure enough this demonstrated that nobody agreed about anything. I told Christofas, seated at my left hand, that I proposed to recognise our incompatibilities, and call it a day. Once more, consternation. On the contrary, I was told, my only proper course was to call for an adjournment, during which I, as Chairman, would be available to receive suggestions for compromise solutions from my colleagues. I did as I was told.

I adjourned to the Presidential suite, where tea was served, and a stream of visitors was ushered in, led by Christopher Tugendhat who, far from being amenable to an acknowledgement of failure, now warned sternly that all sorts of Governments – and most certainly our own – would find themselves promptly in the dock if the Council dispersed without agreement.

Eventually we all reassembled. Taking a line which caused Sir Kenneth Christofas considerable distress, I said that we seemed to have come to an impasse, and suggested that we might as well call it a day. Immediately the French representative asked to be heard. He felt, he told us, that in fact some useful progress had been made, and he suggested that we should adjourn and agree to meet again in three weeks' time, at which point he was confident that compromise solutions would be found. This was a proposition which commanded general support (after all, the more the meetings, the more the allowances properly claimed by all and sundry). And thus it was resolved.

Three weeks later we duly met again. Apparently honour had been satisfied. Another Lucullan feast was digested, and then one and all rapidly acknowledged that there was no possibility of agreement about anything. The Commission would have to do its worst at the European Court. Everybody dispersed cheerfully for the Christmas holidays. At least the threat of an immediate obligation to harmonise our duties upon wine and beer had been averted, and to that extent I had presumably done my duty. But I was left with a suspicion that, as a Community diplomatist, I had left something to be desired.

(Jock Bruce-Gardyne, *Ministers and Mandarins*,
London: Macmillan, 1986)

In due course the Commission did indeed take various member states to court, and in his 1984 budget Chancellor Nigel Lawson harmonised wine and beer taxes, although he took advantage of the economic upturn to cut the tax on wine rather than increase dramatically the tax on beer, to the annoyance of the opposition.

4.a.3   The European Council: enlarging the Union

The Council of Ministers and the official machinery that underpins it constitute the workaday level of EU business, where most matters are settled. The European Council is a later creation which, as it were, floats above the Council of Ministers, acting as a cross between an informal court of appeal and an inner cabinet. It was invented in 1974 when President Giscard d'Estaing of France suggested that the EC's heads of government should occasionally meet informally. The arrangement stuck, and the twice-yearly meetings have acquired important, though informal, status.

A lot of business now gets done at the European Council. For instance John Major reported to the Commons in December 1993 that its recent meeting had agreed a package of measures to encourage economic revival, discussed trans-European transport links and international trade negotiations (GATT), approved a package of measures against drug trafficking, scrapped various outdated EU directives, discussed the Yugoslav conflict, and informally met President Yeltsin of Russia. But many of the issues run on from meeting to meeting, and in between times the country holding the current presidency of the Council must try to broker solutions.

A reasonable example – here greatly simplified – is the lead-up to the December 1984 meeting in Dublin, which was to agree terms for Spain and Portugal to join the EC. This raised problems for both new and existing members, centring on, first, wine, since the Mediterranean countries' huge wine production led Germany and France to press for limitations on production to prevent a glut of the product, and, second, Greece's attempt to use the advent of the Iberian countries to gain extra money for Mediterranean countries – including Greece. Ireland at this time held the presidency, and the then Prime Minister of Ireland, Garrett Fitzgerald, recalled with some feeling the complexity of the horse-trading that led to the summit.

Felipe Gonzalez [Prime Minister of Spain] came to Dublin to discuss the enlargement negotiation with me. In our tête-à-tête I sought flexibility from him in relation both to wine – where he was happy to rely on Italy to fight the battle against production limitations – and fish. . . . The Portuguese were concerned lest a hitch in the Spanish negotiation would hold up, or even perhaps prevent, Portuguese membership – just as our membership application of 1961 had been shelved in January 1963 when de Gaulle had vetoed British entry. They therefore wanted a preliminary agreement that would mark the fact that their negotiation had been substantially successful. During the following weeks we secured the agreement of our partners to the signing of such a document. As soon as Soares [Prime Minister of Portugal] learnt of this he asked for an immediate meeting to sign it, and a couple of days later, on 24 October, he visited Dublin for this purpose.

. . . Meanwhile the lack of progress on outstanding issues had led us to send Jim O'Keeffe (Junior Irish Foreign Minister) on a tour of capitals in mid-October; this helped to secure agreement on a range of outstanding items, which narrowed the field of disagreement to two or three significant issues, including wine. By mid-November the crucial importance of wine to the negotiations had become even clearer. German proposals to deal with the wine surplus by means of a compulsory distillation of wine produced in excess of 100 million litres, which would involve price reductions of one-half or two-thirds on the wine surplus distilled, were rejected by Italy and Greece. Indeed these countries turned the tables on the Germans by pressing for a solution of which one element would be a financial penalty for the sugaring of wine that subsequently had to be distilled. (Producers in Germany and Luxembourg sugar some of their wines, because this artificially increases the quantity of drinkable wine.) Helmut Kohl (Chancellor of West Germany), whose power base is in a wine-producing area, was shocked and furious at this counterproposal.

. . . The final pre-Council meeting of Foreign Ministers took place on 26–28 November, just five days before the Dublin meeting of heads of government. It failed to resolve the crucial wine deadlock, on which the Germans and Italians remained obdurate, and Greece was furious with the UK for refusing to agree that funding for the Integrated Mediterranean Programme, involving substantial financial aid to Greece in compensation for losses expected as a result of Spanish and Portuguese membership, should be additional to normal Structural Fund money from the Community Budget.

Reviewing this situation immediately after the end of the Foreign Affairs Council, I decided I would visit Paris and Rome at once with a view to working out a possible compromise on wine during the weekend before the European Council. Next day I met Mitterrand [President of France] in Paris and also had a technical discussion with Roland Dumas (French Foreign Minister), during which I tried out some ideas on how the Franco-Italian disagreement might be resolved. What I had in mind was a regional wine production limitation system to be implemented by national governments; the

French had been unhappy about allowing such a system to be implemented at a regional level.

The French press comments after my visit were fairly downbeat. If my 'last ditch' efforts succeeded it would be a triumph for Irish diplomacy, they said, but they did not rate my chances highly.

Encouraged by Dumas's reaction to my proposals, however, I flew on to Rome, where next morning I had a meeting with Craxi [Italian Prime Minister], Andreotti [Italian Foreign Minister], and the Agriculture Minister, Pandolfi, who were accompanied by a senior official, Renato Ruggiero. I found it difficult to pin the Ministers down, but from their reactions and Ruggiero's demeanour I judged that the proposals I had in mind might 'run'.

. . . When I returned to Dublin my officials and I put together a concrete proposal, and on Saturday I rang Dumas and Ruggiero to tell them precisely what I would propose at the outset of the European Council. Receiving favourable reactions in principle from them, I suggested that when I turned to their delegations at the Council to ask them to react to what I was suggesting, their response should be a grudging agreement to look at my suggestion with a view to returning to it later, if the Germans and Luxembourgers meanwhile showed a willingness to compromise on the wine sugaring issue. Both Dumas and Ruggiero agreed to this tactic.

When on Monday morning the European Council turned its attention to enlargement, I put forward my compromise on wine and secured the desired responses from the French and Italians. Then I turned to the Germans and Luxembourgers, saying that there was an evident need to take a specific step in relation to wine sugaring that would ensure a contribution to reducing the cost of the Community's wine policy. My concrete proposals towards this end, which involved a version of what had already been tried out in the Foreign Affairs Council, were greeted by Helmut Kohl with undisguised hostility; he stuck to this line for most of the meeting, but agreement was eventually reached on a proposal designed to limit to some degree the cost of distilling German wine whose alcohol content had been increased by sugaring. And when we returned to the enlargement issue on the morning of the second day, the French and Italians accepted my compromise on production limitations, subject to some slight adjustments, as being a necessary step towards enlargement. The other, less difficult enlargement problems were handed back to the Council of Ministers to settle.

(Garrett Fitzgerald, *All in a Life*, Dublin: Macmillan and Gill, 1991)

But the Council did not end without drama.

Hopes that Spain and Portugal would be given a clear welcome to join the Common Market were dashed by Greece at the EEC summit in Dublin last night.

Two days of negotiations by the Community heads of government succeeded in solving all the technical problems standing in the way of Spanish and Portuguese entry, but Mr Papandreou, the Greek Prime Minister, finally insisted on maintaining a right of veto over the applications. Mr Papandreou said Greece would continue to block the entry of Spain and Portugal until it was satisfied that the EEC would adopt a costly programme to safeguard the future of its Mediterranean regions.

This so-caled Integrated Mediterranean Programme has been proposed by the EEC Commission in a move to assist the very poorest regions of the Community with the impact of enlargement. It would also answer some of the specific points made by Greece in its 'memorandum' last year, which, essentially, called for a renegotiation of Greece's EEC entry terms.

The programme would last for six years and would provide about £4 billion of EEC money to help the pooer Mediterranean regions. The whole of Greece would qualify for such aid, along with parts of Italy and France. The Greek share would be about £1.5 billion, but, so far, EEC ministers have provided only nominal funds for the programme. The 1985 budget, as approved by the European Parliament, would give only £40 million towards it.

(*Daily Telegraph*, 5 December 1984)

And so the saga dragged on. Eventually the Greeks got some of what they wanted, and Spain and Portugal were admitted. Unfortunately most European council meetings are like that: a tangle of issues that progress from stage to stage, becoming more and more complicated until some urgent event compels the participants to resolve them. For that reason, despite the huge press attendance, the quality of press coverage is often shallow.

4.b   THE POLITICS OF INFLUENCE

As the introduction explained, one of the most important influences on the development of policy is pressure from outside interest groups. Section 1.f showed the influence of determined and well-organised pressure groups. The two basic rules of lobbying government are: make sure that the right officials and ministers know clearly what your views are; and feed your views into the policy making process at an early stage, rather than waiting until the decision is taken and then making a clumsy (and potentially unsuccessful) late tackle. Even then, these groups can mishandle the opportunities offered to them.

4.b.1   How not to make friends and influence policy: the Scotch Whisky Association

A good example of a pressure group mishandling its relations with the government was the belated attempt by the Scotch Whisky Association to prevent a change to spirits duties in 1982. (This is, incidentally, another case that shows the sway of the EC over Whitehall policy making.)

In the run-up to the 1982 Budget, the excisemen came to me with a proposal for the phasing-out of a special duty on immature spirits. This duty had, I was

told, originally been introduced during the First World War to discourage
munitions workers from drinking red biddy. It was relatively expensive to
collect, and yielded almost nothing. Furthermore the Common Market did not
like it. I was assured that 'the stocks were sold, the press was squared, the
middle classes quite prepared' – in particular there was on the file a letter
from the most important of the 'middle classes' in this context, the Scotch
Whisky Association, saying that, while they were not keen on the idea, they
were prepared to live with it providing the duty (which was a mild deterrent to
some imported competitors for the domestic Scotch market) was phased out
and not abolished overnight – a point which the Customs had conceded. So I
gave the OK.

Two or three days after Budget Day there was a minor explosion. A letter,
written on the very eve of the Budget, had been despatched from the Scotch
Whisky Association not to the Treasury, but to their sponsoring Ministry,
Agriculture, to protest that the phasing-out of the immature spirits duty would
spell the end of the world as the Scotch whisky industry knew it. I was not
particularly surprised. In days of yore, when I had myself represented a Scots
constituency at Westminster, I had frequently witnessed the elephantine
clumsiness with which this particular pressure group endeavoured to defend
the interests of its clients.

The Customs told me that, in their judgement, if we did not move on the
immature spirits duty we were quite likely to be taken to court by the Brussels
Commission; that if we were we would certainly lose; and that if we did lose
there would be no question of phasing out the duty in a genteel manner: it
would have to go in one fell swoop. Which, they reckoned, the Scotch whisky
industry would find a lot more painful.

Nevertheless it hardly seemed worth a serious Parliamentary row, which
the Scotch Whisky Association might easily provoke. So we had them in. I
drew their attention to their earlier letters, and gently suggested that if they
had had last-minute second thoughts they might at least have had the
gumption to get in touch with the Treasury. I pointed out the European
hazard. Now that we had announced our intention in the Budget, the
Commission would be all the more likely to act against us if we reversed it.

They were duly contrite. Yes, they had had second thoughts. Yes, they
should have told the Treasury. But it really was a matter of life and death.
They would happily run the risk of a European prosecution. But would we
please, please, withdraw the relevant clause.

So I said, 'On your head be it. If the Brussels Commission puts us in the
dock, don't come to us for sympathy.' But rather than simply withdrawing the
offending clause, we could at least win brownie points on the Tory back
benches by allowing one of our Scots MPs to put down an amendment to
scrap it, and then yielding gracefully to his persuasive oratory.

Which is what we did. It all went swimmingly. Our Scots colleague got
glowing press notices for sticking up for Scottish interests, and the

Treasury basked in a warm glow of back bench approval. But not for very long.

Some weeks later I discovered, nestling coyly in my overnight red box, an interesting exchange of correspondence with the Rum Importers' Association. First there was a furious letter from the Association, which pointed out that when Customs had first canvassed the idea of abolishing the immature spirits duty round the spirit trade the previous autumn they had responded – copy enclosed – to the effect that, for them, abolition was essential, and could not come too soon. Consequently they had been delighted by the appearance of the promised clause in the Budget – and outraged by its subsequent withdrawal. They had been even more outraged, on perusing Hansard, to discover that I had not even shown a trace of awareness that they had an interest in the matter – even that they existed.

Appended to this letter was a draft reply for me to sign. This had me say that I was saddened to see that they were in such a pet. But of course I had known all about their interest in the matter: it was just one of those occasions when somebody has to be sacrificed for the greater good of the nation as a whole.

I declined to sign. When, I asked, had I been alerted to the interest of the Rum Importers' Association in the matter? So far as I could recollect the Association was absolutely right: I had indeed been unaware of their existence.

My Private Secretary swiftly passed this bad news back to the Customs. He subsequently informed me that they were sure that I had been alerted somewhere, somewhen. Ten days later I found a new draft reply to the Rum Importers' Association sitting in my box. The references to my awareness of their feelings about the immature spirits duty had disappeared. Otherwise the original letter was unchanged.

Once again I declined to sign. I said I assumed that in fact Customs had been quite unable to produce any evidence of my previous awareness of the rum importers' anxieties; and that before any letter went out the whole affair would have to be discussed.

In the end it fortunately transpired that it would be possible to devise a special phasing-out of the duty on rum, and on rum alone. Customs were by no means happy with this: they argued that the rum importers had lived with the duty since time immemorial, and another year or two would not hurt them. Which was indeed perfectly logical. But by now my dander was up, and I was determined that the rum importers should be the beneficiaries of a miscalculation for which I had been expected to carry the can.

(Jock Bruce-Gardyne, *Ministers and Mandarins*,
London: Macmillan, 1986)

4.b.2   How to influence policy successfully: the London boroughs and parking

In contrast to the clumsy efforts of the Scotch Whisky Association, a textbook example of successful government lobbying was the campaign by which London's local councils persuaded the Home Office to transfer parking enforcement in the capital to them. The campaign was run jointly by the London Boroughs Association (LBA), which represented mainly Conservative and Liberal councils, and the Association of London Authorities (ALA) which represented Labour councils.

> London traffic and highway authorities have important responsibilities. How odd, therefore, that having been charged with deciding where to put yellow lines for traffic management purposes, boroughs have never been able to enforce them. That has been the job of the police, who of course have far more serious matters to deal with. Not surprisingly, therefore, the priority given by the police to parking enforcement has gradually slumped. In the Road Traffic Act 1991 it has finally been realised that the authorities responsible for determining the amount and location of on-street parking should also have the responsibility for enforcement. Quite logical really! But what a vast amount of time and effort it has taken to win the new powers.
>
> Traffic wardens, or meter attendants as they were then called, arrived in Westminster on 19 September 1960, shortly after the parking meter. Also in 1960 the Royal Commission on Local Government recommended that all aspects of traffic management including parking enforcement should be the responsibility of the Greater London Council. This did not transpire.
>
> The number of traffic wardens steadily built up with the spread of meters and yellow lines, but the government allowed levels to oscillate widely over the years. Traffic wardens were often the victim of public expenditure cuts. In 1975 the government forced the police to reduce the number of traffic wardens from 2,100 to 1,500 for this reason. This was achieved by 1977 but the number continued to fall and in 1980 reached 1,059. Numbers rose slightly to 1,300 by the end of 1981, but this was nothing like the number needed to do the job properly, and the police were telling the House of Commons Transport Committee in 1982 that London needed 4,000 traffic wardens. This request was ignored and the traffic warden force continued to be a low priority. During the rest of the 1980s the strength varied from 1,400 to 1,900.
>
> Meanwhile the link between London's traffic chaos and illegal parking was becoming clearer to see by the day. Surveys and studies in the late 1980s were showing that 350,000 parking offences were being committed in central London alone, every day; that 149 out of 150 offenders went free; and that improved enforcement throughout London could yield benefits of £100–£200 million per year in terms of reduced delays, casualties and time spent searching for parking space.

April 1987 was crucial for two reasons. Firstly the national and London local authority associations met Home Office and Department of Transport Ministers to express their continued concern at the level of non-compliance with parking restrictions. Secondly, from April to August 1987 the Metropolitan Police carried out an internal study to determine the need for and future role of their traffic warden force. It recommended that 'Responsibility for parking control should be devolved to local authorities . . .'. However, in true British tradition the next stage was a working party – WHOOPIE (Working Party on Parking Enforcement). . . .

WHOOPIE's report surfaced on 17 May 1989. The police and local authorities were unable to agree on the split of parking enforcement responsibilities. The police were happy for authorities to take on enforcement of all permitted on-street parking places, releasing police resources for enforcing prohibited parking – yellow lines and clearways. Authorities, however, wanted the prohibited parking as well. It seemed just a little inefficient to have two enforcement agencies – police/traffic wardens and boroughs – patrolling the same street, one doing yellow lines, the other meters and residents' bays.

To find out the government's reaction to the report a meeting between the LBA, ALA and the Home Office Minister eventually took place on 20 November 1989. There was little joy from this and within a month the government published its 'Traffic in London' discussion document. . . . On parking enforcement the police's views had won through (after all it was a Home Office-led working party). Boroughs would get permitted parking. The perpetuation of two agencies enforcing on-street parking was clearly nonsense, and was only tinkering with the problem. The LBA told the government so, and meanwhile was trying to get parallel powers to the police via a London Local Authorities (Miscellaneous Provisions) Bill.

The Department of Transport published a further 'Traffic in London' document in July 1990. This was a consultation paper about legislative proposals. Their view on parking enforcement had not changed, as the clauses in the Road Traffic Bill in November 1990 soon confirmed. Meanwhile in October the parking enforcement powers sought by boroughs in the London Local Authorities Act were lost. The government again stressed it was not prepared to decriminalise yellow lines.

It was time to take off the gloves. The LBA's long-running campaign, conducted largely behind the scenes until now, became very high profile. A crucial factor was winning a great deal of media attention while at the same time gaining the support of a significant number of Conservative MPs. Richard Tracey, MP for Surbiton, put down an amendment to the Road Traffic Bill at Report Stage to give boroughs powers on most yellow lines.

The opposition supported the case and more importantly so did the two other Conservative London MPs on the committee. Only two Conservatives needed to vote against the government for it to lose its majority. The turning point came when the three Tories spoke in favour of an all party group of amendments inspired by the two London local authority associations.

The committee adjourned for lunch before the amendment was put to the vote and it emerged later the civil servants had seriously feared a government defeat. The minister, who had started his speech bullishly before lunch, ended on a more conciliatory note and the amendments were withdrawn without a vote.

The Conservative London members on the committee were told police opposition had been overcome and the Home Office and Department of Transport had always seen the logic of the boroughs' case.

When a delegation of London MPs met the Home Secretary on 19 February 1991, it was clear that the government had 'come round'. A week later the Minister for Roads and Traffic announced that the Road Traffic Bill would be amended to give boroughs yellow line enforcement powers.

(David Hurdle and Ian Keating, 'The Parking Story', an edited version of an entry in the *LBA Handbook 1992–93*)

In this case the associations did everything right. They submitted a detailed, reasoned case to the department and kept up a dialogue with the officials managing the policy. When officials would not agree, they went to ministers; when that failed, they brought pressure to bear by promoting private legislation; and finally they mustered a majority for their case in the road traffic bill committee. At every stage their approach was reasoned, calm and constructive, and they were careful to win their point without embarrassing the government unduly.

4.b.3   The lone outsider: Bristol Channel Ship Repairers Ltd

Obviously 'institutionalised' interest groups like the local authority associations enjoy a great advantage: they have frequent contact with civil servants, and meet ministers regularly. But the lone, determined individual can achieve a lot with obstinacy, skill and luck, as Gerald Kaufman discovered when Minister of State for Industry.

I was involved for quite a time in a Holmes–Moriarty confrontation – cast the roles as you please – with Christopher Bailey, Chairman of a small ship repair company in South Wales called Bristol Channel Ship Repairers Ltd. Christopher Bailey's company was included in the list of ship repairers to be nationalised by our legislation and he was determined to prevent this. He launched a giant public relations campaign, and by providing information about a form of industrial democracy apparently in operation at his establishments sought to persuade Labour MPs to support him, recognising that a Labour Government with hardly any majority in Parliament was vulnerable to defections. Several Labour MPs were indeed for a time convinced of the validity of his case and put their names to an amendment which would have excluded Bristol Channel from the Bill; later they changed their minds, and the legislation passed through the Commons intact.

Bailey had, however, already set experts to scrutinising the Bill not for policy inadequacies but for technical defects and, much to the chagrin of Department of Industry officials, not to mention Ministers, he found one. This held the Bill up, but only for a time. Christopher Bailey then sent a representative to warn me, most courteously, that there were plenty more defects where that came from, and that it would save the Government a lot of time to remove ship repair from the Bill. We persisted; he was as good as his word. More defects were indeed alleged, and the House of Lords committed the Bill to a dreaded band of Examiners. These, after prolonged inquiry, found that there were indeed certain defects, very few and not very serious, but enough. I, who for some reason had been regarded as being in personal combat with Christopher Bailey, was the one who in the end, to save the Bill as a whole, recommended the exclusion of the ship repair companies from nationalisation. It was without doubt a remarkable victory for Bailey and showed what can be achieved by dogged persistence with the resources, where needed, to back it up. You should never underestimate determined pressure groups.

(Gerald Kaufman, *How to Be a Minister*, London: Sidgwick and Jackson, 1980)

4.c PUBLIC CAMPAIGNS

4.c.1 The police and side-handled batons

One group which Home Secretaries have always regarded warily is the police, given the sympathy on which they can call from most of the public. The arguments over whether or not to issue American 'side-handled batons' to the British police is a good example of a pressure group playing on public sympathy for all it can – although it is worth noting that while the Police Federation, representing junior ranks, demanded the baton to protect their members' safety, the Association of Chief Police Officers (ACPO), representing senior ranks, was more cautious, balancing safety against the possible harm to the police's image. As often happens in debates on police equipment or powers, the debate was sparked by a series of criminal incidents.

The Police Federation is demanding the issue of US-style batons in place of the traditional truncheon.

The federation, which represents junior ranks, renewed its call for the long, side-handled batons in the latest issue of *Police* magazine, after several knife attacks which have left two officers dead and several wounded.

Figures due to be released by the Association of Chief Police Officers today will show several hundred assaults on officers in England and Wales over the Christmas and new year period. But the association said it was opposed to the batons, which did not fit the traditional police image.

However, the federation said the long baton enabled an assailant to be restrained and handcuffed quickly and allowed an officer to keep the attacker out of knife range.

The Home Office said it would consider arranging for the evaluation of any equipment which could help in public order control, if chief officers requested it.

(Independent, 20 January 1992)

Over the next month, chief constables came under a lot of pressure from their junior ranks. While individual chief constables have autonomy in operational matters, ACPO has developed an influential if informal role in co-ordinating their actions and representing their views to the Home Office, and ACPO members were divided on the issue. The Home Office, which has to approve the use of new equipment, took a neutral public stance but stressed the need for any new equipment to be trialled and evaluated before Ministers decided to authorise its use.

Chief Constables bowed yesterday to grassroots pressure and announced that US-style side-handled long truncheons are to be tested by police on duty.

The Police Federation, which represents officers up to chief inspector, welcomed the move. The federation says the truncheon is needed to protect police against the growing number of assaults, running at around 20,000 a year.

Described by senior officers as 'an instrument of self-defence and restraint', the truncheon is 24 inches long, made of toughened plastic and gripped by a five-inch side handle. The length means it has to hang from a belt, rather than fit inside a pocket like conventional wooden truncheons, which are about 18 inches long.

Its supporters reject criticism that the truncheon is dangerous, stressing that it is primarily a defensive weapon, used in a sweeping motion of existing truncheons. It is used in mainland Europe and has been issued to police in the United States for 20 years.

Four or five forces will put the truncheon and a telescoped 12-inch version on a six-month trial.

(Independent, 20 February 1992)

Three months later, however, the trials were apparently cancelled. After the general election in April the new Home Secretary, Kenneth Clarke, seemingly reversed the decision, although there was no public announcement (an interesting if rare example of 'negative presentation').

Plans to test the American side-handled baton have been postponed, according to the Police Federation.

It is understood that the reason for not proceeding with an experiment to test the batons is because they are the same as those used by Los Angeles police officers who beat up the motorist Rodney King [a case which at that time attracted great notoriety].

Officers were to be trained at the central planning unit run by the Home Office in Harrogate. Six forces would then have tested the side-handled batons, which are known as PR24s, and are 24 inches long. Police say they offer extra protection, particularly against people armed with knives.

If the experiments had been successful officers would have been able to use the batons from next year. However, at the weekend the Police Federation was informed that training, which was due to start in July, would not now take place.

A federation spokesman said last night: 'We are puzzled and disappointed. We do not accept that it is sensible to abandon the plans.'

It had been suggested that the new baton was 'too sensitive' because of the video, seen by the public, of the attack on Mr King, he said. 'They say it is capable of being abused but so is the police truncheon and so is the police boot.'

(*Guardian*, 19 May 1992)

The pressure from the ranks did not relent, however, and when within months the Home Secretary changed, the policy changed with him. Michael Howard brought to the Home Office a notably harder line on law and order issues, including side-handled batons.

Michael Howard, the Home Secretary, yesterday reversed the decision of his predecessor, Kenneth Clarke, and told the police service that it could soon test a version of the controversial 24-inch side-handled long baton.

Mr Howard told senior officers at the Police Staff College, Bramshill, that scientific evaluation of an expandable version of the side-handled baton would begin shortly; if tests are successful, the baton will be tested operationally by a number of forces. He also said that the Metropolitan Police would be able to test on the street three other types of straight baton. . . .

The expandable version has been designed to overcome one of Mr Clarke's principal objections: that it would have to hang visibly from the officer's belt and thus damage the police's image. This version, made of hardened plastic and steel, compacts to 13 inches, the length of the standard wooden truncheon. If issued it would hang from a belt loop within a tunic or coat; it would be visible on officers in shirtsleeves.

Mr Howard said: 'We ask the police to do so much for us. When they ask for something from us we should listen. If the expandable side-handled baton is proved to protect police officers, particularly women police officers, from attack, my position is clear. They should have it. The rigid side-handled baton, with its aggressive appearance, is inappropriate for our police officers. The new expandable baton, however, is much less conspicuous to carry.'

But he made it clear that the baton would be issued only after scientific evaluation. Its advocates say that proper training is needed for it to be used effectively as a weapon of self-defence and that in the Los Angeles case the officers had not been trained correctly.

(*Independent*, 17 June 1993)

Perhaps the most notable aspect of Michael Howard's decision was not the reversal of Kenneth Clarke's decision, but rather the fact that Michael Howard only authorised scientific tests, rather than authorising immediate use of the baton. This probably reflected cautious advice from his officials: 'But Minister, what if the baton proves unreliable and someone gets badly hurt? An evaluation in the laboratory will give us a better idea of what it is worth.' Probably both proponents and opponents of the baton expected the evaluation to confirm their prejudices. In the event, the scientific evaluation proved favourable.

An expandable side-handled baton is to be tested by police in 13 forces across the country as a possible replacement for the traditional wooden truncheon, Mr Howard, Home Secretary, announced yesterday.

At 13.5 inches, the polycarbonate baton is slightly shorter than the standard truncheon but extends with a flick to 24in.

It has been on trial at the Home Office police scientific development branch since the summer and Mr Howard has now decided it should be tried out on the streets. . . .

The expandable baton is seen as a compromise. Trials start in January and an evaluation report should be completed by the end of July. . . .

A wide range of alternative batons are being, or are soon to be, tested by officers in 20 forces, including the 26-in rubber-coated cane similar to those used by Far East police.

(*Daily Telegraph*, 24 November 1993)

4.c.2   The campaign to keep Bart's Hospital open

Another public campaign, notable for its skilful handling of the media, exploitation of contacts and presentation of a reasoned alternative course of action is the campaign to save St Bartholomew's Hospital in London, which was threatened with closure by a Department of Health review.

It all began in Budapest. On Friday October 23, last year, the chief executive of St Bartholomew's Hospital, Professor Michael Besser, was listening to the presentation of research work at a conference in the Hungarian capital. He was handed a fax which had arrived at his hotel. It was a summary of a death sentence on the 870-year-old hospital in London's Smithfield.

From that moment, his professional life changed. He ceased to be a man of medicine in charge of a celebrated hospital. Instead he became a full-time public relations figure rushing between radio and television studios, newspaper interviews, campaign meetings, fund-raising events and discreet lobbying sessions with people of influence. Besser was still in the life-saving business. This time the life he was fighting for was that of his own hospital. This week he achieved the victory for which he has struggled so hard.

Bart's is more than just a major London hospital catering for some 400,000 local residents and several hundred thousand more commuters. It is also a national referral centre. Heart patients travel from as far as Wales. The children's cancer services, built up over 20 years, are internationally renowned. The hospital is also nationally respected for gastroenterology, diabetes and the treatment of hormone disorders.

But the Government was determined to rationalise specialties in London, to cut unneeded beds and release more money to improve the capital's dilapidated primary health care services. Sir Bernard Tomlinson was charged with producing a plan to do this. His proposals included closing Bart's and selling the historic buildings. This was the news Besser received in Budapest. 'There had been rumours, but it was all much worse than anticipated,' he said. By the Saturday afternoon he was back at Bart's chairing a small strategy group.

Besser, a commanding figure with an energetic determined manner, decided the group's priority was to present the Health Secretary, Virginia Bottomley, with a financial survival plan for a slimmed-down Bart's. It wanted to preserve its renowned specialist centres, along with emergency services. Once it had agreed these clear objectives, it set about unleashing public support. 'We asked everyone in the hospital and patients and friends to tell everyone,' says Besser. 'Influential friends, your MP, your local newspaper.'

Bart's, on the doorstep of Fleet Street, is not short of media connections and they were quickly exploited. Jane Dacre, a Bart's consultant, alerted her husband Nigel, who is editor of ITN, and her brother-in-law Paul, editor of the *Daily Mail*. Anthony Clare, a former professor of psychiatry at the hospital talked to BBC colleagues. Jane Anderson, a senior lecturer in Aids and wife of the television presenter Clive Anderson, spread the word among her colleagues.

The media was bombarded with argument – any bit of information that might help the cause, such as the fact that the time Tomlinson had spent at the hospital was not more than five hours.

A vital figure in the campaign was the popular Professor Lesley Rees, dean of the Bart's medical school. She was an influential member of Besser's inner strategy group of consultants and managers. She immediately harnessed the loyalty of Bart's medical students and as a member of the Press Complaints Commission was able to use her contacts with editors. 'It was not so much that we wanted to tell people what to write,' she says. 'We wanted them to know very quickly what could happen.

'The idea of closing Bart's to balance the health care books seemed to reflect a general malaise in this country. Quality of care and years of loyalty were left out of the equation. It was like saying Westminster Abbey should be demolished to build MPs' offices.'

Quite separately from the hospital management, another pressure group was established. This was the Patients' Campaign, run by a former insurance salesman, Don Magnus, who had undergone several life-saving heart operations at Bart's. Many of his helpers had similar stories to tell. It was this group which raised the £35,000 to fund the campaign. The hospital is adamant that not a penny of NHS money was spent.

Local self-help groups for children's cancer and retinoblastoma, a potentially blinding eye disorder, mustered support from all over the country to make clear that a national institution was under threat. Meanwhile letters poured in from a vast overseas network of doctors in medical institutions who had at some stage benefited from their time at Bart's. Rees put together a slim but telling volume of the 'International response' and sent it to John Major.

The campaign profited all along from friends in high – and useful – places. Clifford Chance, among the world's largest firms of commercial solicitors, offered free advice. Still, Price, Lintas, a leading advertising agency, gave free creative time to develop an aggressive poster campaign. One ad questioned the absurdity of closing Europe's most up-to-date operating theatre even before it officially opened. Another was headed: 'This is one cardiac arrest you won't recover from.'

The combatants all look back on November 16 as the day of the crucial breakthrough. The visit by Lord and Lady Romsey had been planned for some time. Their five-year-old daughter, Leonora – a god-daughter of Prince Charles – had been treated by Bart's until her death. They came to present a cheque for £43,000 to the children's cancer unit.

Lord Romsey's description of the 'quite exceptional care' and dedication given to Leonora made a huge impact on the media who covered the event, as did his disclosure about an argument he and Bottomley had had about the closure.

The second breakthrough came in later December when a well-briefed Parliamentary Select Committee on Health put Tomlinson through such tough questioning that he visibly wilted. He seemed incapable of answering satisfactorily how closing a site like Bart's – virtually valueless in development terms because of its listed buildings – would provide the millions needed for London's dilapidated family doctor services, or how much would be available to re-site Bart's specialist units.

These unanswered questions and the gathering momentum of public support increased political doubts about the Tomlinson plan. Besser and his colleagues accepted that a rethink of London's health services was necessary, given that the NHS reforms should have led to more patients being treated outside the capital. Nevertheless, the campaigners were able to exploit the winter weather and the approach of a yellow alert when some hospitals found they might be unable to make beds available.

Curiously, Bottomley never met Besser until November 30, when both attended a private cocktail party. It was a courteously pugnacious encounter.

Bottomley: 'I have got to be decisive about London hospitals.' Besser: 'Not over Bart's dead body, you haven't.' It is Besser who seems to have been proven right.

The final political breakthrough may well have been the debacle over the mines [see 6.b.4]. It is reckoned that the Government was loath to risk a similarly expensive one over London hospitals. In the end, Bottomley has decided to give Bart's a partial reprieve, confining it to specialised treatment and research. The site of the hospital close to the levers of power and influence was vital to the success of the campaign. That success is a dramatic demonstration of the powers that can be unleashed when the professional classes exploit their considerable network of contacts and lobbying skills.

(*Daily Telegraph*, 13 February 1993)

In fact the arguments over the future of Bart's rumbled on for some time after this article was written, but eventually the hospital survived in attenuated form.

5   Implementation and policy review

5.a   IMPLEMENTING POLICY

Implementation is the unglamorous end of the policy process, and attracts very little interest. The interesting part of a policy is its development: the pressures that give rise to it and the political conflicts that surround its adoption. Once the political sound and fury are past, the interest goes out of the subject for the politician and journalist, and implementation – although no less vital a stage in the process – is carried out in quiet oblivion. Mercifully so, from the administrator's point of view: a policy that is implemented without fuss is a policy that (usually) is working well.

The coverage of implementation tends therefore to be of policies that miscarry. Of the examples of disasters set out below, one (the community charge) failed because it was fundamentally flawed and gained neither public approval nor co-operation; and two (the graduated fines system and the Child Support Agency) were flawed in practical detail. The success of the council tax attracted a little coverage only because it took the place of the failed community charge. The rare attempts of the Central Policy Review Staff to carry out fundamental reviews of government policy (of which two examples are given) were intellectually acute but not conspicuously successful.

5.a.1   Absolute failure: the community charge

The prime example of a policy that fails disastrously when it reaches the stage of implementation is the community charge, whose genesis within the Department of the Environment was described in 2.a.4. Despite fierce opposition, the community charge was implemented in Scotland in 1989–90 and in England and Wales in 1990–1.

The British political elite is extraordinarily metrocentric. The further away from London a problem is, the less it seems to matter, and for many purposes Scotland is seen almost as a foreign country. It is literally true that London's national newspapers carry better coverage of eastern Europe than they do of Scotland. Had the cabinet looked north of the border in 1989 they would have seen the problems that rapidly developed, especially popular resentment against a 'regressive' tax – that is, a tax whose level is unrelated to people's ability to pay – and the difficulties of collection. A property tax like the rates is easy to enforce because, if the owner fails to pay, you put a charge on the property. A tax attached to a particular person is easier to avoid: people move about, houses do not.

The following series of newspaper extracts from the spring of 1990 illustrates the way in which a serious policy problem can snowball into a major crisis: what should have been a relatively modest change in local government finance spilled over into defections from the Conservative Party, loss of confidence in sterling, and a series of expensive bailing-out operations by the Treasury. What these few extracts cannot reproduce is the volume and stridency of media coverage of the problem which, after a time, built up momentum of its own. This, combining with the inherent practical difficulties of collecting the poll tax, created a tidal wave against the policy.

The core of the problem was that the initial projection of average community charge levels issued by Chris Patten, the Environment Secretary, proved over-optimistic, partly because inflation rose above government predictions, partly because local authorities took advantage of other changes in the finance system to increase their spending, and partly because the government's estimates were based on unrealistic assumptions (like a 100 per cent collection rate). Even the use of 'capping' – a government limit on the size of councils' budget increases – could not solve the problem. This became clear in February 1990 when councils set their first community charges. An editorial in the *Guardian* set out the problem.

The beauty of the poll tax, enthusiasts used to explain, was that it would discipline high-spending local authorities not through the clumsy and centralist machinery of ratecapping and the like, but by exposing them to the vengeance of their electors. Under the rating system, the then Environment Secretary, Mr Kenneth Baker, told the Commons in commending his new alternative four years ago, roughly half the 35 million local electorate didn't have to pay; and even among those who did, three million had their bills met in full through housing benefit. So millions of people could blithely vote for irresponsible councils in the certainty that others would foot the bills. 'The choice before the country in financing local government', Mr Baker declared to Conservative cheers, 'is whether one depends upon constraints operated through the ballot box or whether one goes for more central control.'

But now, it appears, we have both. As the evidence mounts that the average liability under the poll tax will be £100 or more above the £278 predicted by Mr Patten, ministers are moving to protect themselves from the wrath of affronted charge-payers. It was always envisaged that capping might be needed: in the transitional period only, Mr Baker told the Commons four years ago, some control would be necessary to ensure that 'certain local authorities' did not take the opportunity substantially to increase their spending. And sure enough, ministers now confirm that they intend to cap the charges planned by some local councils – though they've yet to make clear how many, or where, or what criterion they will use to distinguish between those 'irrational and excessive' councils whom Mr Michael Howard [then a junior Environment minister] identified last March as possible cases for capping, and blameless (Conservative) victims of cruel circumstance.

But it's already clear that the simplistic division between low-spending councils (good, and almost all Conservative) and high-spending councils (bad, and almost all Labour) just does not work. And that leaves the concept of voter vengeance looking damaged as well. Take Mole Valley, for instance, Mr Baker's own local council, or Epsom and Ewell, or Esher: what are local electors to think as they contemplate poll tax estimates way above what the Government says should be levied in their areas? Should they mutter 'Socialist rotters!' and resolve to vote them out? If they do, they'll be wasting their breath: for these places are all in solidly Tory Surrey, where a man may march for a day and never catch sight of a socialist councillor.

There are various reasons for this mess. One of them is that, just as the Government says, some local councils still will not practise prudence. But a second, whose political impact will be much the greater, is that prudent councils cannot match Mr Patten's unrealistic targets without slashing local services to an extent which even Conservative councillors find insupportable.

(*Guardian*, 16 February 1990, editorial)

The heart of the dispute which led to the resignation from the Conservative whip of West Oxfordshire's ruling councillors lies in the yawning gap between two sets of figures. The Government insists the community charge should be fixed at £270 a head: local authorities, including those controlled by Conservatives, say the real figure, based on their budgets for next year, will be closer to £430.

The councils insist that the gap between their position and the Government's cannot be blamed on bad housekeeping or underhand attempts to use the new tax to boost their budgets.

Mike Grealy, finance under-secretary for the Conservative-dominated Association of County Councils, says the Government's wildly optimistic inflation estimates made last July are by far the biggest cause of disagreement. Its estimates of total local authority spending in the next financial year – £32.8 billion to be raised by poll tax, with £23.1 billion added from central government through revenue support grant and business rate income – were based on inflation rates of 5.5 per cent this year, 4 per cent next.

Even at these figures, the government estimates would mean a cut in real income, as they represent a rise of just 3.8 per cent over 89/90, well below inflation. In September, the Government revised its own inflation estimates to a still-optimistic 7 per cent this year, 5 per cent next year, but held to its original poll tax estimate.

The association believes that by the time district council budgets have been published, including those from the high-spending metropolitan boroughs controlled by Labour, the average level of poll tax will rise to around £430 a head. If the Government tries to close so large a gap by 'capping' local budgets, the cuts that follow will be huge among Tory and Labour councils alike.

Schoolchildren too young to vote are likely to be the first victims. With the row deepening, council officials have begun contemplating deep cuts, and say they will begin with education. 'Schools will have to be first,' said Chris Gray, head of policy review at Oxfordshire County Council, drawn into the dispute following the resignation from the Conservative whip of 18 of the 25 ruling Tories of West Oxfordshire District Council.

'About 60 per cent of our budget goes on education. We have budgeted for the introduction of the new national curriculum and the self-management policy, but it is hard to see how we could expand our programme like this if we have to cut it at the same time.' Roads and social services will also be prime cut-back targets.

. . . West Oxfordshire's failure to meet the poll tax target is a dark portent for the Government, for it boasted the third-lowest rates in the country. With the sort of careful cheese-paring advocated by Whitehall, it even managed to produce a below-target poll tax for its own district requirements. The final level of £412 was caused by the county's budget, and the compulsory £47-a-head 'safety net' charge designed to meet inner-city shortfalls from within local, rather than rational, government funds.

'That in the end is why we resigned the whip,' says council leader Mrs Margaret Frost. 'There was nothing more we could do to meet the needs of our residents within this Government's policies.'

(*Daily Telegraph*, 2 March 1990)

The Tory council at Barnet, which takes in the Prime Minister's Finchley constituency, yesterday announced a poll tax of £338 – £60 above the Government's national target figure.

Barnet has kept its community charge down to that level only by using nearly £12 million from its reserves – worth £53 a head off the poll tax bill – and making budget cuts.

The news came as Chris Patten, the Environment Secretary, complained in the Commons that community charge figures announced so far implied that local authorities were set to overshoot Government limits by £3 billion from April.

(*Guardian*, 22 February 1990)

The Government's political problems spilled over into the foreign exchange markets yesterday with the unrest caused by the introduction of the poll tax prompting a heavy fall in sterling for the second successive day.

At one stage, the Bank of England was reported to have intervened in an attempt to halt the pound's slide, but the downward trend continued in New York after trading in London had ended.

The fall of 1.2 per cent in the effective sterling index over the past two days could, if prolonged, add to the Chancellor's economic difficulties. Inflation is already set to rise above 8 per cent over the next few months and a lower exchange rate adds to pressure on prices by pushing up the cost of imports.

(*Guardian*, 3 March 1990)

At least £2.4 billion of new Treasury money will be needed next year simply to peg poll tax bills at this year's £370 average in England.

The public spending arithmetic reveals the scale of the cabinet battle facing the Environment Secretary, Chris Patten, if he is to carry out his weekend pledge to improve the community charge.

It would cost a further £1 billion for every £30 reduction in the average poll tax bill from this year's level if Mr Patten wanted to prove the popularity of the new tax in a possible election year.

Poll tax protests continued to grow over the weekend with 8,000 people marching in Plymouth and thousands more in Derbyshire and Manchester. There were further resignations of Conservative councillors in Norfolk and the Isle of Wight.

(*Guardian*, 5 March 1990)

Final community charge figures show that the Government is likely to be frustrated in its attempts to deflect public anger by pointing to much higher levels of poll tax set by 'extravagant' Labour councils. The average poll tax in Labour-controlled councils is turning out at £370, which is only 7 per cent higher than the average poll tax of £345 in Tory-controlled councils.

The Conservative poll tax figures are on average 31 per cent above the Government's guideline – not much different from the Labour, Liberal Democrat and Independent councils who are all on average 36 per cent above the guideline.

(*Guardian*, 12 March 1990)

By this stage the crisis had built up a self-sustaining momentum of its own, and a concession announced in the budget by the then Chancellor of the Exchequer, John Major, did little to damp down the fires.

The political impact of the last-minute poll tax 'sweetener' announced by the Chancellor yesterday was marred by further resignations of Conservative councillors in protest at the community charge and by anger at the Government's failure to backdate the concession in Scotland. Tory back-benchers saw the announcement that people with savings of between £8,000 and £16,000 will be eligible for poll tax rebates and housing benefit as a sign that the Government was beginning to listen to community charge complaints.

'This sweetener will ease the pain in Conservative areas where elderly people were feeling they were being treated very unfairly,' said Keith Hampson, a leftwing Tory MP. The measure, which will cost £120 million, will add 250,000 people to the seven million already eligible for rebates.

Nine Conservative councillors in Beverley, Humberside, yesterday resigned the party whip, and in St Austell, Cornwell, the Conservative mayor, George Down, announced he had left the party over the poll tax. The resignations alarmed Kenneth Baker, the Conservative Party chairman, who had hoped the resignation of 18 Tory councillors in West Oxfordshire was isolated. . . . The resignations sent new jitters through the Tory backbenches. Emma Nicholson, MP for Devon West and Torridge, congratulated the councillors.

(*Guardian*, 21 March 1990)

The Prime Minister last night insisted there would be 'no trimming or turning' in government policy in the wake of one of Labour's greatest by-election victories.

The Mid-Staffordshire election, in which Sylvia Heal, the Labour candidate, turned a Conservative majority of 14,654 into a Labour lead of 9,449, was the party's best result since 1935. . . .

Mrs Thatcher admitted last night that the Mid-Staffordshire voters had sent the Government a message about the impact of high mortgage rates and the cost of the poll tax, but she said the seat could only be won back at the next general election.

(*Guardian*, 24 March 1990)

On 31 March a large demonstration against the tax in central London erupted into a riot, with fighting between demonstrators and the police in Trafalgar Square and Whitehall and looting in the West End. In terms of its effect on government policy, it was probably insignificant; if anything, it was likely to stiffen ministerial resolve. But it shook financial and international opinion.

Shares and sterling fell heavily yesterday as the City reacted nervously to the poll tax riot in Trafalgar Square and the turmoil in world financial markets caused by the chronic weakness of the Tokyo stock market. The fragility of the pound was underlined by the response to the clashes between police and demonstrators, which were shown on prime-time television in the United States.

(*Guardian*, 3 April 1990)

There were no similar disturbances elsewhere; the riot had been staged largely by anarchist and disaffected groups, whose impact on public opinion was negligible, if not counter-productive. Had theirs been the only opposition to the poll tax, it would have been insignificant. What really mattered was the inability or refusal of many usually law-abiding citizens to pay the charge, and the belief of an even larger proportion of the population that the fundamental principle of the tax was unfair. It rapidly became clear that the tax was being destroyed by the difficulties of collecting it.

> Magistrates' courts have been told to prepare for a sharp increase in workload to cope with poll tax defaulters, according to a private official circular. The Home Office says it is not possible to estimate the number of default cases likely to arise, but it has urged court clerks to contact local councils to discuss arrangements for dealing with non-payers.
>
> (*Guardian*, 6 April 1990)

> The Government was under mounting pressure last night to make more poll tax concessions in Scotland after new figures revealed the scale of non-payment to be much higher than forecast.
>
> Council leaders bluntly told the Scottish Secretary, Malcolm Rifkind, that their authorities would face a financial crisis later this year if non-payment remained at its present level of up to 20 per cent.
>
> In a report to the minister, the Convention of Scottish Local Authorities (Cosla) calculated that two months ago 850,000 Scots had either not paid the tax, or were well behind. Of these, almost 400,000 had been sent legal warrants by sheriffs' officers (bailiffs) acting for councils, while a further 450,000 were at the 'final notice stage' of debt recovery. Alarmingly for the councils, there appears to have been no significant improvement since January.
>
> (*Guardian*, 7 April 1990)

By this stage the tax seemed to be damaged beyond redemption; one year in Scotland and two bad months in England had sufficed to wreck it. Essentially the reasons for failure were fivefold. There was public resistance to the principle of the tax; it was difficult to implement and collect; the government's underestimate of the level of the charge rebounded on it; there was strong opposition from Conservatives in local government; and as things were seen to go wrong the financial markets became jumpy, which always causes a government great concern. After a while, like an avalanche, the disaster simply gathered a momentum that made it irresistible, and made the policy unsustainable. Margaret Thatcher records in her memoirs that by May 'a number of our backbenchers were in a mood not far short of outright panic'.

Nevertheless, matters drifted on for another nine months, with ever-increasing arrears of payment and queues of defaulters being taken to court. A review of the community charge in the summer led to the pumping of another £3 billion by the Treasury into local authority finance; even then the projected average community charge at 'standard spending' was £379 (compared to the earlier government estimate of £270). The *coup de grâce* was delivered when Michael Heseltine challenged Margaret Thatcher for the leadership on a platform of a radical review of the tax. Once Margaret Thatcher pulled out of the election the other contenders – Major and Hurd – also promised reviews. In March 1991 the new government announced the scrapping of the poll tax and the introduction of a 'council tax' rather like the old rates.

5.a.2 Unobtrusive success: the council tax

This was introduced in 1993 with minimal fuss or complaint, for reasons analysed by one of the few academics who understands local authority finance.

> Whitehall, the local authority associations and individual local authorities made strenuous efforts to work together harmoniously. Local government officers in England, Wales and Scotland were full of praise for civil servants. This feel-good factor was reciprocated.
>
> Professionalism in local and central government, in the local authority associations and in bodies such as the Institute of Revenues, Rating and Valuation was another key element in the successful implementation of the new tax.
>
> The decision to introduce council tax was taken in March 1991, allowing just two years to make preparations and install it. . . . In the event, each authority adapted itself and its procedures to local conditions and produced a council tax that worked. Only in a handful of councils were there major difficulties with implementation.
>
> . . . A number of other factors also influenced the successful introduction of council tax. First, it is clear that the public view it as broadly fair. This perception helped the new tax avoid the popular resistance which dogged the community charge for the whole of its short life.
>
> The importance of this conclusion cannot be over stressed: taxes that do not have public acceptance – and possibly those that do not command a reasonable level of political consensus – are unlikely to be implemented with ease.
>
> A second success factor was the fact that bills in the first year of the new tax were – on average – virtually unchanged as compared with the previous year. Moreover, transitional relief was paid to losing households in such a way as to take the sting out of any significant rises in individual tax bills. In the first year of poll tax, bills in England rose by 30%, with inadequate protection for losers.
>
> A third reason why council tax was a success is surely the fact that it is – predominantly – a property tax. The resilience and adaptability of property taxes is widely recognised. Indeed, for over 400 years up to 1990 – 1989 in Scotland – Britain relied on property as its local tax base. Such taxes are widely used in Australia, New Zealand, Canada and the United States.
>
> (Tony Travers, *Local Government Chronicle*, 29 April 1994)

5.a.3 The devil in the detail: unit fines

It is a popular saying in Whitehall that 'the devil is in the detail'. An idea that seems eminently sensible at face value may prove, when it comes to working through the practical detail, to contain thorny problems. One such was the new sentencing regime introduced by the Criminal Justice Act 1991. This account from the *Daily Telegraph* describes what happened when the practical effects of this reform became apparent.

MR PETER ARCHER   The matter requires much careful thought. If he says that he would like to give it careful thought . . .

MR JOHN PATTEN   (indicated dissent)

MR ARCHER   The Minister is shaking his head; he does not want to give the matter careful thought. So it will be on the record for the future that when we raised the problem, the Minister did not want to give it careful thought.

Hansard's record of Standing Committee A, considering the Criminal Justice Bill, reports this exchange on December 11, 1990. John Patten, then Home Office minister responsible for steering the Bill through the House, may not recall it, but given the shambles which the Bill has engendered, that shake of the head was always going to haunt him.

The Criminal Justice Act 1991 is not quite another poll tax, but the iniquities it seems to be causing in magistrates' courts are proving deeply embarrassing to the Home Office. It is not just that the unit fine system it introduced is causing wild fluctuations in punishment. It is that magistrates – sensible, worthy and restrained – are resigning because they feel it stops them administering justice properly. Recently the Lord Chief Justice added his weight to the criticisms.

The magistrates' objections focus not just on well-documented difficulties with fines, but on confusion over the extent to which they can take into account the offender's previous convictions when sentencing – the 'problem' which Peter Archer, a former Solicitor General, raised with Mr Patten. It is the combination of these factors which has gelled into a sense of unfairness: while a motoring offender with a job may attract a fine of hundreds of pounds, a persistent burglar with no legitimate income, whose record cannot be considered, may have to pay only £50. The Home Office is engaged in damage limitation, and changes are in the air – but how could such a demonstrably bad piece of legislation have passed through Parliament?

One reason is that the Bill was too rich in radical ideas. It flowed from the Government's desire to reduce prison overcrowding (and costs), to make sentencing more consistent, and to introduce more 'proportionality' – making the punishment fit the crime. But it dealt with a number of high-profile proposals: electronic tagging (now discredited), allowing children to give evidence on video, making parents responsible for the offences of their offspring, and privatising the prisons. As debate focused on these issues, two real problem areas tiptoed through almost unnoticed.

The Bill was the result of more than three years of consultation, and there can be few in the judicial orbit who did not forward their views. David Faulkner, then a permanent under-secretary at the Home Office, played a leading part in its drafting, and the ideas of several criminologists were considered. There were green and white papers; more than 200 Conservative members gave their opinions, as did the Magistrates Association, the Justices' Clerks Society, and several pressure groups.

Fines calculated on 'units' of the offender's disposable income were agreed to be a good idea – but a crucial blunder has led to the current anomalies. A similar system, based on daily incomes, has operated for more than 50 years in much of Europe. The idea had been raised in Britain before, but the sticking point had always been the amount of administration a court would have to undertake to determine daily incomes. By the late 1980s, however, courts were already assessing disposable income in order to calculate instalments for fines. The Home Office reasoned it would be possible to use this information to calculate units.

Year-long experiments were established between 1988 and 1990 at four courts: Basingstoke, Bradford, Swansea and Teesside. They were considered a success: fines were paid more quickly, and there was a significant drop in the proportion of offenders imprisoned for default. But to be consistent with what was then the legal maximum for fines, the maximum fine per unit in the experiments was £20, with a maximum total of £1,000.

The seeds of confusion were sown when the Bill came to Parliament; Kenneth Baker was Home Secretary. In the Bill, the maximum for a unit was raised to £100, with the minimum at £4 – so any reasonably-off offender could be fined five times the amount in the experiments, up to £5,000. It is this range which has caused such violent swings. The Treasury must take part of the blame; they were concerned that the new £4 minimum would cut revenue, and were anxious to see a rise in fines, which had been static since 1984.

Hansard reveals that there was little discussion of unit fines, and what there was dwelt on whether £4 would be too high a minimum for the poorest. Only Viscount Tenby in the Lords hinted at any understanding of what might happen: 'We must . . . be careful not to be so obsessively fair towards the lowest income groups that we correspondingly disadvantage others.' But that was it; no one saw it coming.

. . . David Faulkner remains convinced that fine tuning of the system rather than wholesale changes are needed. 'With hindsight one could wish these things had been ironed out beforehand,' he says. 'One of the difficulties is the rush and pressure of parliamentary business. It is very difficult to get the detail right.' And the devil, as someone should have told John Patten before he shook his head, is in the detail.

(*Daily Telegraph*, 7 April 1993)

But in May the Home Secretary, Kenneth Clarke, surprised critics by opting not for reform but for abolition, which he announced in a Commons statement.

> That Act is plainly not working as Parliament would have liked, and it is clearly in the interests of justice that I should move to put matters right quickly, now that I do have this welcome opportunity . . . therefore, I intend to table amendments to the present Criminal Justice Bill which will deal with the problems of the Criminal Justice Act 1991 and also strengthen the powers of the courts in other important respects.
>
> First, we will seek to amend section 1 of the 1991 Act so as to allow the courts to take into account all the offences for which the offender is being dealt with, instead of only one offence, or that offence and one other offence, which is the case now.
>
> Secondly, we propose to restore to the courts their powers to have full regard to the criminal record of an offender and his response to previous sentences when deciding on the sentence for his current offences.
>
> . . . So far as fines are concerned, I am quite satisfied that courts should continue to have regard to the particular circumstances of individual offenders – in particular, to their means to pay – when fixing the level of a fine. I have been equally clear for some time, and I have frequently said, that we should not require magistrates' courts to go through the mechanistic provision currently required under the unit fine arrangements. My hon. Friend the Member for Fylde (Mr Jack), Minister of State in my Department, and I have been seeking for some time modifications that we might make to the rules of the unit fines scheme to produce better results. We have now concluded that it is not possible to do so.
>
> Accordingly, I now propose to abolish the unit fines system and replace it with provisions which will require magistrates fully to consider an offender's means when imposing a fine but which will not require them to fine by application of any mathematical formula. [Interruption.] I get the sense that this change will be widely welcomed, not least by magistrates outside the House.
>
> (*Hansard*, 13 May 1993)

5.a.4   The devil in the detail: the Child Support Agency

Another innovation, generally welcomed at its conception but fiercely criticised when its practical effects become clear, was the Child Support Agency. This article from the *Independent* analyses what went wrong, and in particular the role of Social Security ministers overseeing the Agency, and the Treasury.

> Eight months after its launch, the Child Support Agency – once heralded as the salvation of single mothers and the scourge of feckless fathers – is about as popular as the poll tax and VAT on fuel. It is under fire from divorced

fathers, ex-wives, new wives, women's groups, advice groups, lawyers, Conservative and opposition MPs and even, less vocally, from the agency's own staff.

So why, if the Child Support Agency was set up with all-party support in April, is it now so deeply unpopular? The Child Support Act, which established the agency, was a major social policy change, intended to bring about a fundamental cultural shift so that parents accepted responsibility for the children they produced rather than expecting the state to provide. Before the Act two-thirds of lone parents were receiving no maintenance from the absent parent.

Yet the reality is that family lives in the late 20th century are messy; many people have second or even third families. If the CSA is to survive, two things need to happen: a fairer method of assessing payments must be found, and an appeals system put into place.

. . . The agency's job is to track down absent parents – nine times out of 10, the father – to assess how much child maintenance he should pay and to pass it on to the mother and child. If the mother receives state benefit the Treasury claws it back. If she is not on benefits, she enjoys a real increase in income.

At first politicians gave the impression that the purpose of the agency was to force 'runaway' men – who paid nothing towards the upkeep of the children they had fathered – to pay up. The reality is that the maintenance to be paid by all absent parents will eventually be set by the agency – regardless of whether the mother is on state benefits and even if maintenance has already been mutually agreed or set by a divorce court. From 1997 the courts will have no role in setting child maintenance.

Over the last two months the agency has been working overtime to meet government targets: this year the aim is to take on one million cases and to rake in £530m in savings. The eventual savings target is £900m a year.

By July it was obvious that the targets would not be reached as the rate of sending out forms was slow. It is rumoured that Ros Hepplewhite, CSA chief executive, told Peter Lilley, the Secretary of State for Social Security, that the agency would fall £130m short of the target this year – would this be acceptable? No, he said, it would not.

So in August a 'Closing the Gap' initiative was launched to set the agency back on track. 'Field workers' in the branch offices were enlisted to help send out forms. A leaked memorandum spelled out exactly how they were to help close the savings gap. It caused much embarrassment this week to Ms Hepplewhite and Alistair Burt, the social security minister whose job is to defend the policy, when they were questioned by the select committee.

In the now infamous memo, apparently intended to rally the troops, Dave Moody, divisional manager of the CSA for Wales and Merseyside, said staff should target more profitable cases where the maintenance bills would be high. This was not the time, he said, to be tackling those cases that they knew should be a priority, but which would need a lot of effort to extract money.

'The name of the game is maximising the maintenance yield – don't waste a lot of time on non-profitable stuff!'

Two other revelations this week did not do much for the agency's image, either. A government minister admitted that the Treasury will get £480m of the savings and the million mothers and children will share £50m. And some mothers will get nothing extra: the Government expects 250,000 absent parents (a quarter of all this year's assessments) will not be eligible to pay any maintenance because they are unemployed and on state benefit or very low earnings.

Since the agency stepped up the pace of work – by the end of September it had sent out 527,000 assessment forms – opposition to the CSA (or the CIA as one Glasgow MP, Jimmy Wray, calls it) is on the verge of turning into revolt. There are several groups with differing grounds for complaint.

Some mothers claim they will be worse off because if maintenance takes them just above Income Support level they will lose 'passport' benefits such as free prescriptions, dental treatment and school meals. Some absent fathers say they would be better off unemployed, and therefore not eligible to pay maintenance, because they are left with so little money.

But in the front line of attack are middle-income, mainly middle-class fathers who find themselves targeted by the agency. Thousands of them have organised a network of opposition to lobby Parliament and mobilise the media.

They are mainly divorced and separated men who previously paid maintenance, either amicably agreed or ordered by a court, and who now find these arrangements being overturned by an agency of the state. The CSA says average bills will double to £50 a week from the £25 typically set by courts, but many fathers who have contacted the press face a four-fold increase. MPs' postbags are full of genuine hardship cases where fathers are unable to meet all their commitments. One apparently unforeseen consequence is that some say they will have to reduce contact with their children and cut down on treats.

(*Independent*, 5 November 1993)

Sharp criticism from backbenchers of all parties, including a hostile report from the select committee on social security, and sensationalist press coverage pushed the government into a review of the policy. This time, instead of scrapping the system outright, ministers modified the arrangements.

Absent fathers are to be protected against the full impact of hefty new maintenance payments imposed by the controversial Child Support Agency, under measures announced yesterday.

Mr Major ordered the review after MPs were deluged with complaints that the CSA was targeting those already paying maintenance rather than runaway fathers who paid nothing. The main beneficiaries will be those parents with second families, the poorest parents and those with older children.

From February fathers with second families and who have their maintenance raised by the CSA to £60 or more a week will have the new demand phased in over 18 months rather than having to find it immediately. The phasing will be in three six-monthly steps of £20 or 25% of the difference beteween the old and new demands.

In addition the level of protected income – the amount of money which is set aside before maintenance demands are made – is to rise from £8 to £30 above the amount he could claim in income support for himself and for his second family, where appropriate.

. . . Earlier this month, the Commons Social Security Select Committee joined the growing clamour for changes in the system after an investigation into the workings of the agency. It recommended a number of changes, many of which have been taken on board by the Government.

Labour attacked the moves as 'a political solution to an awkward problem'. Ms Sue Weare of the Campaign for Fair Maintenace said the changes did not go far enough.

(Daily Telegraph, 23 December 1993)

The furore continued, despite these and further changes, although much of the anger was directed against the way the Agency was implementing the policy, rather than against the policy itself. Within a year, it had become too much for the head of the CSA to endure.

Mrs Ros Hepplewhite, head of the widely criticised Child Support Agency set up to pursue absent fathers for maintenance payments, quit her £50,000-a-year post yesterday. She cited pressures 'from an exceptionally demanding job'. Her decision was privately welcomed by ministers striving to give the agency credibility and brought renewed attacks on the CSA by Labour and Liberal Democrats.

An agency spokesman stressed that Mrs Hepplewhite was not sacked. 'It was her decision. She wants to think about her future. She has no specific plans and there is no severance package'.

. . . Mrs Hepplewhite, who with her staff has been subjected to an avalanche of hate mail, decided to quit two months after issuing a remarkable apology for the agency's failures. 'Overall our standards of service did not reach acceptable levels and we did not achieve some of our key targets,' she said in her first annual report. 'We apologise to our clients for the difficulties they have experienced because of our shortcomings.'

Mr Peter Lilley, the Social Security Secretary, who thanked Mrs Hepplewhite yesterday for her 'courage and dedication', had to add £70 million to the CSA's operating budget and sanction the recruitment of 700 more staff when it fell £112 million short of its target. The agency's shortcomings included too many delays and errors in assessing claims, delays in answering telephone calls and letters and failures in collecting maintenance.

Criticism of Mrs Hepplewhite reached a peak when MPs learned her pay could be boosted by the number of cases settled, irrespective of whether they concerned easily traced fathers or those deliberately avoiding payment. The ferocity of attacks on agency staff – they included demonstrations and razor blades sent through the post – took politicians by surprise. One insider said: 'We've witnessed the ruthlessness of the articulate middle-class male who has had to reach down to the bottom of his pocket.'

(*Daily Telegraph*, 3 September 1994)

Why did the Chief Executive, rather than a minister, resign? To some extent it was a matter of personalities: Ros Hepplewhite had taken a higher profile than most public officials. More fundamentally, however, the problem lay as much in the way the CSA was operating as in the policy that it was implementing, which put the head of the agency in the firing line. This could be taken as a sign that the nature of ministerial responsibility is changing: while ministers remain responsible to parliament for their policies and, up to a reasonable point, the actions of their departmental officials, where execution of a policy is entrusted to an agency, then its chief officers must answer for shortcomings in implementation.

5.a.5   The Central Policy Review Staff: energy policy

The previous examples showed policy reviewed as a result of crisis or failure. Much rarer is systematic, deliberate review of policy to see whether it is adequate and working well. A rare systematic attempt at policy review across Whitehall was the Central Policy Review Staff (CPRS), a small multidisciplinary unit set up within the Cabinet Office by Ted Heath, which operated from 1971 to 1983, advising the cabinet on strategy and policy. One of its functions was to review cross-departmental policy issues and, instead of approaching policy in the usual incremental way, to ask radical and fundamental questions. One such was energy policy, where early on the CPRS, drawing on external expertise, foresaw the problems to come.

[The CPRS] approached the planners at Shell and asked to see the results of their analysis of various scenarios involving substantial increases in the price of oil. It consulted some outside economists (including Ralph Turvey and Michael Posner) about energy supply and pricing policy. It began discussions with the CEGB [Central Electricity Generating Board] about the fuel efficiency of different methods of generating electricity, and set up a good working relationship with the National Coal Board, which provided information about its operations.

. . . When the CPRS started serious work on energy, in early 1972, oil was selling at $1.90 a barrel. The price of petrol at the British pumps was 34.5 pence a gallon. The CPRS report on energy policy, presented to incredulous ministers in the summer of 1973, suggested three possible oil-price scenarios for 1985: what it termed EASY ($3.75 per barrel, at 1972 prices), SCARCE ($6 per barrel), and CRISIS ($9 per barrel).

The report itself was in many respects a model for what the CPRS was to do over the next decade, both in presentation and in substance. The style was clear, direct, and jargon-free. Of the report's 65 pages, 30 were mainly statistical annexes. The arguments of the remaining 35 were summarized in a 4-page introduction, followed by a list of recommendations. The report was bound in the striking red covers that were a hallmark of the CPRS's presentations.

The main recommendations in the report were that action in the next two years should assume the possibility of the SCARCE scenario, namely that by 1985 oil could be costing up to $6 per barrel. The major implication of this assumption was that the current policy of shifting from coal-fired to oil-fired power stations should be halted. The situation could be reviewed and followed by more drastic action later if this seemed necessary. There was an extensive list of secondary recommendations. These covered topics such as North Sea oil production (policy towards which should be clarified and should embody a more active approach to licensing); the coal industry (in which new sources should be sought while pit closures concentrated on pits the most expensive in resource, not financial, terms); power stations (where a speedy choice should be made between the two leading types for the next generation of nuclear reactors and research on other types terminated, while the scope for dual coal/oil-fired stations should be investigated); electric vehicles; environmental policy; the tax regime for petroleum products; future Russian demand for, and supplies of, crude oil, and other topics.

The basic theme of the report was simple enough in principle. A national energy policy was needed. Without this, ad hoc decisions would be taken, unrelated to decisions in other areas, leading to incoherence and inconsistency at considerable cost to the nation. In this sense the report was a manifestation of the central role of the CPRS. It drew to the attention of Ministers the need for an overall strategy in order to avoid conflicting objectives or the use of inconsistent means to achieve policy goals. It made manifest the CPRS's central role in two other respects. First, it tried to look ahead, in this case over a ten-year period. Secondly, it brought together a wide range of material on the likely demand for, and supply of, different types of energy, which it analysed in some depth and presented simply and briefly.

The CPRS gave an oral presentation to Ministers of the findings of the report. This caused something of a sensation. Many Ministers simply refused to accept the validity of the SCARCE scenario and accused the CPRS of scaremongering. As a result, most of the report's recommendations were not accepted for implementation. In fact, of course, the CPRS was to prove completely right in principle, even if wrong in practice. The oil price rise came much sooner, and was more drastic, than the report had predicted. Following the Arab–Israeli war of 1973, oil was $11.00 per barrel (equivalent to $9.90 at 1972 prices). It later rose to a peak of $40.40 (equivalent to $19.70); by July 1987 the price was $19.80 ($7.30).

Rothschild [the CPRS Director] and his team were vindicated. Their pessimistic foresight was acknowledged by the rest of Whitehall. This single episode did more to establish the credibility of the CPRS, in its early days, than did any other factor.

> (Tessa Blackstone and William Plowden, *Inside the Think Tank:*
> *Advising the Cabinet 1971–83*, London: Heinemann, 1988)

5.a.6 The Central Policy Review Staff: alcohol policy

Being vindicated on energy didn't save the Staff from being ignored over some of its later reports, however prescient they may have been. One example – future pressures on public spending – was killed off by a cabinet revolt (see 3.c.4). Another was a report on alcohol policy which was ignored not because nobody believed it but because it upset too many established interests.

The CPRS launched a major study of alcohol and its effect on society – almost a model example of an issue which was everybody's business and yet nobody's. As the report itself noted, 'In central government sixteen departments have direct major interests in alcohol production, sale, and the consequences of its consumption.' The number of vested interests involved constituted a powerful reason for not disturbing the status quo. Despite a great deal of lobbying by the alcohol producing interests, the CPRS report, completed in May 1979, concluded that the trends in alcohol misuse justified government concern. The government should make clear this concern in its public attitudes and should commit itself to countering the rise in the consumption of alcohol and to reducing alcohol-related disabilities.

This was clearly not a message which Ministers wished to hear immediately before a general election. If it was true, as the report said, that 'Going out for a drink' was the main social activity outside the home, it would be hard to think of a set of conclusions less likely to attract practical politicians. The report was not published. After the election, the proposal to publish it was raised again. The DHSS argued that this was unnecessary, since they would publish something of their own. They did, but it was a very different kind of document. 'Drinking Sensibly', published on Christmas Eve 1981, stated that alcohol problems were a matter of personal responsibility, and that people who got into difficulties should look after themselves (HMSO, 1981).

> (Tessa Blackstone and William Plowden, *Inside the Think Tank:*
> *Advising the Cabinet 1971–83*, London: Heinemann, 1988)

From these cases it is hard to escape the conclusion that most policy review in British government is crisis-driven, and that radical policy review is apt to founder on a combination of indifference, established interest and traditional preference for the incremental approach.

6 Legislation, legitimisation and control: parliament and the courts

6.a PARTY CONTROL

As explained in the Introduction, parliament is largely a reactive body. The government controls the agenda and hours of times of sitting of parliament. Most policy initiatives originate in Whitehall, and parliament reacts to them.

There are certain limited ways in which parliament can play a positive role in shaping policy. One is through the promotion of private members' bills, like Margaret Thatcher's bill described in 2.b.5. Another way is through select committees: two successful initiatives by the Home Affairs Committee of the Commons were described in 2.b.6 and 2.b.7. And in a more generalised, less co-ordinated way, backbenchers can influence ministerial thinking by representing to them the mood of the public: not just the local demands of their own constituents – keep our local hospital open, build this bypass now – but the unease of the public at large about national issues: something must be done to reduce crime, or to lower interest rates. This anxiety manifests itself through formal devices such as parliamentary questions and adjournment debates, and through less formal channels such as a word with the minister in the division lobby or a drink with his parliamentary private secretary. (The importance of those informal approaches is underestimated.) It is usually difficult to trace a particular policy change to the intervention of a particular MP; rather these interventions cumulatively make up a general political atmosphere that can influence ministers' decisions.

For the most part, however, parliament exercises a negative power: acting as a brake on ministerial initiatives. This can take the form of parliament exercising its right to reject or amend a bill – for example, the House of Commons voted down a bill to allow Sunday opening by shops in 1986 (6.b.2). Equally often, however, it can take the form of MPs on the government back benches making it clear that they will not stand for a proposal. Here the same phenomenon of informal, almost anecdotal influence operates: ministers are told by a number of their own MPs that this is simply not tolerable, and they will not support it. Obvious conduits for this kind of 'backbench veto' are the formal party mechanisms for liaison between the front and back benches: the Conservative

1922 committee, the Parliamentary Labour Party, and both parties' backbench committees.

6.a.1 The Parliamentary Labour Party

Oddly, although the Labour Party is less inhibited than the Conservative Party about criticising its leaders, it is possible to identify relatively few occasions when the Parliamentary Labour Party (PLP) at its weekly meeting has firmly reined in the government. This may owe something to the fact that, at the time of writing, Labour had held office for only thirteen years since 1960, and for seven of those the government enjoyed no majority in the Commons, which rather inhibits backbenchers from outright revolt. None the less the leadership remains wary of backbench dissent, as witness the care that Richard Crossman, when Leader of the Commons, took to stage-manage a PLP discussion of the prices and incomes policy by putting the trade unionist Minister of Labour, Ray Gunter, in to open the debate.

> John [Silkin, the Chief Whip] and I had carefully arranged to put Ray Gunter in as the first speaker. . . . Sure enough he started a long and emotional speech by saying that the Party should be assured that if the Bill was any kind of threat to the trade unions he'd have nothing to do with it. He delivered the goods. He made the impact and I think he has removed any serious danger. But even Ray didn't reveal the whole truth, namely that Michael Stewart [Economic Affairs Secretary] had been forced to make a whole series of concessions to meet the particular demands put by the TUC in his secret meetings with them.
>
> (Richard Crossman, *The Diaries of a Cabinet Minister: Lord Privy Seal and Leader of the House of Commons 1966–68*, London: Jonathan Cape and Weidenfeld and Nicolson, 1976 (7 June 1967))

For all Crossman's apprehension, the PLP failed inexplicably to rise in revolt over such contentious issues as American participation in the Vietnam War or the Labour government's prevarication towards the white government of Southern Rhodesia, which had illegally declared its independence from the British Crown rather than move towards black majority rule. One rare issue that did stir it was the white paper on trade union law, *In Place of Strife*, which proposed to curb wildcat strikes. This had the potential to cause enormous trouble: in the end it split the cabinet and was effectively vetoed by the trade unions. But the PLP reacted far more mildly than might have been expected when a meeting was called to hear the Employment Secretary, Barbara Castle.

> The first meeting of the PLP on my WP [white paper]. Of course, as usual, despite the great outcry against my policy, there were only about 100 people there. . . . I made a good opening speech and an even better winding-up one. Surprisingly, the mood was far from bitter and there were a lot of

compliments for my 'sincerity' – even 'Socialist' sincerity! – and for the great bulk of the WP. But there were almost non-stop objections to the three proposals they dislike most: the strike ballot, the conciliation pause and the attachment of wages, in that order, especially the latter. . . . It is astonishing how much furore that has created! There were still so many wanting to speak at the end that Douglas said we would have to hold another meeting.

> (Barbara Castle, *The Castle Diaries 1964–70*, London: Weidenfeld and Nicolson, 1984 (5 February 1969))

Further meetings showed the same disquiet, but the PLP never really got up a head of steam on the issue, and certainly the disquiet voiced at party meetings never caused Wilson or Castle to consider backing down. In the end the unions, rather than the PLP, scuppered the proposals.

6.a.2   The Conservative 1922 Committee

Within the Conservative Party the main channel for backbench opinion is the 1922 Committee, whose workings were described in a rare article in 1972 by its former chairman.

The main feature of the Committee is to act as a sounding board for backbench opinion and as a bridge between the backbenches and the front with a special duty devolving upon the chairman to act as exponent and interpreter of backbench opinion to the leader of the party, and to invite Conservative Ministers to attend the Committee to explain actions or policies of particular interest or controversy – invitations which, to my knowledge, have never been refused. Ministers attend the Committee only by such invitation, though, since 1952, Conservative Whips have been welcomed at the weekly meetings in an observer capacity. There is a difference in the composition of the Committee dependent on whether the Conservative Party is in office or in opposition, since shadow ministers are eligible to attend if they so wish and Oliver Stanley in particular frequently contributed to the proceedings in the 1945 Parliament. It has in the past sometimes been suggested that junior ministers should be admitted to the meetings, but in 1952 the decision was taken, reluctantly on personal grounds, to continue the practice of exclusion.

Conservative prime ministers, even the most eminent, recognized the power of the Committee, just as the Committee recognizes the limitations of its power as a non-executive body. I remember when in my first parliament I was accompanying, as a member of the executive of the Committee, the then chairman, Sir Arnold Gridley, to see Mr Churchill as Leader of the Opposition, being surprised to hear him suddenly interrupt Gridley's flow with the words: 'And pray Sir Arnold, how did you come to constitute yourselves into this pleasing assembly?' It seemed odd to be unaware of the constitutional arrangements of the parliamentary party on which his political position rested. Of course; as I realized later when I became more familiar with his style, it was part of the Churchillian puckishness.

In fact, Churchill recognized and accepted the position and importance of the Committee. He took considerable pains with his speeches to it and particularly with his speech at the annual luncheon at which we entertained him. He continued, too, to extend to the then chairman of the Committee the traditional privilege of periodical consultation or confrontation, a privilege from which I derived much interest and pleasure but which I never exercised without some feeling of awe and the consciousness that I was in the presence of history. Those contacts and exchanges continue today between the present Prime Minister and present chairman and I hope and assume that they bring pleasure and profit like those of earlier days.

(Sir Derek Walker-Smith, 'The 1922 Committee: A Power behind the Tory Throne', *The Times*, 19 October 1972)

The pits closure crisis, described in 6.b.4, gives a good example of the influence of the 1922 Committee at moments of crisis. Michael Heseltine was summoned before the committee to explain his decision to close the pits; the pronouncement of its chairman Sir Marcus Fox that the scale of closures proposed was unacceptable perceptibly heightened the pressure on the government, and the 1922 Committee executive's later endorsement of the government's amended plans was a crucial factor in damping down the backbench revolt.

6.a.3 Labour backbench committees

Backbench committees are a slightly different matter. Usually they correspond to the main government departments so, for example, both Conservative and Labour parties have foreign affairs and education committees. They have a lower profile than the full meetings of the parliamentary parties and, as a rule, will attract relatively few MPs to their meetings; more than twenty would be unusual.

Conservative backbench committees are open to all the party's MPs. In contrast Labour committee memberships are more clearly defined to the extent that a Labour MP may belong only to three such committees. But it is hard to detect much sign of any influence that they exercised upon the Labour governments of the 1960s and 1970s. References to them in the diaries of Castle, Crossman and Benn are rather sparse, and all three of these ministers were aware of the need to keep in touch with backbench opinion and, if possible, mobilise it in their support. But there is little evidence of much traffic in views in either direction.

Crossman's diary for his spell as Secretary of State for Health and Social Services records four policy meetings with the corresponding backbench groups, none of them successful.

I visited the Social Security group of the Parliamentary Party. I'd offered them pre-legislation discussion, just as I'm having with the CBI and the TUC, if they were prepared to turn up regularly and do the work. We had only seven or eight people there. This gives a nice picture of the attitude of a Parliamentary Labour Party which has pensions as one of its major issues in the General Election. When Ministers offer to have completely confidential discussions with them they simply don't turn up, not because they don't know about the meeting but because they don't want the trouble. It's a grim thing to say but the real truth about the House of Commons is that it loves complaining about itself but basically it likes itself as it is, doing very little work, having most of the debates on the floor and resenting the hard work of the Standing Committees. It certainly doesn't want any more work and it certainly hasn't got any ambition to control the Executive.

> (Richard Crossman, *Diaries of a Cabinet Minister: Secretary of State for Social Services*, London: Hamish Hamilton and Jonathan Cape, 1977 (15 July 1968))

I had been called to the PLP social security group to expound the [pensions] scheme. Being modest, I had said to Tam [Dalyell, Crossman's Parliamentary Private Secretary], 'I suppose I won't get many people, they will all have gone home. Perhaps we will get thirty.' Four people were there when I came into the room and eight were there in total.

> (30 January 1969)

I had arranged to see the Health group at 4 o'clock. I wasn't going to let them feel I had neglected them on the Green Paper and they had put on the whip that I would be at the meeting. I turned up in Room 13 to find Shirley Williams with two other people. Every single member of the group knew about the meeting. It looked a bit silly, and we had to break up.

> (29 October 1969)

I had promised the Labour Party Health Service group a meeting on hospital closures. When I got there at 6.00 there were three people.

> (24 November 1969)

6.a.4   Conservative backbench committees

In contrast the Conservative backbench committees seem to be more formidable propositions. The annual election of their officers is watched carefully as a barometer of parliamentary opinion. Some ministers take elaborate care to cultivate contact with them. Sir Geoffrey Howe as Foreign Secretary met the backbench foreign affairs committee monthly. As Home Secretary, William Whitelaw reputedly met the Home Affairs Committee weekly, and this assiduity could stand him in good stead when tempers run high, as they did in 1982 when the publication of rising crime figures coincided with the shooting of two policemen.

Mr William Whitelaw, the Home Secretary, last night silenced his critics among Conservative backbench MPs with a fighting defence of his rule at the Home Office and an unspecified promise of stronger police powers to deal with suspected offenders.

Supporters of his liberal regime, as well as his personal friends, turned up in force to a meeting of the party's home affairs committee at the Commons to defend him against some who were out for his blood. They had reason to expect trouble.

Recently there has been much private blaming of the Home Secretary for uncertain leadership by MPs anxious about the rise in certain categories of crime. In turn, many MPs whose constituency annual meetings fall at the end of March have been facing questioning by anxious local parties. Ninety-six Tories have signed a Commons motion supporting the Police Federation's call for capital punishment to be brought back.

But in the end there was no contest last night. Mr Whitelaw's protectors demonstrated with applause when he entered the room, and again when the chairman, Mr Edward Gardner, QC, welcomed him.

After he had spoken, only two of 15 MPs who followed were critical – Mr Tony Marlow, Northampton, North, and Mr Teddy Taylor, Southend, East – and neither strongly so. Mr Gardner commented that the meeting was 'one of the most remarkable demonstrations of support for the Home Secretary that one can remember'.

Mr Gardner said that after Mr Whitelaw had given a satisfactory review of Home Office policy, the questioning was 'almost entirely favourable and friendly', something which he, Mr Gardner, found surprising. He thought this was because the Government has provided for an increase in police numbers, has brought in a new legislation for treating young offenders, and has started a new prison buildings programme.

Mr Whitelaw faced the expected calls for the restoration of capital and corporal punishment, to which he is known to be opposed.

The Home Secretary had hoped to legislate for some of the proposals to strengthen police powers put forward by a recent royal commission, but he did not specify. He did indicate, however, that he intends to change the law so that people who have served prison terms will no longer be able to serve on juries, something for which many MPs have pressed.

Mr Whitelaw also told the party that the police were determined to deal with any outbreak of violence which might mark the anniversary of last year's riots in the English cities, beginning with the outbreak in Brixton, south London, last April. He said there was some risk of trouble because of what he called the 'anniversary technique' by which trouble makers promote demonstrations.

(*The Times*, 23 March 1982)

6.b   THE HOUSE OF COMMONS

6.b.1   The Whips

If these informal, party-based conduits fail, however, or if the pace of events is so fast that they cannot be used, the government's backbenchers can apply the further sanction of refusing to support the government on the floor of the Chamber, or voting against it. Backbenchers are always loath to do this: the ties of party loyalty are strong, too many rebellions weaken a government, and the tradition of party discipline enforced by the whips is strong. But the frequency and size of rebellions over the past quarter-century indicate that the government's power to coerce backbenchers through the government whip has been greatly exaggerated.

Each party has an elaborate whipping system by which parties issue voting instructions to their backbenchers and bring strong pressure to bear on them not to disobey. The strongest instruction that can be issued is a 'three-line whip' – literally, a written instruction underlined three times – defiance of which is a serious offence against party discipline. But ultimately if an MP decides to vote against the party line, there is not much the Whips can do. They can wheedle or cajole, but the sanction of withdrawing the whip – suspending the MP from the parliamentary party – is one they are reluctant to use, since they lose all control over the MP and, in any case, will ultimately be obliged to re-admit him or her to the fold. The suspension of eight Conservative backbenchers who voted against their party on the Maastricht treaty in 1994 caused contention within their party until they had the whip restored the following year. Probably a more subtle and effective sanction is a warning that too many rebellions will ruin a backbencher's chance of office (although it never did Harold Macmillan or Michael Foot any harm). It is intriguing, however, that a former Labour Chief Whip, Edward Short, and former Conservative Leader of the Commons (and erstwhile rebel backbencher) John Biffen both write of their jobs primarily in managerial or welfare terms.

> The term 'Whip' was imported in the eighteenth century from the hunting field, where the job of the whipper-in was to keep the hounds from straying and, so far as our MPs are concerned, that remains the basic function of the Whips in Parliament in the late twentieth century – 'straying' in both the physical and political sense! But there is a good deal more to their work than maintaining discipline in the Party. Whips are also welfare officers who must make themselves aware of the personal problems of their Members and give whatever assistance they can, particularly where attendance at Westminster may be affected. Knowing about these problems can often avert the wrath of other Members when colleagues appear to be getting more than their fair share of time off.
>
> (Edward Short, *Whip to Wilson*, London: Macdonald, 1989)

The main purpose of the Whips Office is to have a comprehensive knowledge of what is happening in the Commons. Whips not only transmit the wishes of government to the parliamentary party, they also act as sounding-boards for back-bench opinion. They evaluate and report back to Ministers how policies are being received, what issues are likely to be difficult, and what members of the government are shining or fading on account of their ministerial performances. The Whips are also assessing the performance and worth of back-benchers, and their judgement ensures the initial promotion prospects of those likely to ascend the government ladder. It is the Whips Office, not Ministers, who choose parliamentary private secretaries.

There is, of course, a disciplinary aspect to the work. This is usually carried out in a spirit of regret, even if occasionally accompanied by anger; no penalties are imposed. If a member is in genuine disagreement with his government there is little the Whips Office can do. It is a sensible courtesy for a dissident MP to inform the Whip of his intended vote. The Chief Whip is expected to be able to tell the party leader what will be the size of the majority; and he can reasonably expect to be informed by those intending to buck the party vote.

. . . In the 1970 parliament I had a formidable record of voting against the Conservative government. I opposed three-line Whips on British membership of the European Community and on the Conservative prices and incomes policy. For good measure I also opposed the local government 'reform' which created the artificial county of Avon substantially at the expense of my native county of Somerset. Throughout all this I maintained good and courteous relations with the Chief Whip, Francis Pym.

(John Biffen, *Inside the House of Commons: Behind the Scenes at Westminster*, London: Grafton, 1989)

The central point is that the government wants to get its business through the House as painlessly as possible. Rather than try to dragoon reluctant backbenchers through the lobbies, it is far more effective to avoid fuss in the first place by gathering intelligence about the mood and views of backbenchers to pinpoint troublesome issues (see for example the Whips' report on the child benefit issue at 3.b.2); taking care of the MPs who have some personal problem; and securing the opposition's agreement to the order of business. While the party whip is a dominant fact of life, there is little the Whips can do in the face of a determined rebel, and even less in the face of an organised rebellion, as was shown by splits on Europe within Labour in the early 1980s and within the Conservatives in the early 1990s. And the whip is even less potent in the Lords where there is great independence of mind, the number of peers attending debates varies and most members of the House are beyond caring about the allures of government office.

There are three ways in which backbenchers can defeat the government: an example of each is given below. They are:

- voting against the government to defeat or amend a proposal (the shops bill);
- threatening to vote against the government to force it to drop a proposal (the sale of British Leyland);
- threatening to vote against the government to extract modification of government proposals (the pits closure crisis).

6.b.2   Voting down a bill: the shops bill

An episode which reasserted the Commons' independence was the vexed issue of the shops bill in 1985–6. The law on Sunday trading was widely agreed to be unsatisfactory and riddled with anomalies: the Shop Hours Act of 1960 allowed shops to sell whisky but not dried milk; postcards but not birthday cards; fresh vegetables but not tinned vegetables; and fish and chips could be bought legally anywhere – except in a fish and chip shop. The law was widely ignored, especially in the 1980s by DIY chains who did their best business at weekends. Local councils, responsible for enforcement, frequently turned a blind eye. But over twenty attempts to rationalise the law by private members' bills since 1960 had foundered on the opposition of religious groups and the shop workers' union USDAW.

It was just the sort of issue to excite the free market zeal of Margaret Thatcher's government. In 1983 a Home Office inquiry headed by a QC recommended abolition of all restrictions, and the government announced plans to legislate for complete abolition. At first, the Commons seemed to agree.

> The Government's plan to sweep away all restrictions on shopping hours, including Sunday trade, was backed by a comfortable majority in the Commons last night, despite a substantial backbench rebellion.
>
> Although there was a three-line whip, 26 Conservative MPs voted against the Government and up to 40 abstained at the end of an emotional debate in which the Government was frequently warned by its own supporters that it was threatening the traditional character of the British Sunday.
>
> The vote means that legislation to implement the main recommendations of the Auld report will be introduced into Parliament in the next session and is expected to become law next year, although the size of the revolt last night confirmed that the legislation will be keenly fought.
>
> (*Financial Times*, 21 May 1985)

As the debate developed, business, unions and pressure groups lined up on either side. As shown by these two stories which appeared on the same day in the *Financial Times*, most – but not all – major retailers supported reform, even if not all planned to take full advantage of it.

> Britain's big retailers – with one or two notable exceptions – are strongly in favour of liberalising the laws governing shop opening hours. Yet, surprisingly, few expect the legislative changes to herald widespread opening of stores seven days a week.

A study of 40 leading retailers by the business studies faculty of the Polytechnic of Central London has found no great across-the-board enthusiasm for Sunday opening.

Mr Terry Burke, who carried out the survey, says: 'The majority of high street multiples are cautious over opening and will only do so if they consider it likely to be profitable or as a reaction to competitive pressures and fears of loss of market share.'

(*Financial Times*, 29 May 1985)

Britian's Co-operative retailers, which have almost 6,000 shops, yesterday decided to campaign against the introduction of Sunday trading.

Delegates to the Co-operative Congress meeting in Bournemouth voted overwhelmingly to oppose legislation to allow seven-day trading.

The Co-op's opposition is based on concern that Sunday trading would be against the interests of shopworkers and lead to the breakdown of the traditional British Sunday.

(*Financial Times*, 29 May 1985)

Understandably enough, the trade unions were opposed to the reform.

USDAW, the shopworkers' union, is to spend £100,000 on a campaigning offensive aimed at winning public support for its opposition to Government plans to sanction Sunday trading in England and Wales and radically reform wages councils.

Separate legislation on the two issues – the repeal of the 1950 Shops Act and reform of wages councils to take workers under 21 out of their jurisdiction – is expected in the next parliamentary session.

... The £100,000 campaign fund will be use to finance posters on the London Underground pressing the union's case for the retention of wages councils in their existing form. An advertising campaign in women's magazines will focus attention on USDAW's case against repeal of the 1950 Shops Act.

(*Financial Times*, 2 September 1985)

In late 1985 the government introduced a bill in the Lords to reform shop opening hours – a procedure usually reserved for bills expected not to arouse strong controversy – and, despite criticism from Church of England bishops, it passed through all its stages without significant amendment. At this point the opponents of the bill made a concerted effort to get their side of the case across.

A campaign to persuade MPs to oppose government plans for Sunday trading was launched yesterday by a coalition of opponents to shop hours reform. These included Church leaders, retailers, trade unionists, and social organisations.

The campaign, called Keep Sunday Special, is aimed at coordinating opposition to seven day a week trading. The Government's Bill to abolish all controls on shop opening hours is due to have its second reading in the Commons next month.

The Bill was introduced into the Lords before Christmas.

Opponents of Sunday trading decided to launch their campaign with the aid of specialist public relations advice because the publicity battle has so far been won by supporters of longer shopping hours.

These opponents of Sunday trading acknowledge that some amendment of Britain's archaic laws on shop opening hours is needed.

Dr Michael Schluter, director of the campaign, said yesterday: 'We are not saying that all shops must be shut or that the present law should be left as it is.

'We believe that there are a number of feasible and enforceable ways to maintain regulations on Sunday trading.'

The immediate aim of the campaign is to obtain a free vote in the Commons on the bill instead of the three-line whip planned for Conservative MPs.

The campaign organisers believe that a free vote would lead to the Bill being defeated and force the Government to make alternative proposals for the reform of the shop opening legislation which would still ban Sunday trading.

'The Keep Sunday Special campaign believes that the majority of people in Britain do not want unlimited Sunday trading when they realise the full implications of what is involved,' said Dr Schluter. He claimed that 'the belief that the public wants it has been promoted by a group of just half a dozen multiple retailers who expect to gain most out of de-regulation'.

Retailers supporting de-regulation formed a lobbying group 18 months ago called Open Shop. Its members include the Burton group, Habitat/Mothercare and Woolworth holdings.

Open Shop said yesterday: 'The launch of the campaign is a desperate last-ditch attempt to stop consumers being able to shop when they want.

'The fears the campaign expresses about the consequences of deregulation are entirely without foundation, as the Scottish experience of Sunday trading shows.'

(Financial Times, 10 January 1986)

The public debate grew steadily more vehement. Supporters of reform scored a notable public relations success against religious opponents of the bill when they pointed out that the souvenir shop in Canterbury Cathedral was open on Sunday. But attention turned increasingly to the Commons where Labour, with an eye to its union links, came out firmly against the bill, and intensive local pressure began to have its effect on Conservative back benches. The Whips began to pick up signals that the wind was changing, and in particular reported resentment at the government's refusal to allow its backbenchers a free vote. In the run-up to the second reading of the bill, the government announced a concession.

The Government will offer a free vote to its backbenchers on both the committee and report stages of the Shops Bill which seeks to remove the remaining restrictions on trading hours, particularly on Sundays.

However, there will be a three-line whip on the second reading of the Bill, expected at midnight next Monday. About 50 Tory MPs have threatened to vote against the Government and between 25 and 30 have said they may abstain.

. . . Ministers hope that by offering a free vote on later stages of the Bill, fewer MPs will revolt on Monday and that, in practice, there is such disagreement among the Tory rebels about possible amendments to the Bill that it may survive largely unscathed.

The official belief is that without such a trumpeted concession the outcome of Monday's vote might have been uncertain, especially since Labour will also be imposing a three-line whip, in support of its reasoned amendment and the Ulster Unionists will be making one of their rare visits to Westminster to vote against the Bill.

(Financial Times, 11 April 1986)

In the event, the concession proved inadequate.

The Government suffered its most humiliating parliamentary rebuff early this morning when the Commons rejected by 14 votes the Shops Bill, which sought to remove the remaining restrictions on Sunday trading hours.

Mr John Biffen, the Leader of the Commons, immediately intervened to say that the Government accepted the decision of MPs and had no plans to reintroduce the legislation.

The result of the vote was announced to a packed noisy Commons at 27 minutes past midnight by Opposition whip Mr Ray Powell. With Labour MPs standing cheering and waving their order papers, and ministers, including Mrs Thatcher, sitting red-faced and embarrassed, Mr Powell said that 282 members had voted for the Bill but 296 against.

(Financial Times, 15 April 1986)

After this, the government left the issue well alone. Only in 1993 did the Major government revive the issue, and then it cautiously invited the Commons to choose between five options. Crucially, USDAW changed its stance to supporting limited Sunday opening, and the Commons chose to permit unlimited opening for small shops, and to allow large shops to open for six hours on Sunday. This new Shops Act was passed in 1994.

6.b.3   Forcing the government to drop a proposal: the sale of British Leyland

Some backbench revolts smoulder on for months while the government hopes that they will burn themselves out, or will peter out if the government offers judicious concessions. Other rebellions are sudden and violent, and the government retreats before the violence of the storm. One such occurred in February 1986, when the *Daily Mail* led its front page with the startling and hitherto unsuspected news that the government planned to sell parts of the nationalised car manufacturer British Leyland (BL) to foreign bidders.

American and Japanese car firms are negotiating to buy huge slices of state-owned BL.

The Government is backing the talks, which could herald privatisation, but the plan was already causing political controversy last night.

Labour's deputy leader Roy Hattersley said the implications could be 'catastrophic' for jobs and 'most serious' for defence.

'The Government is planning to sell off the British motor industry to foreign multi-national car makers,' he declared.

The two firms involved are General Motors of Detroit, which already owns Vauxhall and has just bought Lotus, and Honda of Japan, which already has a technical tie-up with BL.

GM is ready to offer around £300 million for BL's commercial vehicle operation, employing more than 11,000 people – trucks, buses and Land Rover. An announcement is expected within six weeks.

The only stumbling block in the talks is Land Rover. There is some feeling in BL that this part of the business should remain British.

(*Daily Mail*, 3 February 1986)

The same afternoon the Secretary of State for Trade and Industry, Paul Channon, made an emergency statement to the Commons confirming that the story was true, although the second bidder was actually Ford rather than Honda.

THE SECRETARY OF STATE FOR TRADE AND INDUSTRY (MR PAUL CHANNON) With the approval of the BL board, discussions are in progress between BL and General Motors with the aim of creating an internationally competitive United Kingdom commercial vehicle industry and improving the long-term prospects for the constituent BL companies. These talks cover Leyland Trucks, Land Rover, Freight Rover and certain related overseas operations. Discussions are at an advanced stage, but a number of important issues remain to be settled . . . .

General Motors would be willing to give undertakings that the majority of the products sold by the businesses involved would be manufactured in the United Kingdom, that the products would continue to have a high local content, that there would be a substantial level of exports, that research and development facilities would be maintained and developed in the United Kingdom, that Land Rover would retain its distinct British identity, and that an appropriate level of investment would be injected into the business to achieve competitive future models and facilities.

The reactions of Conservative backbenchers were mixed, however, as these two comments show:

MR JOHN CARLISLE (Luton, North): General Motors has an excellent record in Britain, and I have every confidence that should the merger take place it will be to the benefit of all the workers concerned.

DAME JILL KNIGHT (Birmingham, Edgbaston): Is my right hon. Friend aware that the future of scores, if not hundreds, of small businesses in the West Midlands depends on their being able to provide parts to British Leyland? May we be certain that their future is being considered in any arrangement to be made?

(*House of Commons Debates*, 3 February 1986)

The *Daily Mail* reported:

When Speaker Mr Bernard Weatherell cut short the questioning after 15 minutes, Tory MP Anthony Beaumont-Dark (Birmingham, Selly Oak) protested furiously and stormed from the Commons Chamber.

Afterwards he said he was prepared to disrupt the work of the Commons if the Government attempted to railroad through the Leyland sale. . . .

Angry Tory backbenchers last night tabled a Commons motion deploring the Government's stance over GM.

(*Daily Mail*, 4 February 1986)

Nor was the opposition confined to the back benches. Norman Fowler, Secretary of State for Health and Social Security, declared his strong opposition within Whitehall, although he did not make it public.

As far as I was concerned, the publicly revealed position was totally unsatisfactory. I was a Cabinet member from the West Midlands whose constituency included many workers and managers who were either employed by Leyland or whose companies relied upon it. However, I had known nothing of this dramatic development of policy. I had not been consulted. I had not even been advised that such developments were in the offing. Yet it was becoming crystal clear that the strategy of sale had been approved by the Cabinet's Economic Committee.

I was a member of the Cabinet but I was also Member of Parliament for Sutton Coldfield. It was not my job to defend local interests irrespective of the commercial and industrial arguments. It was my job to evaluate the proposals on the basis of my local knowledge. After all, it was I who would have to defend the policies locally.

(Norman Fowler, *Ministers Decide*, London: Chapmans, 1991)

On Tuesday 4 February Margaret Thatcher faced a rowdy time at Prime Minister's questions. Ominously, a supportive question from one of her own supporters led to shots across her bows from two Tory MPs.

MR BUDGEN Will my right hon. Friend take this opportunity of reminding all those who are interested in the future of BL that the company has already received over the past 10 years about £2 billion from the taxpayer and that it is unlikely that the taxpayer will wish to provide any more money for BL? Therefore, BL's future may be best safeguarded if it finds allies and friends in the private sector, whether they come from this country or abroad.

THE PRIME MINISTER   As my hon. Friend says, no one can doubt the Government's commitment to the future of BL. The taxpayer has already put in over £2 billion, and in addition there have been £1.5 billion guarantees under the Varley–Marshall assurances. We are determined to create an internationally competitive BL, and that is what the discussions which are now under way are aimed to achieve, namely, to protect jobs in the long term . . . .

MR BEAUMONT-DARK   Will my right hon. Friend accept that many people who have built BL, and in this case Austin Rover, up into a successful enterprise resent very much the implication that somehow or other it is a financial leper? If General Motors and Ford are willing to back BL, why cannot our Government show the same faith?

THE PRIME MINISTER   My hon. Friend should not forget that the backing through the Government by the taxpayer, not the Government, has been enormous. During the lifetime of this Government it has been £1.5 billion. Again he must not forget the guarantees that rise annually. One is concerned for the future of BL. One is concerned, therefore, to have a competitive BL. That is what the talks upon which we have embarked are designed to achieve. . . .

MR JOHN MARK TAYLOR   Will my right hon. Friend find time in a busy day to issue a word of reassurance to 8,000 Land Rover employees in my constituency?

THE PRIME MINISTER   As I have already indicated, discussions are taking place with General Motors with the full support and approval of the BL board. Those discussions are about both Leyland Trucks and Land Rover.

(*House of Commons Debates*, 4 February 1986)

A certain number of 'supply days' are allocated in each parliamentary session for debates on issues chosen by the opposition. Half of the next day was given over to a debate on the affair on an opposition motion. But the most significant opposition turned out to be on the government's own back benches in a vehemently critical attack from the former Conservative prime minister, Edward Heath.

How do we restore faith in our industry by selling out to the Americans? . . . What else will the Government negotiate to sell? Will we get rid of Rolls-Royce to Pratt and Whitney because we still have to support Rolls-Royce? Some Conservative Members say that we are anti-American, but does anybody imagine that the Americans would ever allow their motor, aero engine or aircraft industries to be sold to foreigners? . . . The alternative option is to work for a European arrangement – not a takeover, but an arrangement – which would be a joint operation. We have been successful in defence. There is no reason why we should not have success in the automobile industry.

I wish to be plain and honest. I cannot support the Government's proposition to sell out the remains of the British motor industry to the Americans. I shall resist it in every way possible.

(House of Commons Debates, 5 February 1986)

At the end of a boisterous Commons debate the former Prime Minister and 10 other Tory MPs openly defied the Government by remaining in their seats during a vote on a Labour motion deploring the Government attitude. The Government defeated the Labour motion by 324 to 195, a majority of 129. But on a follow-up Government amendment approving its own 'determination to work towards a viable and internationally competitive automotive industry located in the United Kingdom' the majority slumped to 86, on a vote of 297 to 211.

In such crises, the lobbies of the Commons buzz with rumours. Indeed, what MPs say outside the chamber can be more significant than what they say in it, and it is the job of the government Whips to pick up the gossip and report to the Prime Minister on the state of opinion.

On the Wednesday evening I was told by John Wakeham, the Chief Whip, that there were 'rumbles' in the lobbies that I and Peter Walker (who represented another West Midlands constituency, Worcester) would ride to British Leyland's rescue. I replied that I had talked to neither Peter nor the press. I did, however, intend to raise the subject at Cabinet the next day. I felt strongly that Cabinet ministers with a clear interest should be at least kept in the picture and not hear the news for the first time through the papers.

Early on Thursday morning, I received a telephone call inviting me to join the discussion of 'E' Committee on British Leyland which would follow Cabinet. I was happy to do that, but I still felt that the issue should also be discussed at full Cabinet. Accordingly at our meeting at 10.30am I raised what was rapidly becoming the Leyland row. . . . I raised the central issue of the talks themselves and in particular the position of Ford. I argued that we should recognize the great improvement in industrial relations and productivity that had taken place over the last few years at British Leyland and predicted that we would have very substantial political problems seeing a Ford takeover through. As we went around the table it became evident that there was little support for the sale post Westland. The discussion at Cabinet was short, given that all the major players had now been invited to the 'E' Committee following.

At 'E' the decision was taken to break off talks with Ford. Whatever may have been the Committee's original view, the majority now clearly thought that a sale to Ford was either the wrong policy or not feasible. Even some of those who were sympathetic to the sale considered it 'a bridge too far' in the political aftermath of Westland. There was nothing to be gained in pursuing talks which the majority of the Committee felt were doomed to failure. Rather than allow the row to run on, it was decided to bring the negotiations to an end.

(Norman Fowler, *Ministers Decide*)

The next day's press was not kind to the government.

Cabinet ministers forced the Prime Minister into a sharp about-turn yesterday, vetoing Ford's takeover talks with BL in a signal and rebellious reassertion of collective cabinet responsibility.

Mrs Margaret Thatcher's image of strong leadership was further shaken last night by the whirlwind BL crisis; but she had been left with no alternative but to back down after a clear majority of the Cabinet's powerful economic affairs committee had drawn the line on the Ford talks.

After a mass Commons revolt led by Mr Edward Heath on Wednesday night, Mrs Thatcher, already weakened by the Westland affair, was cornered by the outright opposition of her ministerial colleagues to the Ford option.

... After a one-hour cabinet meeting at No. 10, the economic affairs committee went into session for a further hour and the debate went round and round the table with the Prime Minister being left with no final option but to accept the defeat.

The Secretary of State for Trade and Industry, Mr Paul Channon, who had told the Commons only 24 hours before that it would be 'ridiculous' and 'foolish' not to explore the Ford–BL merger option, was instructed to go back to the House again yesterday to announce: 'We have decided that it would be wrong for the uncertainty to continue and that the right way to end it is to make clear that the possibility of the sale of Austin Rover to Ford will not be pursued.'

(*The Times*, 6 February 1986)

6.b.4　Forcing the government to give ground: the pits closure crisis

The shops bill was an example of backbenchers rebelling in response to pressure from constituents and interest groups. The British Leyland sale was more a case of backbenchers rising under their own steam, stung by what they appeared to find an affront to national dignity, and worried about the country's manufacturing capacity. The coal mines closure crisis of October 1992 was a fusion of all of these motivations. Rather than a slow build up of parliamentary opposition to the point where the government was defeated, this crisis was played out instead as an immediate explosion of parliamentary opposition that had to be appeased by piecemeal concessions by the government.

While the crisis itself broke suddenly, the decision to announce the closure of the mines must have been debated for a long while within the government. Although the closure proposals were formally advanced at the initiative of British Coal, it was accepted by all participants that ministers had been deeply involved: the Prime Minister's Press Office told the press that John Major and other senior ministers had been 'fully engaged' in the decision (as reported in the *Financial Times* and the *Independent*, 16 October 1992). The rationale for the decision was a familiar one, and driven by powerful logic: the market for coal was simply too small for the volume of fuel being produced by the mines. Even so, the violence and breadth of the public reaction to the announcement evidently surprised the government. The following day's lead story in the *Financial Times* summarised well the tone and scale of opposition and, significantly, placed it in the context of other poor economic news.

A nationwide wave of protests hit the government yesterday over its drastic programme of pit closures as several Conservative MPs openly criticised Tuesday's announcement of the loss of 30,000 coalminers' jobs.

With ministers braced for a sharp increase in unemployment figures today, Tory backbenchers joined church leaders and unions to charge Mr John Major's administration with insensitivity and a failure to grasp the human dimensions of the recession.

As the public furore grew, the government suffered a new blow when the European Commission turned down a request for an extra £24.7m to help mining regions hit by the shutdowns.

The depth and savagery of the cuts in the British coal industry also provoked nearly unanimous condemnation from usually loyal Conservative newspapers.

In a full-page editorial, the *Daily Express* accused ministers of 'drifting aimlessly' and being 'too little concerned' by the rising rate of business failures. 'Above all, we deserve and require leadership,' it said.

Coming in the wake of job losses at Lucas Industries and Vickers' failure to win a £1bn tank order from Kuwait, many critics targeted the prime minister for failing to tackle the recession with sufficient urgency. Lord Ridley, former trade and industry secretary, warned that without 'drastic' cuts in interest rates the country faced a slump worse than that of the 1930s.

Mrs Elizabeth Peacock, Conservative MP for the Yorkshire seat of Batley and Spen, called for the reversal of the pit closures, saying dependence on imports was 'strategically dangerous' for the long-term health of the economy. Mr John Carlisle, Tory MP for Luton North, said that, in devastating the lives of thousands, the government was showing it was 'not fit to govern'.

Churchmen added their protests with the Bishop of Sheffield describing the cuts as 'wicked' and Dr John Habgood, the Archbishop of York, condemning them as 'economic madness'.

(*Financial Times*, 15 October 1992)

The Labour opposition tabled a motion deploring the closures, to be debated the following Wednesday. Over the next twenty-four hours it became clear that enough Conservative backbench MPs to imperil the government's majority were willing to rebel. It must be understood that, if passed, the Commons motion would have had no legal force. Strictly speaking, the decision to close the pits was that of British Coal: parliamentary approval was not required. But it was tacitly accepted by all sides that, if the Commons passed a hostile motion, authority to press ahead with the closures would have been swept away and the plans would have had to be withdrawn or drastically revised. This, then, was not a question of parliamentary legislation; rather it was a question of parliamentary legitimisation, by conferring – or withholding – approval of the policy.

In an interview with *The Times*, Michael Heseltine acknowledged the government's difficulties.

About a dozen Conservative MPs have publicly expressed disquiet over the closures and Labour will take care to frame next Wednesday's Commons motion calling for a reversal or moratorium on the closures in such a way as to maximise the chances of government humiliation. Mr Smith [Labour leader] said last night: 'I think Conservative MPs who have joined in the criticism of the action of the government have a splendid opportunity to show that their vote follows their voice.' If 11 Tories and all opposition MPs vote against the government, it would be forced to reconsider its plans. There were indications last night that at least three Conservatives were planning to abstain. . . .

While yesterday's cabinet accepted that there was no alternative to closures with vast stocks of coal building up without a buyer, ministers were clearly alarmed at the backlash inside and outside the party and they agreed that much more had to be done to sell their case to the country and their backbenchers.

Mr Heseltine acknowledged in his interview with *The Times* that the government had work to do in heading off a backbench revolt. Next Monday when the Commons returned, ministers would be talking to backbenchers and 'putting the facts before them'. He added: 'In the end they will see the logic of what has happened.'

But Elizabeth Peacock and Nicholas and Ann Winterton insisted that they would abstain on Wednesday, while William Cash said he would make up his mind on the day. Mrs Peacock, MP for Batley and Spen in Yorkshire, said it was outrageous to throw so many people on the dole and she would be putting pressure on the government to back down. 'If we are debating strictly on the coal industry, I will not support the government on this issue. I have made that very clear.'

Other senior Tories, including Winston Churchill, Sir John Hannam, James Pawsey, Sir Teddy Taylor and Sir Anthony Durant, have condemned the closures. In a sign that Tory Euro-sceptics might exploit the government's difficulties to further their campaign against the Maastricht treaty, Sir Teddy said his attitude would depend on whether the government admitted that the European Commission had stopped it subsidising coal mining. He added that the government was losing public sympathy and that the Coal Board was exhibiting the worst features of Victorian employers.

(The Times, 16 October 1992)

The row overshadowed that Friday's EC summit in Birmingham, called under John Major's presidency to resolve problems over the Maastricht treaty. Late that afternoon, the Prime Minister gave a press conference at which he foreshadowed the further help for mining communities discussed the previous day in cabinet. The same day the government cut 1 per cent off interest rates, despite public statements earlier that week by ministers that this would be premature. The cut was widely described in the press as a response to the coal crisis: as the *Financial Times* put it, 'the right decision for the wrong reason'.

John Major last night moved to restore his government's battered authority with measures designed to boost the economy, help the 30,000 miners who will lose their jobs under British Coal's pit closures plan, and stave off the threat of a Commons defeat over the shutdown.

Mr Major, engulfed in the gravest crisis of his leadership, promised a 'closely targeted' programme to help with the retraining of miners on top of the £1 billion already pledged for redundancy payments. But while he regretted the anguish caused by the closure of 31 pits, he made clear that there would be no going back.

The prime minister had earlier approved a one-point cut in interest rates to their lowest level since 1988 'to help British industry and British families' and last night he announced that Norman Lamont would be holding a series of face-to-face meetings with industrial leaders in the next few weeks to discuss what the government could do to boost business.

Britain's political and economic turmoil had completely overshadowed the special European Community summit in Birmingham and at the end of the day's proceedings, Mr Major took the unusual step of calling a personal press conference to defend the decision to close the pits. He had kept in constant touch with ministers in London – including the chief whip, Richard Ryder – between sessions with his fellow EC leaders, and when he spoke it was in the knowledge that he faces the real prospect of defeat in the Commons next Wednesday, when Labour will call for an inquiry into the closures.

. . . Action to quell the Conservative rebellion became essential after Sir Marcus Fox, chairman of the 1922 Committee, said that a review of the pit closures decision was imperative, adding: 'The scale of the proposals is unacceptable. I am sure there will be a number of answers to the things that concern us – there had better be.' Winston Churchill, another leading critic, said last night: 'If you are going up a blind alley the most sensible thing to do is to make a U-turn.' Michael Heseltine, the president of the Board of Trade, has been asked to address the 1922 executive next week. He also plans to address Tory MPs before Wednesday's debate.

(The Times, 17 October 1992)

That weekend was deeply uncomfortable for the government. Conservative backbenchers returned to their constituencies to find profound resentment, not least amongst party workers. The dependably Conservative *Sunday Telegraph* is worth reading on these occasions.

> The government is prepared to climb down over plans for immediate closure of 31 mines if it fails in a last-ditch attempt to persuade rebel Tory MPs to back its policy ahead of Wednesday's Commons debate on the coal industry.
>
> As Gillian Shephard, the Employment Secretary, battled with the Treasury yesterday for extra money to retrain redundant miners and help set up new businesses in affected areas, Government sources said it would be 'madness' to push the issue to a vote if ministers did not believe they could win.
>
> There are fears that a defeat for the Government in the lobbies on Wednesday would be a further humiliating blow to John Major's credibility, and would also jeopardise Michael Heseltine's future as President of the Board of Trade.
>
> . . . But there were signs last night that efforts to contain the number of potential rebels were failing, as more senior backbenchers joined the chorus of criticism of the Government's plans.
>
> A poll of 100 Tory backbenchers in today's *Sunday Times* reports 44 against the pit closures, 40 in favour and 16 don't knows.
>
> Among the potential rebels, John Watts, the respected chairman of the all-party Treasury Select Committee, called for closure plans to be postponed and demanded a White Paper setting out the Government's case. 'I cannot imagine a decision being handled worse than this and am not going to defend such crass stupidity,' he said. 'There is a limit to how many unpopular decisions normally loyal MPs can be expected to support.'
>
> . . . Mr Heseltine yesterday stuck by the Government's line, 'There is no escape from this dilemma,' he said. 'I believe the Government's case will prevail. There is no escape from the fact that there is no market for coal. I do not believe we will lose the vote.'
>
> (*Sunday Telegraph*, 18 October 1992)

Michael Heseltine's line simply could not hold against the vehemence of criticism from within his party. On Sunday afternoon John Major returned early from Chequers and summoned a meeting of senior ministers. They agreed a package of concessions to backbench rebels. On Monday morning (according to press reports) the cabinet approved the change and that afternoon Heseltine announced it to the Commons.

> Bowing to a wave of public and political outrage, the Government last night lifted the threat of immediate closure from 21 of the mines due to be axed by British Coal. But the biggest industrial U-turn by a Conservative Government for 20 years left the authority of the Prime Minister and Mr Heseltine, President of the Board of Trade, badly damaged and failed to satisfy all the

Tory critics of the closures. After an emergency Cabinet meeting to agree on the climbdown, Mr Heseltine told a crowded and tense House of Commons that British Coal would be allowed to proceed with closing only 10 of the 31 pits on its hit list.

A moratorium lasting until early in the New Year is to be introduced for all the other pits and redundancies. If, after consultation, the closures are confirmed, Mr Heseltine said there would be a 'phased programme' to reduce surplus capacity.

. . . While ministers hoped the retreat would lift the threat of a Government defeat after tomorrow's Commons debate on the pit closures, Mr Heseltine failed to quell the dissent on the Tory backbenches.

Leaders of the Conservative backbench revolt are pressing for further concessions, including a full independent inquiry into the future of the coal industry and the country's energy needs. Some served notice that they were still prepared to vote against the Government, but ministers believe they will scrape home on the night.

The leader of the Tory revolt, Mr Winston Churchill, MP for Manchester, Davyhulme, said that Mr Heseltine had not gone far enough, while Mrs Elizabeth Peacock (Batley and Spen) called for a reprieve for the 10 pits where closure is going ahead.

But Mr Major appeared to have secured the crucially important backing of the executive of the 1922 Committee of Tory backbenchers, who had criticised the speed of the pit closures and the 30,000 job losses.

After an anniversary lunch at the Carlton Club in London, attended by Mr Major, they said they were 'much happier' about the Government's plans.

(*Daily Telegraph*, 20 October 1992)

The government's political calculations proved wrong. These concessions were not enough. A string of Conservative backbenchers announced that they were still not satisfied. On Tuesday, further concessions followed.

The government last night appeared to have headed off defeat at the hands of Tory MPs by signalling that its investigation into pit closures will range far wider than at first thought and throwing a lifeline to the communities.

A series of fresh concessions outlined in public and private statements by Michael Heseltine, John Major, and Lord Wakeham, leader of the Lords and former energy secretary, seemed last night to have isolated all but a hard core of Tory rebels.

In a morning encounter Mr Heseltine assured the executive of the 1922 committee that there would be a full and open review into the closures and that its findings would be published. He was swiftly rewarded after the 90-minute meeting with a statement from the executive pledging support in tonight's vote. Winston Churchill, ringleader of the Tory rebels, said later that he would be supporting the Government 'because of the significant change of policy'.

The prime minister told the Commons that the government would give the 'fullest co-operation' to the inquiry to be launched by the Commons trade and industry committee. Trade unions, including the miners, and independent energy experts will be allowed to give evidence both to the government review and to the select committee inquiry. Emphasising the widened scope of the review, Mr Major is said to have told friends: 'We haven't closed the pits and we haven't closed our minds.'

In a marked change of tone from that adopted by Mr Heseltine in his announcement on Monday, Lord Wakeham told the Lords it would be 'wrong to be too pessimistic'. He committed Mr Heseltine to looking at each pit and considering whether the case for closure had been made; considering and discussing with the electricity generators and regional electricity companies whether the market prospects for coal had been 'correctly assessed'; examining again the switch to gas-fired power stations; and looking again at the level of coal imports to see if they were 'appropriate'.

He said there would be 'little point in having a moratorium on the proposed pit closures if it was merely a device for getting the government off the hook'.

His statement, made after morning talks with Mr Heseltine and Mr Major, was clearly designed to win over remaining rebels. Many had voiced concern that Mr Heseltine seemed to believe that the consultations he promised – he did not even use the word 'review' – would not result in the 31 threatened pits having anything more than a temporary reprieve.

But Lord Wakeham promised that the review would be 'thorough and wide-ranging'. It would result in a 'significantly smaller coal industry' than at present, but it would still be 'substantial'.

(*The Times*, 21 October 1992)

On Tuesday the government was defeated on the subject in the House of Lords by twenty-five votes, but all eyes were on the next day's vote in the Commons. Here the government secured a narrow majority after ministers announced further concessions – notably a review by independent mining consultants – and propitiated the Ulster Unionists.

The Government last night survived the most crucial votes since Mr Major became Prime Minister after further concessions on the pit closures helped to contain a backbench Tory revolt.

But its majority of 21 was cut to 13 when a Labour motion calling for a stay of execution for all 31 pits involved until a review of the future of the coal industry had been completed was defeated by 320 votes to 307.

A Government amendment endorsing the decision to introduce a three-month moratorium on the closure of 21 of the pits while conducting a review of energy policy was then approved by 320 votes to 305, a majority of 15.

Six Conservatives voted against the Government: . . .

Eight Ulster Unionist MPs who were present for the debate also abstained, and Labour MPs pointed accusingly at them when the results of the votes were announced.

The victories bought time for the Government to work out a compromise on the threatened pits and to reassert its authority after an unprecedented chapter of U-turns on economic and industrial policy.

Although the Government survived the critical debate, the revolt revealed a strong undercurrent of concern among Tory backbenchers over the clumsy way Mr Heseltine, President of the Board of Trade, endorsed British Coal's decision to close the 31 pits with a loss of 30,000 jobs.

(Daily Telegraph, 22 October 1992)

This drew the teeth of the crisis, and it disappeared from the headlines for the next six months. When the review was completed six months later the atmosphere was very different.

Twelve of the 31 threatened pits were reprieved for up to two years as part of a £700 million rescue package announced in the Commons last night by Mr Heseltine, President of the Board of Trade. His proposals defused a revolt among Tory MPs, but provided 'no guarantees' that any extra market for coal would be found which would secure a long-term future for the pits saved from closure.

Six more pits will be moth-balled on 'care and maintenance', one will concentrate on developing its reserves; and two will shut in addition to 10 already earmarked for closure.

The rescued pits will be given a new chance to compete against cheaper imports with a subsidy of up to £12 a tonne while the industry is prepared for full privatisation by 1995.

The subsidy would bridge the gap between the price at which British Coal needs to sell coal to the power industry, currently £40 a tonne, and the world price of about £28 a tonne.

But a White Paper on the Government's five-month review of the closures gave warning of a 'substantial risk of further decline' in the market for coal.

(Daily Telegraph, 26 March 1993)

Several days later, the government comfortably defeated a Tory backbench revolt over the plan to reprieve only twelve of the thirty-one pits facing closure. Ulster Unionist MPs, promised help with industrial power costs in Northern Ireland, backed the government, more than outweighing the Tory rebels. The relative ease of the government's success was all the more surprising given the fact that, even as the white paper was published, it became clear that the future of the reprieved pits was uncertain. Two days before the pit vote the *Financial Times* carried a warning as its lead story.

British Coal executives expect to start closing some of the 12 reprieved pits within a year even if the company secures deals to sell extra coal to the electricity generators.

They believe further pit closures and redundancies will be inevitable around April next year because of a fall in sales to generators from that month, and fear they may be forced to act sooner.

'Even if we can negotiate good supplementary deals with the generators, there are severe doubts about whether all 12 can survive a year,' one executive said.

Problems will increase significantly in April 1994 because contracts about to be signed with generators include a 25 per cent sales drop from then, he said.

Similarly pessimistic views were being expressed privately yesterday by a range of senior British Coal employees.

The manager of one of the reprieved mines said yesterday: 'There are two other mines in this area which have been reprieved. At least one of us will close within a year.'

(*Financial Times*, 27–8 March 1993)

And some of the reprieved pits did close later that year.

Why, then, was there not the same outcry as there had been six months earlier? The reasons are complex. The government's tactics were better: taken by surprise in October 1992, it prepared the March 1993 announcement carefully. The fact that the white paper appeared on a Thursday and was put to the vote in the Commons the following Monday allowed little time for a rebellion to gather momentum; and the votes of the Ulster Unionists had been secured.

The intervening period had also served to help the government to win the argument. The review did not just win the government time; it provided material for the kind of informed debate about the future of the coal industry that might usefully have taken place before the October announcement. It became borne in on the government's critics that the prospects for the industry were very poor. The only serious alternative, urged on the government by the House of Commons Select Committee on Trade and Industry, was intervention in the power industry to secure a larger market for coal. The government made it clear that, partly for reasons of public spending and partly owing to EU rules on industrial competitiveness, it would not do this; and amongst the October critics resignation and pessimism began to set in.

Above all, the public mood in March 1993 was different. The kind of public anger that unnerved the government six months earlier is a very powerful force, all the more potent for being rare and unexpected; but it is not a mood that can be kept alive for long. It is difficult for a people to remain furious for six months. By the time the review was completed, the public mood had reverted to the depressed pessimism characteristic of the recession years of the early 1990s, and Conservative MPs returning to their constituencies on the weekend of 27 March did not encounter the fierce resistance from party loyalists they had found in October. As an episode, this odd and short-lived manifestation of public indignation was reminiscent of the 1935 Hoare–Laval pact, an attempt to partition Ethiopia after the invasion by Mussolini. A brief mobilisation of public opinion scuppered the pact, but the mood did not prove durable enough to insist on a firmer stand against the Italians, who ultimately took control of all Ethiopia.

6.c   THE HOUSE OF LORDS

The House of Lords has very noticeably reasserted its role in restraining the power of government since the early 1980s. Although on paper it enjoys a Conservative majority, in practice the substantial injection of life peers over the past thirty years has left a large number of independent 'cross-benchers' holding the balance of power. And as a prolonged period of one-party government implementing radical policies has worn on, the House of Lords has become quite blasé about amending government legislation. Ultimately the Commons has the last word: if the Lords reject a bill in one session and the Commons pass it again in the next, the Commons automatically prevail. But this gives the Lords an effective power to delay a bill for a year, and the government will usually give in – or offer a compromise – to avoid delaying the whole bill for the sake of a few contentious clauses. In this way, the House of Lords has exercised a greater influence over government policy than the Commons.

6.c.1   Voting down a proposal: the school transport charging clause

One particularly memorable reverse inflicted by the Lords on Margaret Thatcher's government occurred very early on, and set the tone for the Lords' behaviour for the rest of the decade.

In 1980, the government tried to legislate to allow local authorities to charge for home to school transport, a proposal disliked not only by opposition parties but by rural Conservatives and the churches (many denominational schools in the shires would have been affected). Trouble over the proposal surfaced in the Commons, where thirteen Tory MPs voted against it, despite a government concession.

> Thirteen Conservative MPs voted against the Government last night in a backbench rebellion against the introduction of charges for children's travel to school. Seven more Conservatives abstained, cutting the Government's majority by almost half to 23 on a Tory backbench move to delete the proposal from the Education Bill.
>
> Last night's revolt in the closing stages of the Commons' consideration of the Bill marked the most serious display of frustration from the Government benches since the Conservatives took office last May. Although it had been preceded by a number of warnings in public and private from MPs who thought the proposal singled out parents in country areas for unlimited school travel charges, Government business managers had not expected quite such a sizeable protest.
>
> (*Daily Telegraph*, 14 February 1980)

Within the month the bill had reached the Lords, and a formidable opposition had begun to coalesce, led from the government back benches, embarrassingly, by that truest of true-blue Conservatives the Duke of Norfolk, and supported by

Lord Butler of Saffron Walden, who as R. A. Butler had marshalled through the Commons the famous Education Act of 1944. The Government Whips in such circumstances usually resort to summoning the many Conservative 'backwoods' peers who do not usually attend, but in this case, according to press reports, they feared that those brought in from rural areas might decide, after hearing the debate, to vote against the clause. So a worried government offered concessions.

The Government decided yesterday to relax the proposed school bus charges in its Education Bill following strong protests from Conservative MPs and peers who said that the charges would discriminate against rural pupils at church schools.

Ministers hoped that the amendments, tabled yeaterday, would placate Lord Butler, the architect of the 1944 Education Act, the Duke of Norfolk, and about 12 other Conservative peers, who were proposing to vote against the Bill. But last night, the Duke of Norfolk, 64, England's premier duke and a leading Roman Catholic, said he would not vote with the Government next week when the amendments are debated. The Conservative rebels are likely to be joined by Labour, Liberal and cross-bench peers on the vote, on Tuesday or Thursday.

Under the amendments, local authorities will be able to charge for only the first two children in any family for school transport. This change is intended to benefit large families and children attending denominational schools, the Department of Education said last night.

Mr Carlisle, Education Secretary, commented: 'In giving local education authorities the power to charge for school transport, the Government has now included four important safeguards for families.'

The other three safeguards are that local authorities can only operate a flat rate charge not related to the length of journeys; that the same charge has to be made whether or not the school attended is the nearest to the child's home; that children from families receiving supplementary benefit or family income supplement will continue to travel free. These were introduced following a change of heart by Education Ministers because of earlier protests from Conservatives.

The Duke of Norfolk, who has five children, one a 17 year old schoolboy, said last night: 'I've tabled my own amendments for next week's debate, calling on the Government to ensure that all children receive free transport to school. The Government's amendments leave me totally unsatisfied in saying that parents will only have to pay for the first two children. Very few families have more than two children these days. One-parent families and particularly people in rural areas, many of whose children go 15 miles to school, will suffer.'

The Duke told the House of Lords last week: 'The church schools were set up in the great Butler Act of 1944 on the express understanding that they would be built in places suitable for church schools and that there would be free transport to them. Inevitably, church schools for Roman Catholics, Anglicans, Jews or Methodists have very wide catchment areas, and it was assumed and promised as a definite pledge that there would be free transport to those schools.'

The Duke added that it was quite extraordinary that the Government and the party to which he belonged should discriminate against the rural community in this way.

(*Daily Telegraph*, 7 March 1980)

The government's concessions did little good. When the Lords came to a vote on the issue, the scale of the government's defeat passed into political legend, although the impact of the news was softened slightly by the fact that it coincided with the Conservatives' narrow retention of Southend East in a closely fought by-election.

Forty-one Conservative peers last night helped to inflict a crushing defeat on the Government when the Lords rejected, by a majority of 104, the scheme to enable councils to charge for school transport. By 216 votes to 112, peers deleted from the Education Bill the crucial clause 23 which would end the obligation to provide free transport for journeys to school of over three miles.

The alliance of Roman Catholic and rural peers and Conservative educationalists who had attacked the scheme appeared to have killed it last night through the sheer size of the majority. Although Mr Carlisle, Education Secretary, said Ministers would have to consider their next moves, it appeared unlikely that a measure which sparked off a Tory backbench rebellion in the Commons would get through a second time.

Were the government to stick to its guns and bring the clause to the Lords again, a fresh defeat in the Upper House would trigger the Lords' delaying power and prevent the scheme from taking effect for a year. The Government's defeat was not solely the consequence of Conservative defections. Had all Tory peers present voted for the measure, it would still have been defeated.

Ministers were clearly staggered last night by the sheer magnitude of the defeat the Lords had handed out.

(*Daily Telegraph*, 14 March 1980)

The government duly gave way, and, despite increasing financial stringency throughout the 1980s, the issue of school transport charges stayed well off the political agenda.

6.d CONTROL BY THE COURTS: JUDICIAL REVIEW

The involvement of the courts in the policy making process is fairly recent. Part of the British constitution is, of course, founded on ancient legal judgements which set limits to the power of the government. But there is no written constitution or constitutional court, and while most government action is taken using statutory powers conferred by parliament, much is also taken under Crown prerogative, an unwritten body of miscellaneous discretionary government power. Consequently Britain has little in the way of mechanism for declaring government actions illegal. This contrasts with the many European countries, like France and Germany, which have constitutional courts whose function is to ensure that laws conform to the constitution. In the United States, indeed, matters are taken to extremes, since decisions of executive and Congress are constantly being submitted to review by the Supreme Court, which hands down dozens of judgements every year on the validity of government actions and congressional statutes.

Since the 1970s the position in Britain has changed markedly with the evolution of judicial review, a procedure under which a citizen may apply to the courts to have an executive decision declared invalid. The number of judicial review cases in England and Wales rose from 160 in 1974 to over 1,230 in 1985, and to over 2,600 in 1992. A similar development has been apparent in Scotland. While the majority are cases against local councils, a large proportion are directed against central government. The reasons for this sudden growth are mixed. On a purely practical level, in 1977 the complex and arcane procedure for applying for judicial review of an administrative decision was greatly simplified. But the change also reflects shifts in social attitudes and political realities. People have become less deferential towards authority and more disposed to argue with official decisions they dislike. The judiciary have openly voiced their concern at what they see as the inadequacy of political control over government, in particular the limitations of parliament as a restraint on government power, and have spoken of the need for a parallel channel of accountability and redress through the courts. Pressure groups have become adept at using the courts to challenge or delay projects they dislike, such as road building schemes. Individuals and groups not part of 'policy communities', and so at a disadvantage in trying to alter policy, can resort to use of the courts. And solicitors and barristers have been encouraged to make greater use of judicial review by government defeats in a number of well-publicised cases (including those set out below).

It is important to understand that judicial review is not an all-purpose appeals procedure for citizens to challenge decisions they dislike. An application for judicial review must be based on one of three clearly defined grounds, helpfully summarised by Lord Diplock in the GCHQ case:

- *illegality*: in other words, the person who took the decision got the law wrong;
- *irrationality*: defined here in a very narrow sense: in Lord Diplock's words 'a decision that is so outrageous in its defiance of logic or of accepted moral standards that no sensible person who had applied his mind to the question to be decided could have arrived at it';
- *procedural impropriety*: that the procedure followed in taking the decision

was somehow faulty. For example a minister's decision to approve a local council's plans to close a school could be declared invalid if it turned out that the local council had not carried out properly the public consultation exercise required by statute.

Even if the courts find the decision invalid, they do not substitute their own decision. They simply refer it back to the original decision maker for reconsideration. Provided that, second time around, the decision is not illegal, irrational or procedurally improper, it is quite possible that the original decision will be reached again. So, in the school closure decision mentioned above, the decision would be referred back to the local council; if, after going through the consultation procedure properly, it still decided the school should close, it could still reach that decision and the minister could still approve it.

Although the grounds for decision appear quite narrow at first sight, the concepts that the courts have to consider are actually rather vague. Two particular angles have allowed judges in recent years to be more adventurous in their interpretation of these principles. Firstly, while ministers' actions are hardly ever blatantly illegal, in the sense of simply ignoring what the law says, often the law gives ministers a discretion, which creates a grey area: many cases like the television licence episode and the Tameside judgement below turn on whether the minister has used his or her discretion reasonably. Secondly, procedural impropriety has been held to occur when a procedure is 'unfair', and, since the concept of fairness is pretty broad, it allows a judge a lot of scope, as the Laker case below shows.

6.d.1   The television licences case

It was in the 1960s that the courts laid the foundations of judicial review with a series of judgements that made it clear that the courts would step in if a public authority acted unfairly or unreasonably. For example, judges held that the Brighton Police Committee had acted unfairly in dismissing their Chief Constable for misconduct without first giving him a hearing to explain himself. But only in the 1970s did the full implications of this legal evolution become clear when the courts struck down a series of ministerial decisions – something they have carried on doing to the present day.

The first of these landmark cases came in 1975, when the Court of Appeal ruled that the Home Secretary had acted illegally by abusing his discretion in trying to stop people renewing their television licences before the licence fee went up. Andrew Congreve, a London solicitor, brought a test case against the Home Secretary. He lost in the High Court, but won on appeal. The leading judgement was delivered by the Master of the Rolls, Lord Denning, a somewhat flamboyant character whose judgements make surprisingly easy reading.

Every person who has a colour television set must get a licence for it. It is issued for 12 months, more or less. The fee up to 31st March 1975 was £12. As from

1st April 1975 it was increased to £18, This increase was announced beforehand by the Minister, but it did not become law until the very day itself, 1st April 1975. Up till that date the Department could only charge £12 for a licence. On and after that date it was bound to charge £18. This gave many people, who already held a licence, a bright idea. Towards the end of March 1975 they took out new licences at the then existing fee of £12. These would overlap their existing licences by a few days; but the new licences would last them nearly the next 12 months. So they would save the extra £6 which they would have had to pay if they had waited after 1st April 1975. To my mind there was nothing unlawful whatever in their trying to save money in this way. But the Home Office were furious. They wrote letters to every one of the overlappers. They said in effect: 'We are not going to let you get away with it in this way. You must pay up the extra £6 or we will revoke your new licence.' . . .

Counsel on behalf of [Mr Congreve] submitted that the demand of the Home Office for £6 was an unlawful demand; that the licence was revoked as a means of enforcing that unlawful demand; and that, therefore, the revocation was unlawful. Counsel for the Minister submitted that, by taking out an overlapping licence, Mr Congreve was thwarting the intention of Parliament; and that the minister was justified in using his powers so as to prevent Mr Congreve from doing it.

. . . Can the minister revoke the overlapping licence which was issued lawfully? He claims that he can revoke it by virtue of the discretion given to him by section 1(4) of the 1949 Act ['A licence may be revoked, or the terms, provisions or limitations thereof limited, by a notice in writing of' the Minister]. But I think not. The licensee has paid £12 for the 12 months. If the licence is to be revoked – and his money forfeited – the Minister would have to give good reasons to justify it. Of course, if the licensee had done anything wrong – if he had given a cheque for £12 which was dishonoured, or if he broke the terms of the licence – the Minister could revoke it. But, where the licensee has done nothing wrong at all, I do not think the Minister can lawfully revoke the licence, at any rate, not without offering him his money back, and not even then except for good cause. If he should revoke it without giving reasons, or for no good reason, the courts can set aside his revocation and restore the licence. It would be a misuse of the power conferred on him by Parliament; and these courts have the authority – and I would add, the duty – to correct a misuse of power by a Minister or his Department. . . .

What then are the reasons put forward by the Minister in this case? He says that the increased fee of £18 was fixed so as to produce enough revenue for future requirements. It was calculated on previous experience that no one would take out an overlapping licence before 1st April 1975 – or, at any rate, that no appreciable number of people would do so. When he found out that many more were doing so, he tried to prevent it so far as he could. He gave instructions to the clerks that anyone who applied towards the end of March for an overlapping £12 licence should be told to come back on or after the 1st April 1975, and thus made to pay the increased fee of £18. His policy would be thwarted, he said, and the revenue rendered insufficient, if large numbers of people were allowed to take out overlapping licences. He said, too, that other licence holders (being the vast majority) would have a legitimate grievance. So he considered it proper to revoke the overlapping licences of those who had acted contrary to his policy.

Are these good reasons? I cannot accept those reasons for one moment. The Minister relies on the intention of Parliament. But it was not the policy of Parliament that he was seeking to enforce. It was his own policy. And he did it in a way which was unfair and unjust. . . .

The licence is granted for 12 months and cannot be revoked simply to enable the Minister to raise more money. Want of money is no reason for revoking a licence. The real reason, of course, in this case was that the department did not like people taking out overlapping licences to save money. But there was nothing in the regulations to stop it. It was perfectly lawful; and the department's dislike of it cannot afford a good reason for revoking them. So far as other people are concerned (who did not have the foresight to take out overlapping licences) I doubt whether they would feel aggrieved if these licences remained valid. They might only say: 'Good luck to them. We wish we had done the same.'

There is yet another reason for holding the demands for £6 to be unlawful. They were made contrary to the Bill of Rights [of 1688]. They were an attempt to levy money for the use of the Crown without the authority of Parliament; and that is quite enough to damn them.

(Congreve v. Home Office [1976] 1 AER, pp. 706–10)

The Home Secretary then apologised, and made arrangements for refunds to those members of the public who felt they had lost out financially.

6.d.2   The Tameside case

The dam had been breached, and two more cases the following year showed just how profound an effect judicial review could have upon government policy. The first, and politically liveliest, was the 'Tameside' case on the question of comprehensive education. Tameside's Labour council submitted to the Education Secretary plans to turn their schools into comprehensives but, when the Conservatives took control of the council in 1976, the council sought a partial delay pending a review of the future of the five grammar schools. The Education Secretary believed that there was insufficient time to hold the selection procedure for the grammar schools that year, and issued an order to the council to press ahead with the reorganisation. His order was made under section 68 of the Education Act 1944, which gives the minister discretion to give directions to a council 'if satisfied that any local authority was acting unreasonably'. So the case did not turn on whether comprehensive education was a good thing, but on the reasonableness of each side's actions.

What was instructive about the outcome was not so much the legal arguments on each side but the highly partisan way in which each side reacted to the judicial decison.

Five law lords decided unanimously yesterday that Mr Mulley, Education Secretary, acted unlawfully in directing Tameside Council to abolish its grammar schools and reorganise them as comprehensives. In a two-sentence announcement Lord Wilberforce, president of the judicial committee of the House of Lords, dismissed Mr Mulley's appeal against a ruling by Lord Denning, Master of the Rolls, that he was wrong to try to compel the Conservative-controlled council to go comprehensive.

The decision was received with delight by Mrs Thatcher, who sent a telegram of congratulations on behalf of the entire Shadow Cabinet to the Tameside Conservative councillors, and with gloom by Mr Mulley. He said in a statement: 'I am naturally disappointed, but I accept, of course, a ruling given by the highest court in the land.'

. . . Mr Norman St John Stevas, Conservative Shadow Education Secretary, said immediately after the judgement that the case was an historic milestone in both education and administrative law. 'Never again will an Education Minister be able to behave with dictatorial arrogance to parents and councillors.'

He urged the teachers who had been in conflict with the Tameside authority to do all in their power to make the system of selection for grammar schools work. The appeal fell on deaf ears. Mr Eric Pilkington, secretary of Tameside Head Teachers, said that he and his colleagues would do no more than was legally required to assist the selection of children for grammar school places.

. . . Conservative MPs last night tabled a Commons motion noting with concern what they alleged was 'the continuing disdain of the Government for the rule of law', displayed in the cases of Tameside and Laker Airways. But Mr Bruce Grocott, Labour MP for Lichfield and Tamworth, tabled a question to Mr Sam Silkin, Attorney General, asking him to ensure in future appointments to the High Court 'a proper balance between those judges who have received State education and those who have been educated privately'. He said the judiciary was 'still the preserve of the elite'.

(*Daily Telegraph*, 3 August 1978)

6.d.3　The Laker Skytrain case

Another case in the same year attracted popular interest because it opened the door to cheap transatlantic air travel. Its constitutional interest, however, was that, first, a minister was, again, held to have overstepped the limits of his discretionary power, and, second, the Court of Appeal showed itself willing to overrule action taken under Crown prerogative if it caused injustice.

One purpose of the Civil Aviation Act 1971 was to allow at least one commercial airline to compete with the state-owned British Airways. The businessman Freddie Laker wanted to operate a cheap 'Skytrain' air service across the north Atlantic. To do this, he needed a licence from the Civil Aviation Authority, and he needed to be a 'designated carrier' under a treaty with the United States. Initially the licence was granted and the British government asked the USA to agree to Laker's designation. But in July 1975 the Trade Secretary, Peter Shore, announced a change in policy. In future the government's general policy would be not to permit competition between United Kingdom airlines on long-haul scheduled services. This policy was set out in a white paper approved by both Houses of Parliament. Shore then used his powers under the Civil Aviation Act 1971 to issue guidance to the CAA saying, in effect, that Laker should lose its licence, and had its designated carrier status annulled. Laker, who had already spent £7 million setting up the route, challenged.

The Court of Appeal ruled, firstly, that the fact that Parliament had approved the white paper was irrelevant. That could not overrule the Civil Aviation Act, which allowed competition. Only a proper Act of Parliament could change the law. Secondly, it ruled that the Trade Secretary's guidance to the Civil Aviation Authority was invalid: because it tried to reverse the competition provisions of the Act, it was not really guidance at all. Therefore it was ineffective.

Thirdly, there was the alternative line of defence put forward by the Government, that the Trade Secretary could use the 'prerogative power' of the Crown to withdraw the designation, because the designation was given under a treaty with the United States, and the treaty was made under prerogative power. No, said the court. Precedent held that prerogative power was abused if it was exercised 'in circumstances which worked injustice to the individual without any countervailing benefit for the public'. At this late stage, when Laker had invested a lot of money and was, literally, ready for take off, cancelling the designation was an abuse.

That last point showed just how subjective these decisions can be. The government wanted to stop Skytrain because it reckoned that, on balance, protecting the commercial viability of British Airways was more important than lower air fares. Effectively the Court was saying that, at this late stage, the injustice done to Laker was more important than protecting British Airways: in these circumstances, an individual's rights overrode the government's view of the public interest.

'Laker Airways Ltd v Department of Trade' threw the government into a state of alarm. In this case, we actually have an eyewitness account of how the government reacted in the face of reversal in the courts. Edmund Dell, who by then had succeeded Shore as Trade Secretary, records the discussion that ensued in a Cabinet committee on the question: should the government appeal further to the Judicial Committee of the House of Lords?

What considerations then would favour an appeal to the House of Lords? The first was undoubtedly inertia. The civil aviation policy, against part of which Laker was fighting, had been approved by the House of Commons after lengthy negotiations with interested parties. It had been accepted, albeit reluctantly, by the major British airlines and by the unions. Nobody could be certain of the effect on existing scheduled services of introducing Skytrain. Even the Civil Aviation Authority had only proposed an experiment. The unions in particular were by no means in love with Laker and might resent a decision not to appeal, especially as there was held to be a good chance of winning. Why undermine a compromise policy painfully worked out after months of negotiation and thereby prejudice relations with the unions, in an era of voluntary incomes policy, when the recourse of an appeal to the Lords remained? One can see that some Ministers might regard relations with the unions as being at that time of much greater importance than whether Skytrain should fly. Moreover, there was the crucial issue, left in some doubt by the Court of Appeal, of the extent of Crown prerogative. Even if we lost in the Lords, the noble judges would perhaps settle that.

What arguments were there on the other side with which to answer these weighty considerations? First, the effect of Skytrain on existing schedule services might well prove to have been exaggerated. The idea of Skytrain was very popular especially in view of the widely received opinion that civil aviation is a racket and that a little genuine competition would do a great deal of good. One would expect governments to be attracted by popularity, but it is not necessarily a decisive argument, and rightly so. Moreover, collective decision-makers are not necessarily enthused at the thought of a colleague gaining approval by overturning previous policy while he still has a choice. Another consideration was that we were in the midst of the difficult Bermuda II negotiations. We were trying to get a better deal in our civil aviation relations with the USA and for our pains were being accused by the Americans of being hostile to competition. To switch policies and endorse Laker would be a nice card to play against the USA which previously had refused to admit Skytrain. They would now be forced to admit it if they were not to drain all credibility from their consumerist propaganda, propaganda they love to use when they feel themselves competitive.

We can then envisage, with an accuracy at least comparable to that of journalists acting our ministerial roles in a television programme, the collective discussions leading up to the decision whether or not to appeal. Minister A says don't bother me with unnecessary problems. I do not want to think again about civil aviation policy unless I am forced to do so by losing in the Lords. B says he is very worried about Crown prerogative. C says that we must keep the unions happy and that trade union official Y, who is involved in this matter, is a key figure in deciding his union's position on incomes policy. D says that the White Paper on civil aviation policy was a first-class document, and E that we all know that the judges are always against Labour governments. Whether that means we should or should not appeal is left unclear. But F says that Skytrain is very popular, that we should at any rate follow the CAA in allowing an experiment, and that to unleash it now would be a shrewd tactical move in Bermuda II; whereas G says that a bit of competition in civil aviation would do a power of good. I should add that H to M are present, but have not read the papers.

> (Edmund Dell, 'Collective Responsibility: Fact, Fiction or Facade',
> in Royal Institute of Public Administration, *Policy and Practice: The*
> *Experience of Government*, London: RIPA, 1980)

The government decided against appealing further. An intriguing footnote is provided by Norman Tebbit, the Conservative politician, who three years later became Under-Secretary of State for Trade, and had to grapple with the result of Denning's decision in the Laker case.

The implications flowing from his judgement were widespread and in my first weeks in office I read the Denning judgement with great care. Having thought about it for a while I asked the Deputy Secretary responsible for aviation policy and the Department's lawyers to see me.

'I've been reading Denning's Laker judgement,' I said. 'He was wrong, wasn't he? Peter Shore [Labour's Trade Minister] was within his powers wasn't he?'

'You're quite right,' they both said. 'But we hadn't expected you would come to that conclusion.'

'Well,' I asked, 'why didn't Peter Shore appeal?'

It was not, of course, a question my officials could answer in that form. The reasoning of Labour Ministers was not a matter they could discuss with me, but it was not difficult to guess that Peter Shore had made a sensible political decision not to fly in the face of public opinion, although I believed he would have had a good chance of winning if the case had gone right through to the House of Lords.

> (Norman Tebbit, *Upwardly Mobile*, London: Weidenfeld and
> Nicolson, 1988. There is a slight inaccuracy: the final decision not to
> appeal was taken by Shore's successor, Edmund Dell.)

6.d.4   The GCHQ case

Although the three pioneering cases described above occurred under a Labour government, the courts have continued to mete out the same treatment to Conservative governments since 1979. One such case, which showed a particularly imaginative judicial approach to the question of 'procedural impropriety', was the GCHQ case.

Government Communications Headquarters at Cheltenham provides signals intelligence to the government for national security purposes. In the early 1980s there had been industrial action that had seriously disrupted GCHQ's work. At the time the government felt unable to act against this, since the existence of GCHQ was not publicly acknowledged (despite the fact that GCHQ recruited openly in the graduate careers market). But this inhibition was removed in 1983 when, following a spy scandal, the existence of GCHQ had to be acknowledged. In 1984 the government announced that in future staff working at GCHQ would no longer be allowed to belong to national trade unions. This action was taken under Crown prerogative power, in this case an Order in Council (in effect, a royal decree) of 1982. This caused a political furore, and the Council of Civil Service Unions challenged the decision on the grounds that the staff should have been consulted beforehand on this change in their conditions of service, in accordance with previous practice at GCHQ.

The government fought the case to the House of Lords (in practice, legal appeals to the House of Lords are heard by its Judicial Committee, a panel of five senior judges). While the government won the battle on the specific issue of national security, it rather lost the war since the Lords' judgement both entrenched unions' entitlement to consultation and extended the principle that actions under the prerogative are subject to judicial review.

The case turned on three issues. Firstly, the government argued that the courts had no right to review either (*a*) the Crown's discretionary exercise of its prerogative powers or (*b*) any action of Crown servants to whom the prerogative had delegated a power. The House of Lords decided, on (*a*), that the Queen's discretionary prerogative was, at least to some extent, subject to review. On (*b*) they agreed that when a prerogative action delegated authority to somebody – in this case, the Prime Minister – the way that person used that power could definitely be reviewed by the courts. In the words of Lord Fraser's judgement:

> There is no doubt that, if the Order in Council of 1982 had been made under the authority of a statute, the power delegated to the Minister would have been [subject to review by the courts]. I am unable to see why the words conferring the same powers should be construed differently merely because their source was an Order in Council made under the prerogative. . . . Whatever their source, powers which are defined . . . are in my opinion normally subject to judicial control to ensure that they are not exceeded. . . . The courts had already shown themselves ready to control by way of judicial review the actions of a tribunal set up under the prerogative [the Criminal Injuries Compensation Board].
>
> (CCSU *v.* Minister for the Civil Service (HL(E))
> [1985], 1 AER, p. 399)

The second question was whether the procedure under the decision was unfair because the unions, having been consulted on such issues in the past, had a 'legitimate expectation' of consultation in this case. The court held that, under normal circumstances, they did. Lord Fraser again:

> [Counsel for the unions] submitted that the Minister had a duty to consult the

CCSU, on behalf of employees at GCHQ, before giving the instruction on 22 December 1983 for making an important change in their conditions of service. His main reason for so submitting was that the employees had a legitimate, or reasonable, expectation that there would be such prior consultation before any important change was made in their conditions.

It is clear that the employees did not have a legal right to prior consultation. The Order in Council confers no such right. . . . But even where a person claiming some benefit or privilege has no legal right to it, as a matter of private law, he may have a legitimate expectation of receiving the benefit or privilege, and, if so, the courts will protect his expectation by judicial review as a matter of public law. . . . Legitimate, or reasonable, expectation may arise either from an express promise given on behalf of a public authority or from the existence of a regular practice which the claimant can reasonably expect to continue. . . .

In the present case the evidence shows that, ever since GCHQ began in 1947, prior consultation has been the invariable rule when conditions of service were to be significantly altered. Accordingly in my opinion if there had been no question of national security involved, the appellant would have had a legitimate expectation that the minister would consult them before issuing the instruction of 22 December 1983.

(CCSU *v.* Minister for the Civil Service, pp. 400–1)

And, because there had been no such consultation, the procedure was unfair. But in the specific circumstances of GCHQ, this was overridden by the third issue: the government's argument that the Prime Minister had acted reasonably in not consulting, because of the consequences that this would have for national security. Lord Diplock, in his judgement, went out of his way to make clear the line between the responsibilities of the courts and those of the government:

The reason why the Minister for the Civil Service decided on 22 December 1993 to withdraw this benefit was in the interests of national security. National security is the responsibility of the executive government; what action is needed to protect its interests is . . . a matter upon which those upon whom the responsibility rests, and not the courts of justice, must have the last word. It is par excellence a non-justiciable question. The judicial process is totally inept to deal with the sort of problems which it involves.

The executive government likewise decided, and this would appear to be a collective decision of cabinet ministers involved, that the interests of national security required that no notice should be given of the decision before administrative action had been taken to give effect to it. The reason for this was the risk that advance notice to the national unions of the executive government's intentions would attract the very disruptive action prejudicial to the national security the recurrence of which the decision barring membership of national trade unions to civil servants employed at GCHQ was designed to prevent.

> There was ample evidence . . . that this was indeed a real risk; so the crucial point of law in this case is whether procedural propriety must give way to national security when there is a conflict between (1) on the one hand, the prima facie rule of 'procedural propriety' in public law, applicable to a case of legitimate expectations . . . and (2) on the other hand, action that is needed to be taken in the interests of national security, for which the executive government bears the responsibility and alone has access to sources of information that qualify it to judge what the necessary action is. To that there can, in my opinion, be only one sensible answer. That answer is 'Yes'.
> I agree with your Lordships that his appeal must be dismissed.
>
> (CCSU *v.* Minister for the Civil Service, pp. 412–13)

The impact of the growth of judicial review on government is three fold. Firstly, it constitutes a direct control by the courts over the government, preventing ministers and officials from acting unfairly or beyond their legal powers. Secondly, it is a psychological check on government: officials are made to realise that they can be compelled to account for their decisions. Thirdly, the very possibility that decisions might be challenged compels government to be a great deal more circumspect when taking its decisions, to make sure that it does nothing that might be challenged in the courts. For example, the GCHQ case brought it home very clearly to ministers and civil service managers that they had a duty to consult their staff before changing their conditions of service.

The importance that officials now attach to the possibility of judicial review can be seen in the training courses in administrative law now made available by departments to their staff, and the publication in 1987 by the Treasury Solicitor of a brief and lucid guide to judicial review under the significant title *The Judge over Your Shoulder*, which sets out legal principles that officials should bear in mind when taking decisions.

The extent to which the possibility of judicial review acts as a constraint on government action has been illustrated in the memoirs of Margaret Thatcher. In early 1990, with the poll tax crisis (described in 5.a.1) at its height, she sought to control the crisis by an extensive use of the government's statutory powers to cap local councils' budgets. But

> the lawyers advised that anything like the scale of capping I wanted to see was unlikely to be sustainable in the courts. Consequently Chris Patten [Environment Secretary] could only announce the capping of twenty councils. This was very disappointing. But a defeat in the courts would have put the whole system in disarray.
>
> (Margaret Thatcher, *The Downing Street Years*, London: HarperCollins, 1993)

Half the value of judicial review is its deterrent effect. It makes governments think twice before acting, and forces them to ensure they are acting within the law. This can be seen as an unjustifiable interference by unelected judges in the right of elected politicians to govern. In the television licences case, counsel for the Crown suggested, 'If the court interferes in this case, it would not be long before the powers of the court would be called into question' – a remark for which he had to apologise to the court several days later, and from which the Home Secretary rapidly distanced himself. Alternatively it can be argued that, in the absence of a written constitution and a bill of rights, the courts are acting to prevent governments from abusing their sometimes ill-defined powers: if governments did not find judicial review a nuisance, it would not be much use. The Conservative MP and barrister Ronald Bell argued in a Commons exchange on the television licence case that the courts were moving into this area because parliament was failing in its duty to control the executive.

Either way, the growth of judicial review and its restraining effect on government make it the most important constitutional development since Britain joined the EC, and it has come to exercise a potent restraint on government policy.

Conclusion

The case studies in this book cannot provide complete coverage of the decision making process in British central government. The span of executive activity is so wide and the possible permutations of forces so numerous that a single book can illustrate only a few interesting facets of the system. Furthermore, any collection of case studies is severely constrained by the availability of published material, especially in a field like central government which, of necessity, carries out much of its business behind closed doors.

None the less, it is interesting by way of conclusion to consider what these case studies tell us about the four dynamic forces operating in the system that I described in the Introduction: partisan, administrative, interest and public. In particular, most case studies exemplify some kind of conflict between forces for change and forces resisting change. To what extent do these different dynamic forces, and the agencies that embody them, act as forces for change, and to what extent are they forces for the status quo?

That is more than just an academic distinction: it has considerable practical importance. Many of the case studies in this volume describe government being overruled by external forces – outvoted in parliament, blocked by interest groups, driven back by public opinion, vetoed by the courts. Is this getting out of hand? In certain polities, effective government has been thwarted by these external pressures. One of the great flaws of the French Fourth Republic, which collapsed in 1958, was said by its critics to be the extent to which powerful interests could block government action. One of the aims of the politicians who founded the Fifth Republic was to break the power of this *régime des intérêts* – the sovereignty of vested interests. Similar forces have been at work in the Italian Republic, both before and since the overhaul of its constitution in 1993 which was designed to eliminate them. There are comparable difficulties, although not as acute, in the United States where, for example, vested interests blocked President Clinton's health and gun law reforms in the early 1990s, despite the then Democratic majority in both houses of Congress.

If we analyse the four dynamic forces defined in the Introduction, we find that the only one of them which is predominantly a force for change is the partisan dynamic, which for most practical purposes means ministers. Time and again we see them in these studies acting as the spur to change. On those rare instances when ministers are seen resisting change, it is for one of three reasons. Firstly, because they believe they will face substantial opposition from parliament or public opinion – the public dynamic, in short – that will prove unpopular. That is why Butler dragged his feet on homosexual law reform. Secondly, because they have a genuine fear that the policy outcome will be against the national interest: hence Clarke's apparent unwillingness to allow the police to carry side-handled batons. Thirdly, because it clashes with political values: hence Margaret Thatcher's Unionist sympathies, which led her to oppose devolution in Northern Ireland. But in most of the case studies, it is ministers who are applying the spur for change. And in an age of manifesto politics, that is only to be expected: parties devise programmes and, if they win elections, their ministers act as agents of change to inject the manifesto commitments into departments.

Note, as mentioned in the Introduction, the almost complete absence of influence of the party machine. Policy making in opposition, so unflatteringly described in the episode of the race relations bill, has improved only marginally since 1964. And you will seek in vain any examples of party opinion exercising leverage on ministers. What does happen – and this is shown in the pits closure crisis and the shops bill affair – is that party activists in the constituencies will exercise influence on their local MPs and this filters through to the government in the form of pressure from the Commons, and hence in the 'public dynamic' (although some MPs, of course, are ministers and so receive this influence direct). But as a regular and significant influence on ministers, the party machine is not significant.

If the partisan dynamic largely pushes towards change, the administrative dynamic, embodied in Whitehall by the civil service – is far more cautious. Shirley Williams, after five years as a Labour minister in the 1970s, described the civil service, without particular hostility, as 'a beautifully designed braking mechanism'. The reasons for officialdom's caution are cogently spelt out in David Lipsey's description of the civil service's reservations about items in Labour's 1974 manifesto at the Department of the Environment. Officials are there to ask the question: will it work?

So there is a tension, sometimes erupting into conflict, between politicians and officials. Is that so surprising? They are two separate cadres of people, serving two very different constitutional purposes. Officials are there to keep the ship moving forward on an even keel; ministers are implanted, as a kind of irritant, to alter the course. The psychological function of both is different. In a sense, the civil service is the rational, technical part of the machinery: cool, analytical but a bit bloodless. Politicians, in contrast, are the 'irrational' element: intuitive and impulsive. This distinction is not absolute. Officials are as much prone to subjective prejudice as anyone: look at the tendency of departments, as described by a former head of the civil service, to develop a 'departmental view': the Foreign Office's pro-European stance since the 1960s, for example, or the free-trade ethos of the old Board of Trade. Similarly ministers are to a large extent driven by rational argument: look for instance at Tebbit's caution when appointed Employment Secretary. But there is a fundamental difference in what makes officials and politicians tick. A career civil service, politically impartial, must be driven by logic. Politicians, in thrall to the public mood, have more an element of gut instinct, alloying logic with emotion. It was beautifully exemplified in 1950 when the acting Prime Minister, Herbert Morrison, refused to sign up to a Franco-German initiative that was the start of the European Community, because 'the Durham miners wouldn't like it'.

How does the interest dynamic cut across the reformist/conservative distinction? Interest groups address issues one by one, and favour or oppose change entirely pragmatically, depending on whether it helps or hinders their particular cause. So we see the police opposing change when the Select Committee proposed abolition of the 'sus' law, but agitating for a change to allow officers to carry side-handled batons. A quick glance at the causes on which the Association of Metropolitan Authorities took a stance shows its attitude towards change dictated entirely by whether it advanced or set back the interests of its members. In short, the interest dynamic is *ex officio* selfish and, while interest groups have a valuable and often expert contribution to make to policy making, to allow them too great a sway over policy decisions is to subordinate the general public interest to the interest of a particular group.

The public dynamic is a far more difficult element to assess. Firstly, it is an amalgam of pressures and, for that reason, is often not well articulated. Secondly, the mass of public opinion is not easily roused: often its expression is left to individual campaigners or interest groups, who may evoke some degree of sympathy from the public. Sudden groundswells of public anger, such as occurred in the coal mines closure affair, are infrequent and short-lived. But a determined campaign to rouse public opinion by an interest group can excite a certain amount of support: the decision of many Conservative MPs to vote against the 1986 shops bill was due to pressure from constituents roused by the 'Keep Sunday Special' campaign, just as many peers voted against school transport charges because school governors, parents and the clergy lobbied them.

The extent to which the public dynamic is stirred to assert itself depends on whether people feel themselves affected, or have a strong feeling about an issue that will not necessarily affect them. So there was much public sympathy for the campaign to keep Bart's open, even in areas which would have benefited from the switch of hospital funding out of London. It also depends on the intelligibility of the issue. Closing thirty coal mines or charging for school transport are easily understood, but the extent of public sympathy for the doctors' objections to their new contracts was attenuated by lack of general understanding about what the new contract actually meant in practice.

Broadly, that puts the public dynamic on the anti-reformist side of the equation. People will rise in defence of something tangible they can see and use – the local bus service, the post office on the corner, the pound note (which the public did not want to exchange for the pound coin). They are sceptical of the possible benefits of what might be put in its place. Even then, only when the policy is implemented and the practical effects of the policy become obvious will the public temper simmer over. The poll tax is a good example of this. There was rather generalised discontent with the old system of domestic rates in the 1980s, but people were moved to anger only when an overdue revaluation in Scotland bit hard on ratepayers there. Public opinion was rather ambivalent about the proposed community change, but when the legislation was being passed no great agitation arose about it. Only when the practical effects became clear did the public lose patience. Even then, exactly why the poll tax had come so badly unstuck was not very clearly understood – the causes of the debacle were complex and are still the subject of some dispute today. But the public does not actually need to know why a policy has misfired to express its displeasure. Unlike ministers, civil servants and pressure groups, public opinion does not need a detailed grasp of the policy to disapprove. It has gone wrong, and the government must put it right. So the public dynamic exercises a mainly negative influence on policy making.

Where does that leave two other institutions considered in this book: the courts and parliament? The impact of the courts on policy making is purely negative, since their role is confined to ruling on the legality of administrative actions. If they rule an action lawful, the policy proceeds as before. If they rule it illegal, it must be reviewed or reformed. The courts have no positive role because they have no scope to substitute their own decisions for the decisions of ministers – a state of affairs that nobody wishes to alter.

The position of parliament is more complex. As argued in Chapter 6, parliament's role over policy making has always been predominantly negative: to block or restrain the actions of a government by rejecting or amending bills, or by bringing pressure to bear on ministers to change course. Some scope for MPs to exercise a positive influence does exist: by amending legislation, through the work of select committees – several examples from the work of the Home Affairs Committee appear among the case studies – through private members' bills and through the private representations made to ministers by backbench MPs (see for example Margaret Thatcher's comments on the attitudes of backbenchers towards the poll tax as it ran into heavy weather). But when parliament does weigh in to alter policy, its intervention is usually a negative one.

Which leads us to an interesting conclusion. Within the policy making process only one force – the partisan, meaning mainly ministers – is usually a force for change. Two others, the administrative and public dynamics, tend to resist and restrain the partisan dynamic. And the interest dynamic throws its energies on whichever side suits its interest. Put that way, it seems surprising that the government manages to engineer as much change as it does. What appears to save us from the kind of deadlock visible in the French Fourth Republic and in Italy is the existence of a central executive with a formidable policy making capacity and the fact that while parliament does exercise quite a strong restraint over government policy, 95 per cent of legislation still goes through as the government wishes. The rather surprising conclusion is that, in the field of policy making at least, when it comes to weighing the need for decisive government against democratic restraint and the protection of private interests, our constitution is rather better balanced than superficial appearances might suggest.

References

(excluding newspaper and broadcast sources)

Association of Metropolitan Authorities, *Annual Report*, London: AMA, 1993.

Baker, K. *The Turbulent Years*, London: Faber and Faber, 1993.

Barnett, J. *Inside the Treasury*, London: Andre Deutsch, 1982.

Benn, T. 'The Mandarins in Modern Britain', *Guardian*, 4 February 1980.

Benn, T. *Office Without Power: Diaries 1968–72*, London: Hutchinson, 1988.

Benn, T. *Against the Tide: Diaries 1973–76*, London: Hutchinson, 1989.

Biffen, J. *Inside the House of Commons: Behind the Scenes at Westminster*, London: Grafton, 1989.

Blackstone, T. and Plowden, W. *Inside the Think Tank: Advising the Cabinet 1971–83*, London: Heinemann, 1988.

Bruce–Gardyne, J. *Ministers and Mandarins*, London: Macmillan, 1986.

Butler, R.A.B. (Lord), *The Art of the Possible*, London: Hamish Hamilton, 1971.

Callaghan, J. *Time and Chance*, London: Collins, 1987.

Castle, B. *The Castle Diaries 1964–70*, London: Weidenfeld and Nicolson, 1984.

Castle, B. *The Castle Diaries 1974–76*, London: Weidenfeld and Nicolson, 1980.

The Civil Service Code, London: HMSO, 1995.

Crossman, R. *Inside View: Three Lectures on Prime Ministerial Government*, London: Jonathan Cape, 1972.

Crossman, R. *The Diaries of a Cabinet Minister, volume I: Minister of Housing, 1964–66*, London: Hamish Hamilton and Jonathan Cape, 1975.

Crossman, R. *The Diaries of a Cabinet Minister, volume II: Lord President of the Council and Leader of the House of Commons, 1966–68*, London: Hamish Hamilton and Jonathan Cape, 1976.

Crossman, R. *The Diaries of a Cabinet Minister, volume III, Secretary of State for Social Services, 1968–70*, London: Hamish Hamilton and Jonathan Cape, 1977.

Dell, E. 'Collective Responsibility: Fact, Fiction or Façade', in *Royal Institute of Public Administration, Policy and Practice: The Experience of Government*, London: RIPA, 1980.

Dell, E. 'Some Reflections on Cabinet by a Former Practitioner', *Public Administration Bulletin*, 32, April 1980.

Donoughue, B. *Prime Minister*, London: Jonathan Cape, 1987.

Edwardes, M. *Back from the Brink*, London: Collins, 1983.

Fitzgerald, G. *All in a Life*, Dublin: Macmillan and Gill, 1991.

Fowler, N. *Ministers Decide*, London: Chapmans, 1991.

Gordon Walker, P. *Political Diaries 1932–71*, London: Historians' Press, 1991.

Heffer, E. *Never a Yes Man*, London: Verso, 1991.

Hindell, K. 'The Genesis of the Race Relations Bill', *Political Quarterly*, 36(4), 1965.

Home Affairs Committee of the Cabinet, minutes for 29 November 1957, CAB 134 (HA(57)26), Kew: Public Records Office.

Home Affairs Committee of the Cabinet, minutes for 24 October 1958, CAB 134/1972, Kew: Public Records Office.

House of Commons Debates, 26 November 1958, cols. 44, 437 and 369–71 passim.

House of Commons Debates, 29 June 1960, cols 1490–8 passim.

House of Commons Debates, 5 June 1980, cols 1767–78 passim.

House of Commons Debates, 19 January 1981, col. 21.

House of Commons, *Second Report of the Home Affairs Committee*, session 1990–91.

Hurdle, D and Keating, I, 'The Parking Story', *LBA Handbook 1992–93*, London Boroughs Association, 1992.

Lawson, N. *The View from No. 11: Memoirs of a Tory radical*, London: Bantam Press, 1992.

Lipsey, D. 'Who's in Charge in Whitehall?', *New Society*, 24 April 1980.

Kaufman, G. *How to be a Minister*, London: Sidgwick and Jackson, 1980.

Part, A. *The Making of a Mandarin*, London: André Deutsch, 1990.

Patten, J. (Minister of State for Home Affairs), letter to leaders of British Muslim organisations, 4 July 1989.

Playfair, E. 'Who Are the Policy-makers?', *Public Administration*, 43, Autumn 1965.

Plowden, W. *The Motor Car and Politics*, London: Bodley Head, 1971.

Prior, J. A *Balance of Power*, London: Hamish Hamilton, 1986.

Questions of Procedure for Ministers, London: Cabinet Office, 1992.

Report of the Committee on Homosexual Offences and Prostitution (the Wolfenden Committee), Cmnd. 247 (London: HMSO)

Short, E. *Whip to Wilson*, London: Macdonald, 1989.

Stapleton, G. 'Beyond the Thin Green Line', *MAFF Bulletin*, October 1985.

Tebbit, N. *Upwardly Mobile*, London: Weidenfeld and Nicolson, 1988.

Thatcher, M. *The Downing Street Years*, London: Harper Collins, 1993.

Travers, T. 'The Council Tax', *Local Government Chronicle*, 29 April, 1994.

Wakeham, Lord. 'Cabinet government', *Contemporary Record*, 8(3), Winter 1993.

Wass, D. Government and the Governed, *BBC Reith Lectures 1983*, London: Routledge and Kegan Paul, 1984.

Whitehall and Beyond, London: BBC, 1964.

Whitelaw, W. *The Whitelaw Memoirs*, London: Aurum Press, 1989.

Wilson, H. *Final Term: The Labour Government 1974–76*, London: Weidenfeld and Nicolson and Michael Joseph, 1977.

Wolfenden, Lord *Turning Points*, London: Bodley Head, 1976.

Index